STRAIGHT UP

STRAIGHT UP

Ruby Tui

with Margie Thomson

ALLEN&UNWIN
SYDNEY•MELBOURNE•AUCKLAND•LONDON

Note: some names and identifying details have been changed to protect the privacy of individuals.

Allen & Unwin
Level 2, 10 College Hill, Freemans Bay
Auckland 1011, New Zealand
Phone: (64 9) 377 3800
Email: auckland@allenandunwin.com
Web: www.allenandunwin.co.nz

83 Alexander Street
Crows Nest NSW 2065, Australia
Phone: (61 2) 8425 0100

A catalogue record for this book is available from the National Library of New Zealand.

ISBN 978 1 99100 614 1

Design by Megan van Staden
Set in Tiempos 10/16
Printed and bound in Australia by the Opus Group

10 9 8 7 6

MIX
Paper | Supporting
responsible forestry
FSC
www.fsc.org   FSC® C001695

For anyone chasing a dream:
I see you

Contents

Prologue

ass, hit, bounce, catch.
  I'm down at the Ilam rugby fields in the early morning,
no one else at training yet, and I'm throwing the rugby ball,
that tricky egg, against a pole. Again. Again. Up to a hundred.
More. It's my second season playing summer sevens, my second
year of rugby. I love this game, everything about it. I think I could
be OK at it, but right now I'm the worst in the team, and I don't
really know how to go from worst to as good as I can be. *Pass, hit,
bounce, catch.* But this is one way, surely, and as I do my passes
the others slowly arrive, cars pulling up, women getting out, tying
on their boots.

  Pass, hit, bounce, catch. I fell in love with rugby the previous
year, at 18, in my first year at the University of Canterbury. I was
living in the university hostel just over there on the other side
of the fields, and in fact I could actually see the rugby fields
from my window. I'd been told by my palagi family that going to
university was all about trying things out, seeing where they take
you, so when one of the other girls in the Uni Halls said, Come
and check out the women's rugby, just come for a run-around,
I thought, Yeah, I'll try it. I didn't have any boots but she was like,

Someone'll lend you boots, and I thought, That's a cool culture. I'd played netball for years, and in my head I was going to be a Silver Fern, but even though I hardly ever had the right shoes, and sometimes even had to play in bare feet, no one ever said they'd lend me some.

So I took my chance and went down, and I couldn't believe it. I'd never met anyone like the women I met there on that field. Women rugby players. It was a revelation. Newbies like me, experienced ones — even some Black Ferns, who to me were mythical beings, like magical creatures from a fairy tale. I'd been told they existed but I'd never seen one before.

And the women were like, Come, stand here if you want to, if you're willing. Their arms were open, and I was like, Bro, I've been looking for something like this my whole life. Of course I'm here.

I bought a pair of boots off Trade Me for $20, which I thought was a lot of money, and joined the Uni team.

I just absolutely fell in love with the start line, the potential of something new. I wanted a purpose, and I fell in love with the purpose of the team. I'd always been sporty — quick and fast — although learning to pass that oval ball was a whole new challenge. But our coach Ernie said, Just keep doing it.

Then a few months in, with winter sports ending for the year, some of the girls moved over to rugby sevens. Rubes, you going to play? the other women asked me. I'd only just learned what fifteens was, but — Yeah sweet, I'll follow the team. And I found out that sevens was the game I was born for — but so much harder, fitness-wise, and again I was the worst in the team.

This year we're coached by Mere Baker, famously abrupt, really honest, never says anything for fluff. I'm really trying, but it seems like nothing I ever do is good enough for Baker.

And here she comes now, pulling up in her car, and I'm so proud of myself because look at me, I'm working at my passing. *Pass, hit, bounce, catch.* I keep going like I haven't noticed her.

Nonchalant. Keep doing it, keep doing it. More than anything in the whole world, I want to get good at this game.

Baker gets out of the car and walks towards me and I'm waiting for her to be like, Good job, Ruby.

She walks straight past me.

Doesn't look at me. Doesn't care. She walks over to where the other girls are mulling around in a group and barks, Get on the line. Oh, man! I drop the ball, go over on the line. I thought it was going to be a good morning, but this is not a good morning, because *get on the line* means you're about to die.

Sprint out to there, back, sprint out to there, back, sprint there sprint back ten times. Oh, whatever. I don't care. This is my attitude. I feel like there's no point in fitness because I'm just going to be shit anyway. Baker blows the whistle and everyone takes off for the run round the field. Tess and CJ are the fittest in the team, and they sprint off. They've done a lap before I even blink. After them are a couple of other fast ones, then there's the big middle group where most people are, and then there's a few stragglers at the back, and then there's me. One lap and I'm not even running or jogging — I'm plodding, filled up with this feeling that I hate fitness.

Baker's at the side and I see her staring at me. Go on, I think, just yell at me, I know I'm the worst here . . . Now I'm going past her, and she steps off the side and starts jogging with me — although I'm thinking she could be walking because that's how slow I'm going.

But Baker's experienced, a long-time player herself, and she can tell something hasn't clicked for me yet. So we're jogging together, and then she says: See that next group? Up ahead of us, at the back of that middle group, are Lucy and Birdie. Yeah, I gasp. See Birdie and that?, she goes: If you catch them I'll make you the greatest sevens player in the world. And she says it loud enough that I'll never forget it, but quiet enough that no one else hears.

Are you frickin' serious? I've found this brand-new exciting thing I think I'm alright at — I *can* be, I *could* be, if I could only figure out how to do it — and then she goes, all I have to do is catch Birdie. All I have to do is catch Lucy. *That* was the link between me now, and me being the best in the world? They're 20 metres ahead of me, but *that's* all I have to do to get to be the greatest in the world? Why didn't you tell me that sooner?!

So all of a sudden, I change. Baker stops running with me as I pick up my speed. Lucy and Birdie . . . I make it up to them and inside my head I'm like, *I can. I can go past them.* I do it. And I get up to the middle group. Holy . . . ! And I pass that group, too. What the frick! What the frick! Oh man this is so cool! I feel like my legs have been lying to me all this time — they told me they couldn't go any faster when all this time they could. You liars! I'm running fast now. I leave the middle group behind me, and pass another person.

Up ahead of me, CJ and Tess cross the line, then I cross, and everyone else comes in after me. I drop to the ground. I'm shocked, just absolutely gobsmacked. I've discovered the secret gearbox in my body — a gearbox controlled by my mind. It's my first true moment of mental fitness.

It clicks. I've got this massive goal — to be the best rugby player I can be — and to get there, all I have to do is just take this one little step *here*.

So from now on, training has changed for me. I'm never throwing away another session with my *I hate fitness, I'm no good at it anyway, I'll just go through the motions.* I can feel the change in me. How far can I push myself? Suddenly I want to know. Baker's over there looking at me like I'm a frickin' idiot, but maybe she knows this is a turning point. I'm different. My life is different.

So much has happened to bring me to this point. And I've got so much further to go. I don't know if I believe her yet about where my mental fitness might take me, but it turns out she's right.

PART ONE

LOVE

Sometimes I don't want to be in front of the camera; sometimes I don't want to take selfies and put myself out there on Instagram. Sometimes I don't want to write a book about my life.

But you know what I want more than anything?

I want people to know they can have a messed-up background and use it to fuel themselves forward; that they can use their struggles to create their purpose.

I want people to love themselves so much they can go out and be proud of their whole selves — so proud and grateful they would write a book about it.

Love, greatitude (see page 112), communication. These are my values.

So here I am.

1. No kidding around

There's a photo Mum took when I was about three — maybe it's a birthday, or maybe I just had some friends around at our house. It's a group of us little kids, mostly boys, and I've got my top off and I'm wearing pink shorts. My thick, dark hair is in pigtails. I remember looking at that photo and it struck me for the first time that I had brown skin and all the other kids had white skin. *I look different to the other kids*. It was a self-discovery.

I grew up in polar opposite worlds. Two worlds, two cultures, each with their own good and bad, and not better or worse but just different. Mostly, I got the best of both worlds. I was taught so much by my palagi mum, but then I also learned so much from my Samoan family on Dad's side.

Other times, I noticed I wasn't full brown like my Samoan cousins. Not white enough to be white; not brown enough to be brown — like I was an outsider in both places. I struggled with those feelings all my childhood. But my mum never made me feel different to her, and on my Samoan side I was just another cousin. I was never treated different in either family, but it was just that realisation: *Oh wow, I look different*. It was hard to

understand what it meant. When I went through my hard times
I thought I was out of place in both worlds, but then I realised
I actually have two places.

Later still, I realised there are so many people like me, who
bridge different worlds. There are many Samoans who grew up
in New Zealand and so they're not Samoan in the same way the
older generations were — they don't know Samoan village life;
they may never have been there. They are Kiwi, like I am Kiwi,
and it's a whole new space, the combining of two massive worlds.
I think this is the future of the world, the coming together of
cultures.

———

I've got this memory from when I was about four. By that stage,
my parents weren't together full-time and me and Mum were
living in a house she'd bought in Newtown, in Wellington. But
Dad still often came over, and there would be good, fun times for
a bit, until the yelling started.

My parents are chalk and cheese, completely opposite.
Mum is tall, skinny and white; Dad is short, stocky and brown.
Mum, whose name is Marion, is open-minded, very honest and
trusting, soft and kind. Dad is a ladies' man, the most talented
musician I've ever met, and although he has an alcohol problem
I legitimately thought he was Superman when I was growing up.
His name is Kovati Tui, but everyone calls him Vaki.

I learned early on that some people just aren't supposed to
be together, and my parents were two of those people. Dad just
couldn't articulate his emotions calmly, and he would scream
aggressively and scare Mum.

I watched, like you watch everything as a kid — Mum's
yelling, Dad's shoving, Mum's running away, Dad's chasing her.
It doesn't take much to figure out who's going to win the fight.
They're screaming and Mum's going, If you don't stop I'm gonna

call the cops, and then he's like, Call the fuckin' cops, I don't care. And then she's like, I bloody will then, and then she calls the cops and then, you know, I'm crying and they're all shook up and the cops arrive and they make Dad bugger off.

When they fought like that, I was afraid and I didn't like it — but I was never scared for my life or for Mum's like I would be in the coming years. In those early years, while it wasn't always nice for Mum, the context for me was generally still one of love. I knew I was loved, and I guess because I loved them both I was more like, Oh, the bloody eggs. I knew Dad was an egg, but Mum knew Dad was an egg even more than I did — and Dad was still often there, so they were both eggs. I knew there was a time limit on how long they could handle each other's company, and I'd be able to tell, Oh, you're gonna have to be careful guys . . .

Anyway, this particular memory is of a day when Mum and Dad were all lovey-dovey. It must have been in the early period of yet another fresh start and they were embracing each other, and then they were like, Oh come here Ruby, come and have a hug with us. I honestly wasn't even five and I was rolling my eyes like, Guys come on now, be realistic about this.

So I went up and joined in the hug like we're playing happy families, and Dad looked down at me with a huge, encouraging grin and said, Hey bud, do you want us to get married? Just say the word, do you want us to get married?

I looked up at these two grown-ass adults, and I thought, Who do you think you're kidding here? Honestly, with these two you could flip a coin on any day of the week to see if it was going to be good or bad. I looked straight in Dad's eyes. I felt a little bad because I could tell he wanted me to say yes and be part of this romantic moment. But instead I shook my head. No, I said. I don't want you to get married.

I think I'd always known it: I won't have parents if you stay together, but if you're apart, I've got a chance of being able to love you both. And then it won't be scary.

So I killed their moment with my bullshit detector. But that's why I always say, a kid knows when you're just playing pretend. I knew, at four years old, that it was best if these two did not get married. As a kid with parents who broke up early on, I know it's so much better to leave a hideously volatile environment than to try and force it to work. The kids know when it's not real. Staying together just for the kids and not changing anything makes the nights long, lonely and scary. Trust me, I've never forgotten the terror.

Keep it real. Be honest. Otherwise, the kids are gonna grow up thinking, We'll just bullshit our way through relationships too.

It was awful for Mum. I think she still held on to the fantasy of them being together. She had a kid, so of course she wanted things to work out for my sake. But it was never going to. And meanwhile the time between each argument was getting less and less.

It's quite buzzy growing up and realising that your parents were just doing the best they could with what they knew. After working through all the emotion, you just want to thank your parents for everything they got through. My parents were never meant to be forever and I've always known that.

————

They met at a music gig. Dad was the lead singer of a funk band — they'd do stuff like 'Mustang Sally' — and he's crazy talented. He was always in his own bands, but he was so good he always used to get called up to fill in for other bands. Often, the night before the gig the fill-in bands would send him the cassette tapes of all the songs they were going to perform. I remember him lying on the floor playing his bass guitar to the tapes all night, not reading any music or anything just listening and learning. He would kill the performance every time! To me he was always the best on stage by far.

But all his adult life he's had a problem with alcohol. He's an absolutely raging alcoholic, and he acknowledges that. It's just something he accepts. If he's happy he drinks, if he's sad he drinks. He used to do heaps of drugs as well, he was a real rock star, but now he's content with his lagers.

As I tell my story here, you'll see how this affected me through my childhood, but where I've got to now is that I've found a way to love him, even though so many people have washed their hands of him. We talk on the phone, but I don't let him call me when he's drunk because that's my boundary. I tell him, I love you when you're sober, Dad. I'll talk to you then.

When I was little I thought he was the coolest guy, and even though I always knew he had problems, and that he could be aggressive and didn't treat Mum right, he was always loving to me. He always said, I love you. You're the best, bud. My whole life he told me that.

So on that night they met, Dad would have been putting on the charm, centre of attention, controlling the room. He was cool as, in his leather jacket that he used to wear everywhere. He was the man, and Mum — herself so pretty, so lively — was captivated.

She was from that world of books and education and she had a university degree; he was an immigrant Samoan who'd been born in a village and for whom English was a second language. But when you're in love you're in love, and Mum was always too good at seeing the best in people.

Dad was trying his best — but it still wasn't easy for Mum. When Mum got pregnant with me, she had no parents and her only two siblings felt worlds away. I was born at home in Mum's flat in Island Bay in December 1991, two weeks after my due date. In the lounge was Mum, Dad and their midwife along with a small paddling pool, all waiting for me.

There were no complications and when I came out I didn't cry or make a fuss, I just peered around the room wondering who the heck woke me up from my sleep-in. Not much has changed there.

A few years later, when I was still a little kid, I heard that song 'You are my sunshine', and it gave me this real weird feeling of familiarity. I didn't know the song, but I *knew* the song. I asked Mum about it — Is it from a movie, Mum? And she was like, Oh, your dad sang that to you every single morning when you were in my belly. Holy, I thought. That's so buzzy! But it makes sense because I always felt very loved as a small child.

I think what brought them together was their sense of humour. It was a massive part of their relationship. There would be laughs and jokes and I remember Mum laughing till she cried — she really loved to do that, and it was quite common for us all to be laugh-crying at the same time.

Mum tried to see the good in him for a bit longer. But then Dad slipped back into his old bad habits, started drinking again which led to him being aggressive and unreliable, and eventually, Mum made him leave.

RUBY'S TRAINING BAG
Don't stay together for the kids' sake if it
means sacrificing your happiness and health.
They feel it and will do for years to come.

2. Beauty is in the eye of the beer-holder

Sunshine's streaming through the windows, Mum's blasting TLC's album *CrazySexyCool*, and we're cleaning the house together. I'm three, four, five, six, seven, maybe even made it to eight, and most of the time it's just me and Mum living here in the house. It's my favourite-ever house, one Mum bought for us — a beautiful old villa in a narrow, steep street in Newtown. I remember when we went to see it for the first time: me, Mum and her best mate, Carol, standing in the massive hallway — big enough to play soccer in — and Mum was so happy and proud. She was independent, had a great job, and I went to Wellington South Kindergarten on Owen Street, and then to Kilbirnie School. It honestly seemed like my whole childhood was there in that house, and it was only when we moved, that's when everything went bad. But that was a few years ahead.

Right now, in this memory, I'm with Mum, just me and her, cleaning . . . it's a weekend afternoon, and I'm helping and we're happy and we've got no problems. Mum really appreciates music — she actually named me after the singer Ruby Turner — and cleaning is fun when you do it together, to music. When you're a kid it's cool when they say, Oh, can you help with the dishes or whatever, or with a big job like using Jif on the bath. I love the feeling that we are achieving something together.

I've always loved doing anything if it's with other people.

I felt like everything was going to be OK because Mum was OK. I had my mum. She was the smartest person in the world. We used to laugh and joke a lot. You know, it's weird as a kid because people go, You're not allowed to swear — and yet the adults are all swearing everywhere, and on TV people are all swearing. So I'd say to Mum, Can I swear? And she'd be like, Yep, you can swear, so I'd sit there maybe for ten minutes going Fuck, fuck, fuck, fuck, fuck, just to get it out of my system. Then she'd be like, Are you finished? I'd say, Yeah. And then I wouldn't swear. Whatever swear word I'd heard, whether it was the F-word or whatever word, I'd just say it, like a hundred times, and she'd be laughing. It was cool and fun and I felt safe to do that and I wouldn't get into trouble. She was just the absolute super role model for me.

Mum is fifth-generation Kiwi from Scotland and Ireland. Her family settled on the West Coast all those generations ago, and that's where she's from. So I'm sixth-generation New Zealander on Mum's side, and the first generation born in New Zealand on Dad's side.

Mum's mum, people called her Sue, was a nurse and for a while they lived in Whakatane and Rotorua, which was such a contrast to the mostly white West Coast. Mum was always interested in cultures outside her own. She did her seventh-form year on an exchange in Thailand, so she's got guts, and has this real ability to empathise. I didn't know how to articulate this when I was little, but growing up I was often aware of a weird attitude from a lot of palagi people I met, but Mum was never like that. I felt like she was one of the only non-racist white people I knew, always open and receptive to anyone different to herself. She was just so, so lovely.

Mum went to university and studied English, then went to Polytech and studied for a diploma in graphic design. When I was little she had a great job as a graphic designer in Wellington, and it seemed so flash to me in her office, with white Mac computers and polished wooden floors.

She was a super-hero to me in that she was so super-smart — like, any word in the whole world, my whole life, I'd be like, Mum what does this mean? and she would always know without even having to look it up. Every single night she buried herself in a book when she got into bed, and it made me look up to reading, and that's the reason I am still a reader. I got *Harry Potter and the Philosopher's Stone* one Christmas, and it was just the best to have my very own novel to read.

At the back of our house, the property dropped away into a gigantic secret garden, as big as a rugby field I thought, and it was so cool — I learned to ride my bike there, practised my soccer skills. I went back when I was about ten, just to have a look, and I couldn't believe how small the back garden actually was. Turns out it was tiny — but to me then, it was a whole world.

Dad came in and out of our lives, unreliable — often didn't come when he said he would — but there often enough to have some good experiences, although it was never long before Mum would be throwing pizzas at him or something. When I was turning five I had a pirate-themed birthday party and he built me a pirate ship in the back yard, so for the next few years I had this big pirate ship to play in, swinging between two trees. I used to sit out there and rock in it for ages, imagining I was on the sea, sailing the world, just in my own little space. People are always asking why I have time for Dad now, and it's because of those years when to me he was a superstar who played soccer and was the strongest man on Earth.

At that time, Mum was completely on her own. Her dad died when she was quite young and her mum died when she was in her early twenties. She had one brother who lived down on the West Coast, Uncle Neil, who I sometimes stayed with in the holidays, and one brother over in Australia, Uncle Pete, but day to day she was doing it completely by herself. She was doing such a great job, and I was happy and confident. I felt I had everything I would ever need.

———

When I was maybe three, I got chicken pox. And then I passed it on to Mum and suddenly she couldn't cope. She was too sick to look after me, and she had no family of her own to call on, and Dad wasn't consistently on the scene.

Up until then Mum hadn't really reached out to my Samoan family unless it had to do with Dad. There are many photos of me being held by my aunties or cousins when I was a baby. My aunties always loved me like their own. Me and Mum had been to some family events, but Dad had mixed feelings towards his family. He was a bit of a black sheep, always chasing girls and drugs and the band and not wanting to go to church. All my aunties and uncles go to church still, but Dad doesn't.

He wasn't going to help Mum get to know his sisters. But when Mum got sick, she was on her knees. She had no choice but to reach out to my Samoan family. Mum went out on a limb and called this woman she'd only met once, and one of Dad's five sisters came straight round and took me. Later, Mum remembers saying to my Aunty Tala, I'm so sorry, I've got no money, do you mind . . . and Aunty just said to her, Marion, when are you going to understand I will never ever say no to Ruby? You don't even need to ask. It's family.

Aunties are like that, eh? They just want the baby — they're like, Oh come, come . . . and there were five of them waiting for me in my Samoan family. Even Grandad's sisters were alive at that time, and they all wanted to steal me and all the other cousins away. My middle name is Malae, after Grandad's sister, my dad's Aunty Malae Tuimavave (née Tui), who always cared deeply for me when she was alive.

So that was the first time I went to stay at my Samoan grandparents' house in Strathmore, just ten minutes' drive away from where Mum lived in Newtown.

Wellington has always been a place of love for me, and Grandad's house in particular was always full of people. All of Grandad and Grandma's kids lived there at one stage or another over the years, all ten of them, and they all had partners and kids. Every room had a whole family in it, parents and kids all in together. It's part of loving your parents, to stay with them for a bit. So it's kind of like they all did their bit in a way for Grandad and Grandma. I don't know if it was ever hard for the adults, living all together, but for the cousins it was so special.

When I started spending lots of time there, five of my father's siblings, and their partners and children, my cousins, were living there with Grandad and Grandma. And from that day on I pretty much had eight other parents, twenty other siblings — it was just a whole new world that opened up for me.

Mum, who'd been struggling to pay kindy and then after-school care, and always aware of being so alone, often says, Ringing Tala was the best thing I ever did in my life. Dad had been so much trouble for her, and she hadn't realised that in Samoan culture you've got all this family at your disposal. She fell in love with my aunties and uncles, and she loves them to this day.

And as for me, I remember being at after-school care a couple of times and it was dumb, running around with carers who didn't really care, so if I had a choice — that or hanging out with my cousins — I knew what I would choose.

Aunty Tala treated me like her daughter. She had five kids — the first, Sammy, died when he was three, a few years before I was born — but she took me in and I was particularly close to her son Hemi James who was around the same age as me. I learned that someone can love you like their own. Just so beautiful. She'd usually do the school pick-ups, collecting me with her kids every day. You don't understand the details as a kid, but I just know I was always there, always happy, always laughing and always fed.

Sometimes we'd get picked up from school by Grandad and Grandma, and Grandad would say, What do you wanna eat? And we'd scream, McDonald's! And he'd be like, Do you wanna be like Jonah Lomu? And we'd say, Yes, Grandad. And he'd say, Well Jonah didn't have McDonald's. And then he'd say, What do you want? And we'd just look at each other and we'd scream again, McDonald's!

I was the only cousin that had a European mum. Grandad called me the palagi, and one other cousin had a Māori mum and he called her the Mauli — out of the twenty cousins we were the only two who were not full Samoan. Grandad would go, Hey, where's the palagi? And I'd be like, Here, Grandad! I just always felt like part of the family, and there were always other kids around, and I loved it like that.

My Samoan family stuck to their own. There could be 40 people on a family trip, or going to church, but while they hung out only with Samoans, they never said anything bad about anyone who wasn't Samoan. Grandad and his family had all lived through the era of the dawn raids, when Samoans and other Islanders were spoken about badly, and blamed for everything that was wrong with New Zealand even as they took the poorest-paid jobs, but I think they would've just had the attitude that only God can judge other people — just put your head down, go to work. But then at the same time, nothing's talked about properly.

————

Dad might not have been full-time or diligent, but he was around, and while I was with Mum most of the time I'd go see Dad on the weekends, and I was fine with that, especially because Dad was by then living at Grandad's so I saw my cousins and aunties and uncles too. So I was fine with them living apart and me going from one to the other.

But Dad was going downhill again. One time Mum dropped me off, and I was racing in the door, up the stairs and straight into his room, but when I opened the door, I hit his head . . . what the hell? He was lying on the floor with this blonde lady that I'd never met. He was like, Oh sorry, give me five minutes, bud . . .

He stopped prioritising the weekends with me. The drinking was big, and he was seeing a lot of women, but the saving grace for me was — Oh, whatever then, I'll just run to the next room and play with my cousins. And they were always there, like they were always, always there — Aunty Pele and Uncle Tai's kids Oriana, Davis, Samuel and Hennie, and Aunty Tala's kids Teri Josie, Hemi James, Jamon and later on Merci.

There was one thing that I always did with Dad and that was wait in the car, often for hours. I would rather wait in the car than miss my weekend with him. I didn't care what he was doing. I was in the car; I was with my dad. I guess I genuinely thought that was quality time.

Looking back, I don't know how I did it — there were no phones in those days, so I had no games to play, nothing to do. He'd be going to the pub, doing the drug runs, picking up some weed or whatever, and he was never the kind to just grab it and go. It's always have a cup of tea, have a sesh. I'm like that, too — I can never just go to someone's house. I'm always late because I sit down and talk and I want to give people time, so I understood about Dad taking so long. If I got scared I'd just lock the doors. When he got back to the car late at night, I might get a fright and then I'd let him in and he'd be like, Oh, good girl, bud. If you get scared you lock the doors, good work. And I still loved it, like I wouldn't change it for anything.

One time, when I was maybe five or six, we were parked outside a pub. I was sitting there waiting, Dad was in there getting drunk, and next thing Aunty Tala was banging on the car going, Ruby, Ruby! She'd just happened to drive past with her son Hemi James and he'd spotted me in the car. It was cold and getting dark and I wasn't dressed warmly. She was like, Oh my gosh. She said she was going into the pub to find Dad. I didn't want Dad to get into trouble because of me. Aunty, no . . . She said, Don't worry, I won't say anything too bad. But when she got into the pub and she saw him playing pool, drinking, laughing, she saw red and she blew him up in front of everyone.

I didn't realise it fully at the time, but Dad let me down a few times back then. I still loved him and so it was like a confusing thing, but it was still love. There was another time when Dad had done something wrong and Aunty Tala took me to McDonald's, and once we'd got our food and were sitting at a table, she just started to cry. I didn't understand why because it was turning into an awesome day for me. I was getting some one-on-one time with my aunty, and going to McDonald's. She kept saying things like, Your dad tries, it's not his fault, and all of this, and I was just eating my burger like, I'm not sad, I'm happy.

Sometimes it seemed that Aunty Tala was the only adult in the whole situation.

It was around that same time when I got the first clue that I wasn't an only child. I loved Dad, but man he used to just yell sometimes, tell me to do things, yell and scream until I had to do it. So one day when we pulled up outside a random house, and he said, Go knock on that door, I got a sinking feeling because I knew I was going to have to do what he said.

I don't want to knock on someone's door, I said.

Go knock on that door and say I want to see my sister.

Why, Dad? I don't want to . . . I thought it was a prank. He hadn't started yelling yet, but that could happen at any minute. In fact, he was laughing. Do it.

I had to do it. I went up to the door of this house I had never seen before. My sister told me, years later, that she was ten when this happened, so that means I was five. I think he sent me because he thought I was cute and so the woman who lived there would be nice to me. Anyway, I knocked and eventually this lady answered the door. A complete stranger. I looked back towards the car, and then at her, and I said, Hi, my dad told me to come and knock on your door and ask to see my sister.

The lady went from confused to furious. She was looking for Dad, but she couldn't see him from where she was standing in the doorway. *Oh my gosh what am I doing?* And she said to me, You go and tell your father to go away and never ever come back here, OK? And I was like, OK . . .

I took off back to the car. I told Dad what she said, and he laughed. He didn't tell me who she was or whether I really had a sister. I decided it must all have been a joke. It wasn't that unusual. He used to make me go and talk to people, to ask for things. Even at Grandad's, we'd be hanging out in his room and he'd be like, Go ask Grandad for a smoke.

I don't want to . . .

Go!

I did wish he'd hang out with me a bit more. And this is the thing about love. Dad loved me, and I never doubted that, but just because someone loves you it doesn't mean they know *how* to love you.

Obviously, as a parent you can do things to help. You can be ready when the kid turns up, you can plan better, and not be hungover or wasted. Obviously I think like that, but I also think that, in Dad's weird way, he trusted me with those things. He took me everywhere, and I was like his little mate, and that's just how he was. That was time with my dad. This carried on all those early years when I was with him for weekends and then all the years after me and Mum moved away but I was with him for holidays. It wasn't very many years before I was joining in with him, going into those houses where the action was all about drinking and drugs, and seeing a side of life that for a while seemed to offer something I wanted.

But for now, as a small child, I got to spend the whole weekend with my dad, even if five hours of it was in the car, and even if he sometimes made me do things I didn't want to do. I knew he loved me because he took me with him. He didn't take anyone else. You're the best, bud, he'd say.

And there were such good times, like when Dad and I were driving from Wellington over to Masterton for a family birthday. We went up over the Rimutakas and then instead of going straight to the event, we drove all the way up to Palmerston North and went the long way round, just to spend time together. We picked up a hitchhiker. Dad's like that and I'm a bit like that — you don't do the logical thing, you do the fun thing. I do that a lot — if it's for fun and it includes someone, I'll do the long route or do it the hard way or the expensive way because then that person will have a great time, and it was like that with Dad, too.

With everything I have said about my dad, this is just how I saw it as a child trying to find their place and understand the world. Now, as an adult, I understand the huge culture shock and adversity my dad went through, both as a child and as an adult. He dealt with extreme racism, physical abuse, and an unsettling language and identity crisis as a child immigrant who wasn't given much explanation at all. My dad did whatever he could to survive and get through it. Although he struggles at times, I have found a way to love him as best as I can. Alcoholism is like a sickness you have to deal with and manage. Dad's sickness has forced me to find ways to love him, and this has actually made me a stronger and better giver of love. I wouldn't recommend growing your love skills this way, but I am still grateful for it. Because of Dad I try to look at all humans with an empathetic lens: There must be something good about this person somewhere, there must be something I can learn from them. Dad taught me so much about love.

As I got older I sometimes got irritated with all the waiting. Oh bro, I could've planned something else. But as the years went by, as I turned five and six and seven, I had fewer cousins to hang out with, because bits of the family kept moving, so I had less choice about who I spent the weekends with. Me and my cousin Hemi James were inseparable as kids, but one day he showed me a map of the world. He pointed at a tiny little spot, and he goes, We're here in Wellington.

Yeah, I said.

He pointed to another spot a few centimetres away. And we're moving all the way here, and he pointed to Perth.

What? What do you mean?

We're packing our bags and going here, and he pointed at Perth again.

They were moving away. My best mate, my favourite aunty.

With fewer cousins around, Dad's antics became less fun. He would be either laughing with me or yelling at me; there was no in-between. And I was getting so over the yelling. Sometimes he'd be like, Do you wanna come? And I'd be like, Not really.

RUBY'S TRAINING BAG
Just because someone loves you, it doesn't mean they know *how* to love you.

3. Samoan Superman

G randad, Tu'uga Tui, is the absolute king in our family,
a real pioneer of his generation. He has three matai
(chief) titles, Namulau'ulu Tai Tui, but he is mostly
known as Tui and has a great standing in his village. He was born
in 1933 in Samoa in the village of Vailoa in the district Palauli
on the island of Savai'i. He is one of fourteen children to Senele
and Sau Tui (née La'ulu). Us cousins have a nickname for him —
Grandman, because he's the grand family man. He's approaching
90 now, and has made another huge shift, to Brisbane where he
lives near Aunty Pae, his oldest daughter.

But back in the 1960s, in Samoa, he and Grandma, Avali'i
Tui, dreamed of taking their family to New Zealand for a better
life, with more opportunities for their children. In 1969, when
they were in their early thirties and already had seven children,
they achieved that. But at this time the New Zealand government
only allowed four children per family to enter the country, so
they brought their four eldest children — Uncle Fa'afetai or Tai
(whose name literally means 'Thank you' because he was their
first blessing of a child; he has since accepted the chiefly title
Autagavaia), Aunty Paepae, Kovati (my dad), and Aunty Teletala,

who wasn't the next oldest, but she'd been injured in a fire and so she skipped ahead of Aunty Tauava'e. Over the years Grandad did as he had promised and went back to get the rest of his kids.

It's not an easy thing to move a family from one country to another, and to begin a completely new way of life. Grandad and Grandma went through so much to give us all that better life. For them, as for many other families from Pacific Islands, it wasn't just that they were adapting to a new kind of society, new rules, new cultural understandings — there was also the added shock of racism. It wasn't long after they arrived that the New Zealand economy went into a downturn, and Pacific people, who had been encouraged to come to New Zealand to fill labour shortages in the post-war boom times, were targeted and blamed for everything from increasing unemployment to crime. They were the rogues who were ruining the country.

From the early 1970s it became horrible to be Samoan in New Zealand, and people like my dad grew up embarrassed and ashamed of being Samoan. For Dad, it was a really hard dynamic. He arrived in New Zealand when he was eight and it was a massive culture shock. He really wanted to be Kiwi, to fit into the palagi world, but he was still so young and new to so many things, and he got mocked and bullied at school for all the things he didn't understand.

But Grandad and Grandma would have just expected their kids to be grateful for being here and to appreciate how much of an effort it was. Nevertheless, with the move to New Zealand, all sorts of differences got created that wouldn't have been there otherwise. In that family, which eventually included ten kids, there were real differences — that first group of four moved with their parents from Samoa and so shared that experience from the beginning; others got left behind for years while Grandad and Grandma worked hard to get them here — that was Aunty Tauava'e, Aunty Pei'u and Uncle Seunape — and then others were born in New Zealand and never had that experience of Samoan village life: Uncle Hemi, Aunty Tala'ave, the late baby Tui and Uncle Ulimasao. That's a lot of stuff going on, and a pretty crazy dynamic between different family members.

I realise how lucky I am to have been born here, and to know my place so securely. I know where my dad comes from and I know where my mum comes from. And as a kid, if I wasn't good at the Samoan language, or didn't know everything about the culture that I should have, I had a 'get out of jail free' card — because, Oh, fair enough, you've got a palagi mum.

When Grandad arrived here he got a job at the Optoplast plastics factory in Miramar and he worked there for 25 years, 7 a.m. till 7 p.m. Monday to Friday, and then 7 a.m. till noon on Saturdays. Then he worked at another factory for ten more years. That's 35 years working his fingers to the bone for the family, and that's how he bought the house so many of us lived in. He was always working, at the factories or at his beloved Church, and if he wasn't working he was at home in his overalls gardening in the huge back yard at the family house — my placenta is buried out there, along with a couple of the cousins' — where he kept a massive vegetable garden. Any kind of vegetable, he'd grow it. We loved it when he was out there, because we could be on the tramp or on the swings and he was just there with us.

Nothing happened without him. Everything had to be run by him: Did you ask Grandad? Is it alright by Grandad? Not just the kids but even our parents' generation. To us, he was pretty much a god.

Living in Wellington, he continued to earn respect — he played the organ at church, Pacific Islanders' Presbyterian Church in Newtown, and anyone who visited from Samoa would come to his house, have a cup of tea and talk. Right into his seventies he was like Superman — looking after everyone, able to hold on to the doorframe and do a pull-up. Do it again, Grandad! He'd bought into the New Zealand definition of success, and he smoked like a chimney and drank Coke every day.

Grandma's job was to look after the kids, cook, clean. She was always feeding everyone; I could never understand how she fed so many mouths. I have lots of good memories of Grandma. The late Avali'i Sesela Tomuli was also born in 1933, on the island of Upolu, and was one of nine children to Sesela Tomuli and Fa'aulu Tomuli. There were a few of us cousins that got to know her softer side. Grandma was pretty much after-school care for all us cousins, looking after us, feeding us all.

Towards the end of her life she got a bit less mobile and had trouble moving around. One time I was the last grandkid left at the end of the afternoon, waiting for Mum to collect me, and me and Grandma were playing with a ball in the lounge. The lounge was huge, and she was lying on a couch, and she'd throw it and I'd have to try and catch it. She would throw dummies and make me step the wrong way, and we would both laugh loudly. We played right up until Mum walked in to pick me up.

Everyone thought Grandma was angry a lot, especially Dad, but I got to know this other side, and her smile was so warm to me. She loved to give us hugs and kisses, but it was just so hard for her to move. She died in 1999 of a brain haemorrhage from a fall. That was a real tragedy. I sometimes wish I'd grown a bit older before she passed. Maybe I could've helped a little with her eating or something, knowing what I know now about nutrition.

When I think about what my whole family went through to make this new life here in New Zealand, I feel it so strongly down into my soul: I'm not going to waste my life, I'm not going to just sit here on my laurels. The generation before me went through heaps of trauma, but us, the next generation, we can be so grateful to them, and so proud of our Samoan heritage. We know we can have happiness here. We can do whatever we want and we don't have to work in a factory. We were born here, but we know where our parents came from, and we know who we are. I have never felt embarrassed for being a Samoan New Zealander — I've got the best of both worlds and I know my culture on both sides.

Come on, Rubes. I'm going to do something with my life. How dare I not do it? How dare I not try and be the greatest I can be with this Tui name on my back?

————

Oh my gosh, the prayers. There was nothing that showed that Grandad was the head of the family so much as our nightly loku (prayers). My grandad's a devout Christian, like all Samoan grandads are, so every morning he'd do a prayer that seemed to last for hours, and then every night, every single night, the call would come, words you never wanted to hear if you were halfway through the last level of fighting in Tekken 3 on the PlayStation: Sau fai le loku. Come and do the prayer. And we would all groan, because that means you're about to sit with your legs crossed for two hours.

At those words, everyone in the whole house, out of every corner, no matter how young, no matter how old, has to come into the lounge. You really don't know how many people are in the house until this moment, but you all squeeze in, one after another, sitting on the floor in a circle, and then we kick off singing 'Fa'afetai I Le Atua', the same every time, and then Grandad talks about the Bible. Grandad studied at Bible college but didn't become a pastor, but every night he gets to run his own church service. He does his testimony, he talks about the Bible. If there are enough kids there it turns into a quiz.

You know how during Samoan language week you learn how to say things like Talofa lava (Hello) and What is your name, and How are you? Well, my first words in Samoan were not these. Mine were:

O ai na faia oe? (Who is the lord?)
    O Le Atua (God)

O ai lou Faaola? (Who is our saviour?)
   Iesu (Jesus)

O ai na fau le va'a? (Who made the boat?)
   Noa (Noah)

There were many more questions like this, and I knew them all by heart. It became a game among us cousins to see who knew them best. As the only palagi, Grandad was always so impressed when I knew them.

Then, after the quiz, it was time for us all to take our turn praying.

If you can talk you can do a prayer, and when I was the littlest, he'd start with me. Right, Ruby, you go first, and I'd be like, Thank you for the food, Thank you for this house, Thank you for my cousin, she's the best. Then the next youngest cousin would go — it moves through the ages. By the time I was seven or eight I'd learned that there's actually a way to pray — later on I remember Dad telling me the rough sequence to go in. There's the acknowledgement where you honour and praise God; then you ask for forgiveness for your sins; next comes gratitude; and then there's the requests, like Dear Lord please look after my family. Then it's amene, and it's the next person's turn. As you get older, it is expected that your prayer gets longer. Finally it comes back to Grandad and he is the grand finale — and believe me, he can grand finale for ever.

I'm getting pins and needles in my feet, and some little kids cry and if they cry too much they get taken out. If I get restless there are death stares. Ssshh, Ruby! I look around and I see that some of the aunties and uncles are asleep, even though they've been telling me to concentrate.

To be fair, one thing I always remember about Grandad's prayers is that in the final part, the requests section, he would always pray for God to be with every member of the family and he would say everyone's names. He never forgot anyone, including my mum — I remember him always asking God to watch over Marion.

And then — finally! — Grandad says the words that everyone's been waiting for: Lo matou Tamā e, oi le lagi . . . the first line of the Lord's Prayer. Everyone sits up, sparks back to life, and we complete that prayer together. One more song. And then it's finished.

Sometimes I would think of the missionaries who brought Christianity to Samoa, and I would think, Stuff you, man! But obviously there's all the good values you learn, like patience and being quiet for two hours in a row, and you also learn to be a really good orator. You're used to speaking in a room full of people, and you learn about the chiefly, sacred Samoan language which is quite different to ordinary Samoan chat — it's more theatrical, more poetic. One thing I'll never forget about Grandad is how he could hold a room full of hundreds of people in the palm of his hand because he was such a good orator. In the hall of the church in Newtown he would have them all silent and then all roaring with laughter, and all without a microphone. So there are really cool parts to it, don't get me wrong. But when you're six years old and you just want to play and eat and you have to sit there for two hours, that's not fun.

———

I'm a tiny baby, dressed in my best baby clothes, being held by my mother as she stands up the front of the Pacific Islanders' Presbyterian Church in Newtown, next to my father. I'm screaming. Any minute now Mum will have to hand me over to the pastor so I can be baptised and she's scared about how I'm going to react. Grandad and everyone are in the church. It's a huge moment in our family, like these things always are, and Dad's going, It's OK, it's OK, but I just won't stop screaming. The moment comes and Mum says sorry to the pastor and puts me in his arms. He's a huge man, hot inside his long clothes, with beads of sweat on his generous forehead. Maybe I feel his heat and his bulk and it comforts me. But whatever, a miracle happens. I stop crying. My eyes find his face and I stare and I relax and I'm happy.

Because of the back and forth of my life I wasn't as constantly involved in church as my cousins were, but whenever I was in Wellington I would tag along. And while my fa'a Samoa is not good enough, it's the church and the loku, the evening prayers, that's kept it alive in me. The repetition, the singing. Tagging along to Sunday School, White Sunday, church in general — I know many people think that sounds boring, but honestly it wasn't. Everyone in that church could have been a top ten singer. There were so many young people and they'd always be performing, singing and acting scenes from the Bible, really amazing showmanship.

The women in their fine dresses or their puletasi and their hats, the men in their lavalavas with shirts and ties. Grandad was over there playing the organ, not even looking at the instrument but laughing, my cousins were in the choir, the church would be on its feet because the music is that good.

Here in New Zealand, the church is a focal point for Samoan people in the same way the marae is for Māori — everything happens there, in the church and the hall and the kitchens, and you've just got to find something fun to do, and you muck around there all day. It was an amazingly inspiring place and I found out how much I was capable of through my family pushing me.

If you wanted, you could go to church every single day, and it probably was a saving grace for the Samoan community, a safe place when times were tough — a place to celebrate being Samoan, and all the talents and glories of these amazing people. When I was staying at Grandad's we'd go to the 10 a.m. English service on Sunday, then go home for Tona'i, the big lunch, and then there was the Samoan service at 3 p.m. and Grandad and

Grandma would go back for that, but I always tried to get out of that one.

I'm three. My older cousin Oriana is dressed up and she's performing the siva, the traditional dance, and she looks like a Samoan goddess and I'm awestruck. I look up to my older cousins so much; I always wanted an older sibling. My aunty has made me this cool-as Samoan outfit for the occasion, a little red dress and headdress, and a shell necklace, and she's swiped the red lipstick across my cheeks, and now she's pushing me out onto the floor. Go, go. So I step out and I don't know how to do the dance but I just copy Oriana, shaking my hands around, and everyone is coming up and throwing money at us. I'm not doing it right but it must look cute, this three-year-old trying to copy this thirteen-year-old. I don't know where else in my life I would get an experience like that at such a young age.

Grandad made me learn a long Samoan verse to say at White Sunday one year, and every night he'd make me practise it. Why do I have to? I'm not good at this . . . And he'd go, It's fine, if you make a mistake it doesn't matter. But I stood up in front of the church and I said it and I knew the whole thing and that was so buzzy to me. I absorbed the message: Samoan is in me and it *is* me, and I am proud of it.

Back in the day Grandad made my dad and all his siblings perform in a band; it was called Feedback. They had to practise for hours — they could all harmonise perfectly, probably got hidings if they didn't do it properly, but that was their role. In my generation it was the same — my cousins who came from big families were always playing together in bands that anyone anywhere in the world would recognise as top ten standard. But whereas in the palagi world talent is celebrated as an individual thing, in the Samoan world it's about something different: what can you offer to this community, to your family? It's kind of like a village where everyone has a role to play. It's a duty in that you need to play some part. If you can't sing the lead you harmonise, if you can't harmonise you do the piano, if you can't do the piano, you do the guitar — there will be *something* that you can do well enough, and you don't do it because you want that centre-stage attention but because you want to be part of everything.

My role was more about jumping in to support the lead singer. I can jump in well enough where it's needed. I'm good enough to feel OK about doing a singing item when our family went to Samoa together, but there's no question I'm definitely not the best in the family musically. I'm not like my cousins, but they always made me feel safe enough and welcome enough to always be able to do that.

I'm in awe of my family for all the things they can do.

Dad never came to anything at church. He hated it. And yet, he was how people knew me. Oh, you're Vaki's daughter. How is he? The history of our genealogy isn't always pleasant, but it can still help us make sense of why we are the way we are. It helps us understand identity. My family isn't perfect, but neither am I. And I'm absolutely OK with that.

RUBY'S TRAINING BAG
I'm going to do something with my life.
How dare I not try and be the greatest
I can be with this Tui name on my back?

4. When Tui worlds collide

Playing sport was always something I associated with that warm family feeling of doing things with my cousins. They were all really good at sport. I had heaps of boy cousins, not many girl cousins my age, and I remember we loved WWE, professional wrestling — well they did, so I pretended I did, too. We'd play it on the tramp, and my first concussion was when we were flipping each other and I flipped right off the tramp and onto my head. I sat up and there were bright lights spinning around my head. Holy . . . But then I jumped straight back on the tramp and we just kept going.

I got my first rugby uniform when I was three, the red and black of the Poneke Rugby Club, and that was because my Uncle Tai, the oldest of Dad's siblings, was coaching Samuel and Davis, my older boy cousins, in the under-6s. Hennie, who was my age, started going along and he got the uniform, and so to Mum I was like, Can I? I wanted the boots and everything. I wanted to be involved and be the same as the others.

So we got the uniform and the boots, but then I didn't enjoy it at all. One of the boys pulled my hair, and I didn't understand what was going on. The crowd of kids with the ball would be over there and I would be over here picking dandelions.

I was never a sports freak for the sake of the sports — it was always about the inclusion. I would do anything to be part of the group. My cousins were all doing karate, so I started that too, but then they all stopped and Dad wouldn't let me quit. I was only doing it to be with family, but he and Mum both wanted me to know that sport isn't just this Sunday lunch. If you want to do it, you have to do it properly.

Dad had been really good at rugby when he was younger, and he won't be quiet about how he could have been an All Black if he didn't have to go to church. But by the time I was about five he had moved on to soccer, and he was pretty good at it. I watched him, and I thought: I'll play that. And it turned out I was pretty good at it, too.

Despite everything, I looked up to Dad and wanted to be like him. At that time, in my first year of school, I had long hair that I wore in these big pigtails. I would cry every morning when he brushed out the tangled knots. Dad's hair was shaved at the back with just a bit on top, and I wanted to be like him, so one day I asked him through my tears if I could get it cut like his. He took me to the hairdresser and I got it cut just like his, and we also got a cross shaved into the back of my head. I thought I was cool as. My poor mum. When she saw it she was like, What the heck? Every school day she coloured in the cross with a felt-tip so no one could see it.

So when I joined a soccer team, the Island Bay Hammer-heads, to start with everyone thought I was a boy. This was the time when more and more of my cousins were moving away. I didn't have so many to hang out with after school, and now sometimes I had soccer training after school anyway, and I started to love that — I loved the oranges and the half-time and the high-fives and the way we all came together, and I felt like I had heaps of new mates, although in reality I think the other parents forced their kids to be friends with me — the weird-looking brown girl/boy — because I was such a good player. But for me, this was like another set of cousins: This is awesome, I love this. And the better I played, the more mates I had.

I would do anything to be a part of the team. There was one day when I had a tummy bug, and as we were driving to soccer I spewed into a plastic bag. For Mum it was obvious. You can't play soccer today, she told me.

I couldn't believe what I was hearing. What the heck! Yes I can!

I pleaded with her. Please let me go, please let me go. In the end, I was so adamant that she gave in and drove me to the game. I ran on, played, ran off and spewed my guts out on the sideline, ran back on and scored a goal.

Honestly, I just loved it: I don't care if I'm sick, this is awesome, I'm with my team.

———

Food and eating, sleep and solitude, work and aspiration, love and discipline — it didn't take long for me to figure out that there were some really huge ways my two worlds were different from each other.

When it came to food and eating, Mum taught me about nutrition, about correct portions and different food groups. She always provided a good, healthy, wholesome meal with carbs, meat and veg. Porridge in the mornings. She even got me those vitamins for kids. Tick all the boxes. She helped me understand that food fuelled my body. Fizzy drinks are a special treat. It's not that you can't have them, just don't have them all the bloody time. Which was real weird because then I'd go to my Samoan side and there'd be fizzy everywhere. Those big dollar-each bottles, all the time, all day. If you're thirsty, just go get one. It's cheap, probably cheaper than water; go get it. I'd be like, Oh Aunty, it's only for special occasions, and they'd all laugh and roll their eyes, Oh, Marion! they'd say to each other. But they respected it.

On my Samoan side, food is more about an experience you enjoy together. It's an event. McDonald's is gourmet in Samoa, KFC is unbelievably gourmet. The Tona'i, the big Sunday feast, is an absolute sight — lu'au, kalo, pisupo, sapasui, and nobody does coconut rice like Grandman. There was so much food and just eating, eating, eating all the time, eating all the leftovers, everything, to celebrate being here in this land of plenty, being here together, being family. Dad would inhale it all — all the bones, the tails off the prawns. Grandma would eat till everything on her plate was gone, even the carcass of the crayfish. At breakfast time you made a couple of towers of buttered white bread, and eggs, eggs, eggs. There was always more than you need but that's because it's an experience in itself. Eat whatever you want because we're eating all together and it's mea'ai time. Have it all, have whatever, just eat to your soul's content. And I remember the sounds of everyone enjoying their food too — the uncles licking their knives, chewing with their mouths open, cracking bones, slurping, using their hands — it's pure enjoyment, the way food is supposed to be experienced.

The whole sense of personal space and structure was very different between the two worlds. At Mum's, I had my own room, my own big, green bunk and, because I was the only child, my own toys. I went to bed at a set time.

But at Grandad's, there was never any *mine*, no such thing as having your own bedroom. Everything was everyone's and I had to learn to share. There might be twenty people in the house, every room filled with a family, and at night the lounge became this gigantic bedroom with mattresses put down next to each other, joined up as if they were one mattress with what seemed to me like unlimited blankets and places to sleep. They put the TV on and you just fell asleep while you watched. I felt so safe and loved and warm. The snoring would start and the heavy breathing and I would be the last one awake, watching movies all night. There were no bedtime rules. The TV was on all night and the aunties would get up really early, so it was like the house was awake 24/7.

There were more subtle differences too, such as the attitude to education, work, life and happiness.

Out of all my cousins only a couple of us went to university. That wasn't too much of a focus — we talked more about getting a job and starting to contribute to the family. That's changing now as fresh generations come up, but in those earlier years the whole point of coming to New Zealand was to earn a living. That's why Grandad and Grandma left their village to come here — they were ambitious for a better life. You had to have a job, and it was never: Do you enjoy your job, are you happy? It was just: Do you *have* a job? And someone had to have a car so that everyone could get around, and everyone contributed towards buying that car, so there was always this commonality of purpose, a sense of a joint venture. *Our* venture.

The matter of whether you were happy in your job was never talked about because there was so much else. The family days, the food, the playing together outside . . . it's like you had so much love around you, you didn't need your job to make you happy.

Whereas for Mum in those days, a good job was a personal achievement. It was important to have a good job, and to enjoy what she was doing. Her pay was her pay, just as her responsibilities felt like hers alone. I understood that having a good job was part of what made someone feel good about themselves.

And then my mum's brother, Uncle Neil, had his own business in the tourism industry on the West Coast, and that was something else again. I saw how on the one hand you might work your ass off for 70 hours a week for minimum wage, and if you want more money you work more hours; or you can own the business, start your own company. Of course, as a child I wasn't so conscious of those options and possibilities, but now I see clearly what I was given through my two families.

In my Samoan family, love was massive and fully expressed, but so was the discipline, and both those aspects were very different to my palagi side. I vividly remember my cousins getting massive hidings, punched in the face and scary stuff like that. It was different for me. Dad associated that kind of discipline with Samoan culture and he was embarrassed about it and rejected it. Sometimes he got really upset at what would happen to my cousins.

One of our cousins snuck out at night from Grandad's house where she was living, put pillows in her bed, but she got caught and man . . . Grandad really laid into her. In Samoan culture, you've got to just take it. You go down and you beg for forgiveness and you take it. You're not supposed to hit back or argue about it. My cousin was going, Forgive me, and Grandad carried on, and I was just like, *Holy* . . . Dad tried to tell Grandad to stop.

There's a lot of love in Samoan culture, but the hidings drove me nuts. A cousin the same age as me got hit real bad, his dad would just full-on punch him in the face like an adult, and he'd go down and have to stand up, take another. And whatever he'd done wrong, I knew he didn't even mean it. But the violence is so closely tied to the loving side that you can only really understand it from deep inside the Samoan culture. And maybe you only see it clearly when you step away and get a different perspective.

The bigger the hiding you get, the more you must have deserved it. And rather than being something that alienates you from the family, the hiding actually draws you tighter, in a way. If someone's getting a hiding, the attitude is never, *poor you*, it's like, *what did he do?* He dishonoured the family. That's what people think.

And then when it's over, it's over.

In contrast, Mum and Uncle Neil were never touchy-feely or said I love you, but they could sit there and talk really well together about all these technical and political theories, and their conversation had real substance. I never heard raised voices in Uncle Neil's house, not once. On the Samoan side they didn't articulate ideas in that same way, but there were always hugs, kisses, food — oh my gosh, amazing love actions; but then, when they got upset, they couldn't sit down and have a conversation about that either. It was action again. It was physical.

You go to church for hours with your family, then you sit there and eat, *eat*, for three hours straight and then you wash your hands and have a cup of tea and you laugh and you sing. And then when it's bad, you just smash. You smash this up, use this, anything — smash, smash, smash. So it's all a very visceral experience. When you're loved, you feel like you have everything. When you muck up, oh my gosh, it's so scary. But it is tied up with honour. In Samoan culture, you have to physically go through pain to wash yourself of dishonour, just as you have to physically experience the abundance if somebody loves you.

To palagi, that's sometimes considered barbaric. In palagi culture, to dishonour someone you write a letter or you have a meeting or you get a lawyer and have a judicial hearing; to honour them, you write a recommendation or be a referee for a CV. It's different worlds.

But there is so much important change going on. My generation — people that were born in New Zealand, who are called New Zealanders on their passports — have to try and get it right. The context has changed for our people and our practices. There are whole new ways of disciplining people — for instance, in the old days you might bash a kid because they didn't go to school, but now there are detentions in place, a whole new system. The danger is that we might lose the good things along with the things we don't like. This is such an important time in our culture.

The good side of Samoan life that we never want to lose is: family never says no. It's an unbreakable bond. In the palagi world, people often talk about being alienated, about not knowing who they are. In the Samoan culture, we know where we fit; we know where we're from, and that we're loved.

Growing up in two worlds, oh my gosh, now I'm so grateful. So grateful, because I feel like it's a little bit easier for me to be kind to other people. I understand more about why people do the things they do, and that there's always more than one way of seeing things.

———

I learned from the world around me. I observed the effects that certain behaviours had on people, and when I got told off by the people I loved or I saw something happen to people I loved, I really took it in. Perhaps it's that I've always had empathy. But I do feel that all kids know the difference between right and wrong.

Dad was really trying hard not to treat me like his parents treated him, so he didn't want to bash me. Sometimes he'd slap my ass, quite hard, and this one time he got real angry with me. I was crying, and I ran to Mum. Dad broke down, his head in his hands, crying that he was so sorry, he didn't mean to and Mum was like, Bro, what the hell! And I remember knowing he had gone too far. *You went too far.*

It was the same when they were arguing and the cops had to come. That's too far. I just knew. I was learning what wasn't right.

Another time it was me that didn't do the right thing. My Aunty Tala took me and my cousins to see a Spice Girls show — not the real Spice Girls, but a look-alike show — and I knew the one who was playing Posh Spice because she'd been in the same band as Dad. So when I saw her on stage I was so excited, and me and one of my cousins left our group without telling anyone, and we ended up getting backstage. He got nervous and said he was going back to his mum, but I didn't want to. I was about five or six years old, and I didn't think about how worried Aunty Tala would be. But when I finally did go back to where she was, she was so upset. She normally never yelled or got mad at me, but this time she really went off: *I didn't know where you were! If you do that ever again, I'm never taking you with us ever again* . . . And I realised how what I'd done had affected her, and I would do anything rather than lose the best part of my life.

I also learned about good behaviour. There was a time when Dad lost a wad of cash. He'd just had it, and now it was gone. He was beside himself, looking everywhere. And then I found it — it had got tangled up in the sheets on my bed, and when I gave it to him he was so happy he broke down. Immobilised with gratitude. Do the right thing, give the money back — whoa, I thought, that was the right thing to do! And I saw how when you do the right thing it actually affects people hard out.

I loved those early childhood years in Wellington — my school, my soccer, my cousins and friends. It was my home, it was where all the good stuff happened. I learned so many important things. I wanted to stay there forever.

RUBY'S TRAINING BAG
There's always more than
one way of seeing things.

5. Can't fight 'em maul

But then Mum met her next partner. We'll call him Rick. I was seven or maybe nearly eight at the time.

There was a pub she and Dad used to go to in town where they played pool. Mum loved it — she had cool mates there and sometimes I'd go with them and play pool, and sometimes Mum went with just her mates. One night she met this new guy there. She'd been trying to break up with Dad, and she got together really quick with Rick and almost straight away he was talking to her about how he wanted to gap Wellington.

To begin with, Rick put on his good behaviour. He'd come for dinner and be kind of jokey with me. He wasn't funny but I laughed just to be polite. Even though he was being nice, I always had a weird feeling that he didn't really like me. He told Mum he was a landscape designer — although he never did any landscape jobs the whole time he was with Mum — and he started doing things in the back yard to add to the value of her house.

The first thing he did was take my pirate ship away. He built a pond where the pirate ship had been, and he put fish in it. He built a small outdoor fireplace, and that night we had our dinner outside, sitting around this new fireplace. They began arguing, and I went to sit on the steps that went from the back yard up to the kitchen, watching them. It got heated, and then he pushed her. She fell backwards.

Well, I thought, that's the end of him. Mum will break up with him now. My logic made sense to me. She broke up with my dad because he yelled and pushed, so why would she put up with the same stuff from this random new person? Never mind, Mum, you'll find another one. And I went inside and left her to tell him it was over.

The opposite happened. He moved in. It quickly got worse. Of course it did — those first signs were red flags. It's complicated in the adult world, but from a kid's point of view it seems pretty simple. Mum changed. She had always been a strong woman, happy enough, but now she was in an abusive relationship again. Like most women in those circumstances she probably blamed herself.

It wasn't long at all before I found out I was going to have a sibling. She was pregnant. I was so excited — it was all I'd ever wanted. By the time she was showing a little bit, Rick had convinced her to leave Wellington, and in the blink of an eye we sold our house, the house I loved and wanted to live in my whole life, and moved to what felt like the middle of freakin' nowhere — Tākaka in Tasman.

It feels shocking to write about it like this, but it did seem shockingly fast to me. One minute I had my old life that I loved; next minute everything had changed.

Now we were far away from Wellington, from my Samoan family, from my school and my soccer team and my mates. Mum was far away from her job, her mates, and her support structures. I now know that this is what abusive men do — separate their partner from other people, isolate them so there is no one there to witness, to criticise and to tell them this isn't good.

With the money from her Newtown house, Mum bought

a business on the main road through Tākaka township. It was a clothing shop, Heavenly Bodies, at the front, and there was a house at the back. As she got bigger and bigger, bulging pregnant, she worked every day in that shop and running the house while Rick, it seemed, did nothing except get stoned. He collected a sickness benefit — said he'd been knocked out when he was a teenager or something — and he said he was an artist, so he spent his time in the shed, supposedly being an artist. As far as I could see, he didn't contribute in any way, but now that we were in Tākaka he was always criticising Mum, telling her she was stupid, shouting at her from morning till night. I found it very confusing, and I hated being at home when he was there.

While at the very beginning in Wellington he was all jokey and nice to me, he didn't bother with that any more. I now had no doubt that he didn't like me, and he took any excuse to tell me off. A palagi, he was openly resentful of Samoans, and eventually told me he believed Samoans were criminals, that they stole and raped and were the scum of the earth, and when I heard that it made sense of the way he was towards me. He didn't say that stuff when Mum was around, only to me.

I knew that my best plan for fitting in to my new school was through sport. I wanted to join the soccer team, but the coaches weren't interested in the fact that I knew how to play and was a good striker, so they put me on the bench, only letting me into the game part-way through in a backfield position. But I got the ball and dribbled it up, passed all these people, and was trying to tell the strikers where to put themselves. Then I did a mean-as pass through to one of them, and they got a shot right in front of the goal.

I remember the coaches running on the field going, Oy you, you get off — Ruby, go to the front, go out there, and I was like, Bro, I frickin' tried to tell you, I'm not bad at this game.

As soon as people discovered I was good at sport, they started to take me seriously. It could be any sport — and especially in this shocking time when I suddenly wasn't happy in my home, I loved how it connected me to other people, gave me mates who respected me. I tried a bit of rugby but it wasn't serious as it was such a little school, and athletics. Whatever it was, I always tried to win.

When it came time for the baby to be born, there were serious complications and Mum had to be helicoptered to Nelson hospital, and we sped over the Tākaka hill to be with her. The birth seemed to take days — I'd be with her, then I'd go to sleep, and when I woke up it was still going on. I found out, as an adult, that the complications were so bad during labour she nearly died giving birth. I held Mum's hand to help her, and in the end they had to pull the baby out, and I remember watching him come out and the panic because he wasn't breathing. They rushed a long tube down his nose and started pumping it right in front of me, then the baby started screaming. Then I got to cut the cord, and that was really cool. And there was Dane, my little brother, born in the midst of so much drama. From then on he was my little buddy. But from then on, things between Rick and Mum got worse and worse.

I didn't understand at the time, but Mum had postnatal depression and was really struggling, and Rick got louder and louder with her. It was so stupid. Like Mum would buy the wrong sugar or something and he would scream at her endlessly.

Rick couldn't not be stoned, and while he did other stuff every now and then, the dope was his main thing. I thought it was normal for adults to smoke dope, so when I was in the township one day and I saw one of the guys Rick smoked with, I said, Are you going to smoke some dope with Rick? I didn't think it was a big deal. I didn't think it was any different than drinking a beer. But when I got home, Mum and Rick sat me down and told me, Look, you cannot talk about it in the streets like that. I had embarrassed that guy. I was real pissed off about that. I was thinking, I'm not the one breaking the law, I'm not smoking the weed. If you're embarrassed, don't do it. I just thought they were stupid, and that this whole situation was stupid. Come on, Mum, I thought. You just got out of one bad relationship; now you're in this one.

Rick must also have been up to something, because he ended up pissing the wrong people off. We came home one day and our whole house had been turned upside down by the cops — everything was everywhere, as if we'd been robbed. Mum was really upset, but it just made me more pissed off. Like, what do you *think* is going to happen? And we couldn't even ring the cops, because it was the cops who'd done it.

So pretty quickly we had to move out of that town as well. Poor Mum had poured all this time into her business and I had made a place for myself with the sports, and then we had to move again. We hadn't even been there a year.

———

As far as I'm concerned, Mum should've left this guy ages ago. Should've left him in Wellington when he pushed her, should've left him in Tākaka when we got raided by the police. But instead, we headed further into the wilderness with him. We moved to Canvastown, an even tinier place in the Marlborough district, the kind of place that's defined by how far away it is from other places, with those other places also being far away from anywhere: 10 kms from Havelock; 17 kms to Rai Valley. A middle-of-nowhere place where Rick could do all the drugs he wanted. And we weren't even actually in Canvastown, we were five kilometres out of town in a house on a huge section, and on every side of us was farmland. There were no other houses in sight, no neighbours — just the road going past, and the dark-green Wakamarina river on the other side of the section. He could push her around and scream at her and do whatever he wanted, and there was no one who might hear something going on and call the police. No one to help. As soon as I saw that house, I knew what it meant.

His outbursts weren't an occasional thing. They were frequent. When I heard it starting, I'd grab my little brother and I'd take him to a far corner of our section or into the sleep-out, as far away as we could get from the house. I'd take toys to distract him, or my little radio to block the noise of the screaming. When the screams got loud, I'd get louder too. My job was to hide my little brother from what was going on. I didn't very often actually see it, but I could hear it — the sound of shoving, the screams, the yelling. Once, though, and my memory of this is very vivid, I could see it because they were in the kitchen, and the kitchen window could be seen from where we were outside. The kitchen was a galley — that is, a dead end — so she was stuck at the end and he was coming at her, and I saw she grabbed the kettle to try threatening him with the hot water so he'd back up, but he wouldn't, and he hooked her around the face. She's tiny, my mum, skinny, and he was roaring at her, roaring like he wanted something, but I don't even know what he wanted — and that was the frustrating bit, like, What do you even want? I couldn't make any sense out of it at all. And yet it could go on for hours. Five hours. It seemed endless. And obviously Mum was in no state to take care of Dane after that.

My mum, who had done so much to build her life, and tried so hard to get out of her relationship with Dad, had ended up with someone even worse. Rick never hit Dane, but I worried a lot about what was going on for Dane when Rick was screaming at Mum, because it was impossible to shield him from it all the time. Kids know when something is wrong.

Meanwhile, Mum never stopped working. *He* never worked, and Mum was supporting all of us. She had bought the house with her own money, and then she went out and got any job she could. She waitressed at a cafe in Havelock and then had another job after that. She quickly became the person her boss trusted, because she's such an honest person, so she worked longer hours, staying behind after the shop closed to count the money. I sometimes saw her, exhausted after being on her feet all day, and I'd remember how she had been in Wellington, a hugely respected graphic designer — she was flash, her job was flash and she loved her job. And now she's a waitress in a cafe, at her wits' end. Rick was always yelling about how useless she was and I would think, Why are you calling my mum useless when you don't even work?

I'd get up before her to catch the bus to school, and then when I got home, she would still be at work. Rick would be there waiting and as soon as I turned up he was like, Sweet, and he'd go out to his shed and leave Dane with me. He would only speak to me to tell me off, or to tell me to do something. My job every day after school was to do the dishes and look after Dane, change his nappy, keep him happy. I was nine and then ten, then eleven, and it was honestly just me and the baby at home all the time, and I felt very strongly that his care was all on me.

Then Mum would get home. By this stage it was often after dark, and she would make dinner, feed us, and get ready to do it again the next day. All of us on eggshells in case he erupted. And he often would. It would begin with a niggle about how useless she was, and turn into hours of ranting about how she'd bought the wrong thing or left the paper on the table, or anything. Anything at all. She was very depressed, I think, but she survived by constantly working, and in the weekends we'd do the grocery shop, driving an hour to Blenheim to the nearest supermarket where we'd buy the absolute cheapest stuff. Ninety-nine-cent shampoo, conditioner and budget soap all in one — and you had to be real sparing with it. We just had no money.

I hated that life, and I hated that I hated being at home. I wanted to love being at home. I hated being home by myself with the baby, even though I loved Dane. But in myself, I was sad and lost, not wanting to exist yet so scared of what would happen if I wasn't there. What would happen to Dane? Who would look out for him? And if something happened to Mum, no one would know.

At that stage I didn't exactly fear for her life. I feared for her safety. But really, I just couldn't even think. I was just a child, and I didn't know enough to know exactly what to fear.

Towards me, Rick was rude and abusive and never kind, but he wasn't usually violent, although it was scary sometimes.

He's yelling at me, and I yell back and I'm crying, and I turn and run into my bedroom and climb into my bunk, and he follows and grabs the end of the bunk and starts shaking the bed, violently shaking so I feel like I'm in an earthquake, and he's yelling, You fucking . . . He's so angry I don't know what will happen but eventually he goes away.

But then one day I'm with Dane and we're being silly together, play-fighting. I'm sort of hitting him and pushing him, and he's biting me. But I'm not *really* hitting him. We're just playing around, being kids. And then suddenly Rick is there, looming in front of me, furious, and he punches me full in the face, and I feel like I'm flying across the room from the force of it.

It hurts. I run to my room. He doesn't follow me. Blood in my mouth. I don't know what to do with the blood so I spit it out the window. After a while I go to the bathroom and clean up my face, then I go back to my room. And it seems like ages later, after night has fallen, Mum arrives home. I hear her car pulling up and I run out to see her. I need to tell her before Rick does, what I did to Dane. Mum, I say. Mum, I'm so sorry. I hit Dane. We were playing and I probably got too rough. I'm sorry. She's so busy getting things out of the car that she doesn't even really look at me. Her arms are full and she is in a rush to get inside. She seems confused I'm even telling her. That's fine, honey. I know you'd never hurt him. Don't worry. And she lugs her bags inside.

I don't tell her Rick punched me. It's his responsibility to do that, and I hope that when he tells Mum, Mum will know it's time to leave.

So I go back to my room and wait for her to come in and hug me, and check on me, and tell me everything will be OK — but it doesn't happen. He doesn't tell her what he did, and nothing is said and nothing is done, and her plate is too full for her to notice that something has happened to me.

RUBY'S TRAINING BAG
You're never to blame for the way
an abusive person treats you.

6. Missed the bus

When we moved to Canvastown I just wanted to find a sports team to be part of. I knew it was my best way of forming bonds with people outside my family, now that I didn't have my cousins nearby. But on my first day of school, I couldn't believe it. Twenty-six kids — in total — across all the ages of primary school. I could hardly take it seriously. It was so different from Wellington where there were hundreds of kids, or even Tākaka. How am I gonna get in a good sports team at this school? There was no soccer. No netball.

The only thing was rugby, but it was all boys. I remembered my early experience of getting my hair pulled, and I just thought rugby was stupid. But there wasn't much option. There was a boys' rugby team that drew from the area, rather than just the school, so I convinced two other girls to come with me and in my second year living in Canvastown we played for the boys' team. There were good things about it — oranges at half-time, getting told I was good . . . and I knew I was good, and pretty handy with the ball. But my girl mates didn't love it, and it was always a mission for Mum to get me to the games — we had to drive hours to get anywhere.

But the thing I remember most about that experience was this moment at the end of a game, and we must have just played a good game, because the coach was saying to my team-mates, the boys, You guys could be All Blacks. And then he said to me, You could be a Black Fern, and I thought, What the hell? Who the heck are the frickin' 'Black Ferns'? I literally had no idea what they were. I'd never seen them play on TV. When my friends and I wanted to play netball, we wanted to be Silver Ferns! Everyone knew about the Silver Ferns. We could watch them on TV. I knew what they looked like, I could see their faces. But Black Ferns? It pissed me off more than anything, because here I was in this life that I hated, and he was offering me something that scarcely made any sense at all. It seemed hopeless. There was no possible pathway. It just wasn't a realistic concept at all. What an idiot.

———

We lived in that house for three years. Everything associated with that time of my life is . . . there's no simple word for it. I can just say, we were miserably poor, we were in the middle of nowhere, I had no help, and there were times I wanted to die. There was not a single moment when I felt like I had parents that made me feel safe — not in the morning, not at night. Even when Mum was home she was getting yelled at. I felt alone. I was alone. And as well as hating the house and everything that happened in it, I turned a lot of those feelings onto myself. I couldn't help Mum. Rick was telling me horrible things about Samoan people. I was helpless, useless, a waste of space.

Adults don't always understand how much kids blame themselves when things in their families are bad.

I woke early so I could get my breakfast and make my lunch and be out on the road in time to get picked up by the bus. I never missed the bus. But one day, I did miss the bus. Instantly there was fear in my stomach — I would have to go into their bedroom and wake them up. I didn't want to. I knew the risk. But I had no choice. It was a massive walk for a ten-year-old — five or six kilometres — but it wasn't just the distance. It was a country road with many blind corners and no footpath, and cars whizzing along at 100 km. I opened their door as quietly as I could and crept in there and tried to wake Mum. I touched her arm. Please Mum, I whispered. Please can you take me?

She quietly got out of bed and started getting ready. I went out to wait, but a minute later I heard the raised voice, him yelling at her for spoiling me, and soon she came out and told me she couldn't take me. I'm sorry, Ruby. You'll have to walk.

I would have run all the way to school for Mum, but the fact that she listened to him over me in that moment really hurt.

So then I was out on the road, lugging my schoolbag, kicking at stones, cars zooming past me. After a while, one pulled up beside me, and I saw it was the family from a couple of houses up the road from us, two kids from my school and their dad.

What are you doing?, he asked.

Missed the bus.

Yeah, it was ten minutes early today. They made you walk? He looked stunned. Hop in, he said. You shouldn't be walking along this road. And to myself I went, I knew it! Sometimes I felt like I was going crazy, but now I thought, No I'm not crazy, they're just assholes.

My friends didn't like coming to my house. Maybe they'd come once, and then not again, and sometimes they'd say they weren't allowed. Word was out. People had learned what he was like. One Saturday, one of the girls came round to play and it wasn't long before Rick began popping off — it happened so often, him exploding and screaming at Mum and then the thumping, that I hardly saw it as a big deal. I just went into normal flight mode, grabbed Dane and we all ran to the sleep-out, which is where I often went.

My friend's eyes were big and round. What was that?

I shrugged. I no longer realised how shocking it was. Oh, he just gets angry sometimes.

Her face, I'll never forget it — like, we're ten, but written all over her face was, What the heck! This is not good! And that was the last time she came to play.

The other parents at the school, they must have known, even though in my kid brain I didn't think anyone did. But I guess when kids tell their parents there was screaming and thumping going on, then parents probably pick up on the situation. It wasn't hard for them to know Rick was a criminal. It seemed like he was always getting done, and then he'd be down at the school doing PD hours, cleaning up, doing the lawns. I knew what PD meant because my dad had to do it too when I was little.

One time, as I got off the bus at the end of the day, one of the girls called out, Oh, you going home to smoke dope with that guy?

It was a kick in the stomach. I felt so shamed. So embarrassed. So judged. If I was ever in a dark spot, that was it.

So afraid.

So sad. There was no adult I could rely on, no support or validation coming from any of my relationships. I felt like I was the only one who could see the situation for what it was. I loved my mum, but I felt like I couldn't rely on her for anything. She was definitely extremely depressed in those years . . . I found out later she had severe postnatal depression. But I was depressed too. I cried all the time at night, but never in front of anyone.

So defeated.

———

There's a cross-country competition coming up, and everyone's saying I'll win it. I love sports, and I have a good feeling when I get chosen for things, but in another way I'm coming to hate it. People are like, You're so awesome; you're going to win . . . but it doesn't feel good any more. It feels like pressure I can't deal with. It feels like shame — to represent my mum and her boyfriend; to have that attention when I'm so embarrassed about Rick, who's doing horrible things at home but also shaming us in the community.

If I'm sick I won't have to run, I won't have to go to school, I won't have to feel that pressure, that shame, so all I'm wearing is my shorts and a singlet, even though it's bitterly cold and raining, and I wait in the rain and do my best to get sick. I'm shivering and miserable but I don't get sick.

Sport is usually the only thing that rescues me from these bad feelings, but now even sport feels like overload, and I am completely overwhelmed.

RUBY'S TRAINING BAG
Adults don't always understand how
much kids blame themselves when
things in their families are bad.

7. Getting smoked

From the moment I debuted as a Black Ferns Sevens player in 2012, right up until we won silver at the Rio Olympics in 2016, I didn't touch a drop of alcohol with the team. I'd seen so many dreams ruined with that stuff, and there was no way I was risking mine. To me, the difference between a really good rugby player, and a great rugby player, is the addictions. It's the drugs and alcohol and the adultery. So I kept alcohol right away from my rugby life, and it was funny because all my new rugby friends thought I was straight and narrow. They assumed I'd never drunk anything, and I was happy for them to believe that. I didn't tell them otherwise.

But the truth is that I knew a lot about the drinking life. I was very young when I learned where that path led.

From nine to eleven was a massive time in my life, and not only because of everything that was going on in Canvastown. Every holidays, I was out of there. I would gap either to my uncle's place on the West Coast or to my dad's in Wellington. And if I stayed with Dad, I got up to all sorts. That time of my life, my hardest period, also became my experimental stage. Dad's life was all about drinking and drugs and partying, and of course for me it was either sit in the car or . . . I didn't want to sit in the car any more, I wanted to be with Dad. I needed to feel I belonged somewhere, so wherever I could find to belong, I would go.

Dad was living at Grandad's but he'd made really good friends with this young woman called Hailey. She and Dad kept in touch and they bonded over drinking and all the rest of it. Hailey's mum had died when she was young and she'd inherited the house, and it became the place where we always hung out, and Dad could drink and cook for us, away from Grandad's eyes.

It was like our second home. For as long as I could remember I had always wanted an older sibling, especially with all my cousins moving away, and then all of a sudden it was like I had one. Hailey loved having me around. She made me feel loved and cared for and popular, because she was the head honcho of her house and her scene, and I was like the queen's little helper.

She called Dad 'Dad'. She turned to me once — we were driving along in her car, blasting Eminem's new album — and she was like, I've always wanted a little sister, Ruby. With a lot of the people in her life, she didn't know if they actually liked her, but she knew I thought the world of her. She was often in scary situations, and I definitely think my presence made her feel better.

I would happily take this little bag of white powder to this creepy-looking guy and take the cash and give it back to her. It was awesome, and I was in with the cool people in this cool place. And I could drink with my dad, and we could do whatever we wanted. If he bought a box of beer he'd always be like, You want a four-pack? I'd always had access to alcohol — I can't even remember the first time I had it.

So Dad would cook for us and then he'd go off and see someone else — he was always chasing the party life — and I'd stay with Hailey. She had a fancy-as TV, and Sky, and I could sit up till whenever watching TV.

Slowly and surely Hailey was getting more involved with the

wrong people and then all of a sudden it wasn't just our halfway home, it was all these other people's halfway home, and there were more and more drugs. Weed, NOS, P — any time of the day or night there would be people sitting around drinking and doing drugs. The first time I smoked weed was at age eleven.

One time I'm sitting there with these guys who are all enjoying some NOS. I'm maybe ten, the youngest in the room by at least ten years. It's daytime, so not exactly a party like at night, but this stuff just happens at any time. They're filling balloons off the nitrous oxide container and then inhaling it, and I'm watching as one by one they're off their heads for a couple of seconds. I see them disappear from their usual, real selves, their eyes rolling back in their heads, and then they come back and they're like, Oh that was mean, and they all clap and be like, You didn't faint bro, like it's a cool thing. Then they hand me the balloon and they're like, Do it, do it, do it! Frick, what do I do? Like what happens if I do it, 'cos I just watched them all leave their everyday selves, and I'm like, What if I faint? I won't be able to handle it like they do. So I get a bit embarrassed and they're still going, Do it, Ruby, do it! And I think, If Hailey says do it, I'll do it. So I take my balloon full of NOS and I tell them, I'm gonna do it with Hailey. I go into the other room where Hailey is. She's the head honcho, and I'm lucky because I'm always allowed in with her. I show her the balloon and I say, Can I do this? And she stares at me, like, Oooh, and then she says, Actually, give it here, I haven't done it yet. And she takes it off me and she does it with ease, like it almost has no effect on her compared with the guys in the other room.

I've walked into the other level of the house, like the top level, and Hailey and this guy are passing around a glass pipe. The guy puts his mouth up to one end, lights the bottom of the rounder end with the white powder in it, then inhales the thick white smoke. To me, cigarettes, weed, P, it's all the same because you do the same thing with it. I grab it when it comes past me and

I pretend I know what I'm doing, because what will this make me do? I think it's cool. I don't really understand anything about what I'm getting into, but I'm learning.

Hailey takes me to all her parties. One party we go to, everyone's smoking something or other and doing drugs, wasted as, lying around on all the couches — nothing unusual about all that. Some people are with it enough to double-take that there's a ten-year-old at their party. But this party, we go into this guy's room — it's his house, his party — like he's the head honcho here, and we sit down and he's so out of it, and he says to me, Come here, come watch this with me. So I go and sit with him, and I look at the screen, and he's sitting there watching beheadings on the internet. The internet was pretty new then and I actually had no idea you could watch that kind of stuff online. I pretend it's all good, but inside my mind I'm a bit freaked out and thinking, So if you get to the top of this game, you end up in a room by yourself watching real weird stuff.

I wanted to say to him, Bro, are you sure you don't wanna try soccer?

Hailey was dealing P, of course. One day we were in her room with her supplier, and she had a gram of P in a packet, and the guy took it and poured some of it into the pipe and she was going, No we can't smoke it, they'll find out. And he was like, No, no, don't worry . . . So there were the three of us and I watched them handing round the pipe, and then they sealed the packet back up and me and Hailey drove down to the docks, and she gave it to me because I was a kid, so less likely to get attacked. She was in the driver's seat and I was in the passenger seat, and she told me to wind my window down just a bit, and these guys came over and I handed the packet out, and they asked, Is it all there? She was like, Yeah, yeah, and she told me to wind the window up. A little while after that — holy wrecker — they came around to Hailey's and they were smashing at the door, yelling, You ripped us off, you effing this, effing that. I was not surprised. I wasn't even a teenager yet, and I could have told you that was going to happen. Obviously they were going to weigh it. Those guys wouldn't leave and I was scared they could actually kill Hailey. That house was getting crazy and I felt the danger of it.

Hailey took me around to all those places, but she also protected me because imagine if I'd inhaled all the P, or done all the NOS . . . I might still be where all those people are.

Hailey didn't protect herself, though. She spiralled downward and got into debt and ended up selling her house, so we couldn't go round any more, and after that it wasn't the same. She'd lost her way and the people around her got real scary. She started losing all her stuff, and it wasn't fun any more.

I saw her once more when I was about fifteen or sixteen. I was at a party with Dad and she burst into the room and was pushing the door shut behind her, and I was like, Hailey! And she was like, Oh hi, Bub, how are you? She looked different — hollow cheeks, her eyebrows all thin — and I was like, Whoa, that's not the same Hailey. She was holding the door because this fella was trying to get at her, and she was trying to get away from him.

I'll never forget what I learned from Hailey, and how much she loved me in her own way.

———

I've got a surprise for you, Dad said one day. I was eleven years old. We were driving around in his van, and I just looked at him. OK . . . And he dropped a bombshell.

You've got a sister. She's sixteen and she works at KFC. Do you want to go see her?

Oh my gosh! Yes!

An older sibling, just like I'd always wished for. I remembered that weird time when Dad made me go and knock on that woman's door. It suddenly made sense.

We went to KFC and Dad sat down and he made me line

up to be served. And there she was behind the counter. I was so excited and nervous and shy and I didn't know if she knew who I was, and I didn't know what to say. I said hi, and she and Dad must have been talking because she did seem to know who I was, and she said hi, too. I ordered whatever I ordered and pushed my money across. She was shy too, she didn't know what to say either, but when my order came she brought it across to me herself, and she'd added a chocolate bar and a drink to the tray.

No one had ever given me free stuff before. I felt so cool.

We were just smiling at each other and not really saying anything, and Dad said to me, Do you want to hang out with her after she finishes work? Of course I was like, Oh yes please!

So later that day me and Dad waited for her outside KFC. Dad had a van at the time, so we all had to squash up together on the front seat — Dad, me in the middle and then my sister, Lesh, on the side. Squashed between my dad and my sister: it was the best feeling in the world. Adults had told me it was impossible to get an older sibling, but here she was. My older sister. I couldn't believe it. I couldn't say a word I was so nervous, but inside I was wearing the biggest smile. Then Dad said, Do you want to hang out with her without me? Of course!

So Lesh took me to Glassons and bought me a top — a white, fleecy top and a matching white belt. Matching! I felt so cool. I looked real funky.

Then we went and got our noses pierced together. Cool! But when I got back to Canvastown, Mum was so mad. I guess it reminded her of the time Dad got the cross shaved into my hair, and she made me take it out. Oh, I wanted my nose piercing. Me and my sister got it, matching. So at night I would secretly re-pierce it — so sore, but it was my connection to my sister.

That day with Lesh, it still stands as one of the best days of my whole life — like God had heard me and gifted me this new best friend. She was connecting with Dad for the first time, so suddenly she was like an addition to my life with Dad.

Of course, Dad's an alcoholic, and she was young, so how we bonded was through drinking. I didn't have the skills to say to her, I don't need to do this. Honestly, I loved her so much, we could have just sat in a room doing nothing and I would have been happy. But I guess Dad and her were also trying to figure out their relationship, and so drinking was what we all ended up doing.

I started drinking hard out around age eleven. Grandad and his wife Sani helped me out sometimes when I got hungover, they would be rolling their eyes but they were real loving to me. They didn't make me feel alone. They were like, Oh, her dad . . . They knew it would have been Dad giving me the alcohol. Dad being the black sheep saved me in a way because everyone kind of looked out for him extra and therefore me too.

They did try to love him. I heard from my aunty that when Grandma died she said to Grandad, You have to look after my son, Vaki. But Dad was always arguing with his family because he had been through so much, and I think that because he rejected his family's love, I got that little bit of extra love from them — like I got his share too. I got away with heaps, and I really felt that.

Down in Canvastown I was a loser, bottom of the heap; but in Wellington I felt cool. I felt better-than — more grown-up than the other kids at my school. No one else was going out and drinking yet, getting stoned.

I needed an escape, and I needed to feel like I fitted in somewhere, and I found that by drinking with Dad and sorting drugs with Hailey and their friends.

I felt like I was Dad's bro, his mate, and that's how he always treated me. I didn't understand that I was any different to him, that I was just a child. I didn't see any difference between me and Lesh, even though she was five years older than me.

Later on, Lesh ended up living with Dad at Grandad's house. She took over part of the basement, covered the walls in drawings and quotes and made it her own — she's a real incredible artist.

I loved her being there. We hung out there in the basement and I'd just want to be with her all the time, whatever she was doing. Lesh, like me, wanted happy families, but it was never that simple with our dad.

———

Even though things weren't perfect when I was little, I love both my mum and my dad dearly. They are such different people, and for a little while I was a bit sour at them for various reasons. But then I grew up a bit, I worked on my empathy and now I am just so thankful to both of them.

Parenting is both the hardest job in the world and the most important, yet there is no training or qualifications required to do it. You are just trying your best each day to learn and do the best you can. And that's what my parents did, the best they could with what they had. My mother didn't have parents to lean on and my father went through an earth-shattering culture shock. I got their best, which is all I could ever ask for. I will forever be grateful for the little things my parents did when they could.

I love them both very much.

———

To complete the picture of my siblings, fast-forward till I was 23, and Dad called me to tell me his girlfriend was pregnant. And not long after that, Nikki was born. She's my baby sister, and she's gorgeous, and she loves me and Lesh dearly, so whenever I have spare time I fly down to Wellington and spend a few days. She texts me, or calls me, and I always answer any questions she has and I make sure she knows who she is and who her sisters are, always.

I love all my siblings and even though there has been drama, there's always been an unbreakable love. Technically they are all half-siblings but to me there's no such thing. I am close with them all and treasure our relationships. And when I'm with my sisters and my brother, I'm not a Black Ferns Sevens player, I'm just their sister. Just Ruby.

RUBY'S TRAINING BAG
My family may not be perfect but the love between us is deep and real.

8. 'I'm sorry, she's gone'

It's another day hanging with Dad . . . and he's always got friends, always got girlfriends, and this time he's going to Meredith's house, up in the hills above Wellington.

We pull over on the side of the road and he's like, Do you wanna come in, but I say nah. Sweet, he says, lock the doors if you get scared. So I sit there waiting. It was light when we got there, but slowly it's getting dark. I don't know how many hours, but time is getting on, longer than usual. He usually would've had his sesh and his cup of tea by now. Why is he not out? Sometimes when it's long he checks on me, like, Are you all good? Maybe brings me a pack of chips or something. And I'm like, Sweet, all good, and then he goes back in.

But this is longer, and when he comes back out he says, Oh bud, something's going on. I'm gonna be a while tonight. Then he says, Maybe you should come in.

OK. I'm feeling good tonight because I'm wearing a brand-new white puffer jacket that Dad just bought me.

Come on, get out of the car, come help me, he says.

I never know what's gonna happen, what I'm walking into — is it a party, is everyone wasted? — but when we get inside the house there is no one there. No one in the lounge or the kitchen. Come here, come here, Dad's saying, and I follow him into the bathroom and there's this woman, naked in the bath. She seems only semi-conscious and she's making groaning noises. I've seen people wasted before, but this is somehow different. Something different is in the air.

There's just a little bit of water in the bath and Dad's trying to wash her. He tells me she spewed on herself. Get a towel, he says to me.

Is she sick? Is she sick, Dad?

She'll be fine.

Should we ring the ambulance, like, is she in trouble?

Nah, nah, nah, it's fine.

So we dry her, and as we dress her — it's not easy because she's not helping us at all — he's talking to her like, You're OK, Meredith, and she's groaning back at us, and at least it seems like she is reciprocating a little bit. I keep saying, Dad, Dad, let's call the ambulance. That's what I'd been taught at school, but he keeps saying, No, no, no, it's OK, it's OK.

We get her into the lounge. Dad's holding her and rubbing her and talking to her. I'm standing there watching, and if Dad needs a towel or water or anything, I run and get that.

I start begging Dad to call the ambulance. Obviously, they've been smoking and he doesn't want her to get in trouble but I'm getting really, really freaked out. My dad is trying to protect her . . . he is so stubbornly loyal. He doesn't want her to get in trouble. But then quite suddenly she deteriorates. She goes from kind of normal breathing, sort of moving her head and groaning, to a point where she stops making noises with her voice and her breathing turns into gurgling. I will never forget the sounds she was making. I can still hear them many years later.

Dad, I don't care, where's your phone? I say, and I grab his phone. I don't care if she goes to jail at this point. She's gonna die.

And now Dad's getting upset.

He's tearing up, and going Meredith, no! Meredith, Meredith!

I get through to the ambulance. Dad, what's the address? But he's getting hysterical. Finally, he manages to tell me. And I'm telling the ambulance people what's happening, and in my little-kid world it's like, She can't die. She can't die. She can get sick, but she can't die.

Now Meredith is gasping, but there are these gaps between her breaths. Oh my gosh. And I'm still on the phone, but then they say, Go up on the road now, so I run up to the road, and I'm thinking, *Those frickin' drugs*. Is this what happens to everyone who has P? And I'm thinking about how I gave the P to that guy down at the docks, and to other people when Hailey asked me to. I have given it to people. Did I give Meredith the P? Of course in reality I didn't, but I was a kid, I was freaking out and all this stuff was going through my head. Where did she get it from? Was it me and Hailey? I feel blame, like I am going crazy, even though it has nothing to do with me — it feels heavy and dark and scary.

The ambulance pulls up and I'm waving at it frantically, and I'm probably in shock. Come, I shout to them. Come quick. And I run back down the path with the ambulance officers behind me.

They try everything, and Dad is crying, and they are using the defibrillator on her. Boom. Boom.

Me and Dad are standing in the kitchen, watching. I took my jacket off when we were trying to help her in the bathroom, and now I'm shivering and Dad has his arm around me. I feel like it's my fault, all my fault, and Dad probably feels like it's his fault. Boom. Boom. And she isn't changing, and her body is limp.

Then the ambulance officers stand up, walk over to us, and one of them says to me — and I'll never forget it — I assume this is your mum?

It stuns me. My little-kid brain puts it all together: you take the P and you've got kids, and then you OD, you're dead and your kids lose their mum. The ambulance officers have assumed that Meredith was the mum, I am the kid and Dad is the dad, and I'm like, That's what happens. It's somebody's mum, it's somebody's daughter. It really hits home. And I can't answer because my mind is whirling.

But I wasn't the daughter. And Meredith didn't have any family with her when she died.

I carry that now, and I'll never forget: *That's somebody's mum.* No matter how bad they are or what trouble they're in, that's somebody's mum, that's somebody's dad, that's somebody's daughter. Everybody is somebody, and if you take things too far you will die. This is my first interaction with these truths.

Meanwhile, in the kitchen, Dad is crying and telling them, No, we're not her family, I'm a friend. I don't know any of her family. And the ambulance people are saying, We're so sorry, we couldn't save her, she's gone. There's nothing more you can do now.

Then they tell us we have to leave and not touch anything, and that the cops need to come.

And next we're back in Dad's car and driving away, and it hits me that I left my jacket there. And it's such a small thing, but it's one more thing that I lay at the door of that kind of life.

So I've seen the whole thing play out, from the *Oh, this feels cool, I've got friends*, to doing the NOS, to smoking the crack, to dealing it, to having the parties and then you get through the popular phase and you're in this isolated phase where it's just you and you're alone in a room watching weird shit on a screen, and then you do more drugs and then you die. That's what it feels like. That's what I know.

I see the end of the line.

Wow, I think to myself, what else is there? There's gotta be something else. Where's the other path? How the hell do I get out of this one?

I don't tell anyone about what happened to Meredith. I don't want to get my dad in trouble, and I instinctively know it is a secret for him. I don't want to tell my mum, because she doesn't know all that's going on, and she's got enough already.

Me and Dad talk about it a bit and I say, That was crack, eh? And he says yes. And he says, You were right, bud, I should've called the ambulance.

My poor dad. He didn't know what to do. He was trying to clean her up, and he thought she would just come to. But when he says I was right about the ambulance, I think perhaps I could trust myself when it comes to right and wrong. And with that comes another little feeling that I don't articulate, even to myself: how did he *not* know that that was the right thing to do?

It was years before I told anyone about Meredith. Now it seems so obvious that it was traumatising for me and it shook me. At the time I just told myself it was nothing compared with what kids see in other countries where there are wars.

And the thing was that the moment the ambulance officer said I assume this is your mum, I realised: there are kids out there that this happens to. So I felt lucky in a way, that at least I wasn't watching my mum die.

———

Meredith's death played on my mind.

When mental adversities happen, emotional reactions build up. This is something I know because that's what I lived with in my childhood, although of course I didn't understand that at the time. When I was eleven, I genuinely thought I was a burden to my mother's life. Thanks to Rick, I thought I was the scum of the earth. And on top of that, I thought I had actually contributed to Meredith's death that night. All it took was one more abusive argument, hearing my mother get screamed at for hours again, and I just couldn't take it any more.

I turned it all on myself. It must be my fault. What's wrong with me? I felt like a monster.

I had heard that if people cut their wrist they might die. If I was dead I would no longer be a burden for Mum. It would be

better than living. I was invisible; no one would even notice if
I was gone.

So I go into the kitchen and choose a steak knife with a
serrated edge and a white handle and I take it outside. We've got
a hectare of property, and when I want to run away I run away
into it, into the bushes, among the trees, and I hide and pretend
I'm somewhere else. That's where I go now with my knife, into
one of the bushes that I know is a good place to hide. I hold the
knife in my left hand, and I look at my right wrist, at the thin blue
veins snaking there. Is that what I'm supposed to cut? Will I just
drop dead if I cut it? What if it hurts? I put the blade on my wrist
and apply a timid amount of pressure and drag the knife across
the vein. For a split-second I wait for something to happen. Then
the sharp pain, and the cut turns red as blood finds its way out.

I absolutely freak out. I'm gonna die! I'm gonna get into so
much trouble! All of a sudden I am terrified of dying. In that split-
second, with blood escaping from the cut, I go from thinking that
death is better than living, to freaking out that I might die.

Suicidal thoughts, I believe, are a lot more common in
minors than we would all like to think. I was so captured by
wanting to end all this pain that I had my first, and only, feeble
attempt at suicide. That is hard to write, and I bet for people
who care about me it's hard to read — yet suicidal thoughts are
important to acknowledge so that we don't belittle the magnitude
of a child's feelings, so that we can recognise when a child might
be in danger and we can help.

I truly believed it was the end of the road for me. The raw
emotion, the pain of that time, was very real. Children who are
lost, as I was, feel those feelings at least as intensely as adults do.
A child who gets to the point that I did, of trying to take their own
life, does it because they think it's the only option they have.

There's nothing for me.

The truth is that, as a child, I had no sense of the future or
of hope. When you're a kid, you don't know that the future can

be different to the present. I have since grown and learned that there are many things you can do at a dead end. Now when I hit a hopeless dead end in life I know that I just have to change one thing to change my route. I know that change is possible and it begins with one step.

I am so happy to now truly understand that there *is* hope, and if I hit a dead end, I can always choose to do a U-turn out of it.

Now as an adult I go into schools and talk to kids about mental health, and the thing I feel is most important to say to them is, If you've got no support, it's not your fault. You feel like it's your fault but it's not your fault. It's probably the one time in your life when you truly have no choice over what's happening to you. It's out of your control. But there is hope, because one day it's going to be in your control and you're going to choose — Do I want to live here? No. Do I want to be talked to like that? No — and it's the greatest. One day you get to choose. You'll get to choose a better life. You'll get to choose the things that make you feel cool, and that can eventually become your life.

That was the hardest time of my life. I got through it, but I might not have.

Now, in my adult life, I can still go through periods of emotional accumulation — maybe I'm stressed out because I haven't performed well in fitness testing with my footy, and then my partner starts to mention how I've been pretty slack around the house, and then my mum needs something urgent, and then we lose an easy game we should've won, and then I have an argument with a good friend — all of this stuff I can easily handle individually. But cumulatively, one on top of the other, the pressure increases and then all of a sudden I can find myself absolutely losing it or breaking down at the smallest thing.

I completely disagree with the stereotypical view that crying is for the weak. To be able to cry to release emotional build-up is such a useful tool. I admire people who can openly and freely cry when they feel like it — it's a healthy release of an emotional backlog. I find healthy ways — ways that don't harm myself or others — for myself to release those feelings, and sometimes it's just about getting really clear about what my feelings actually are.

There's so much crazy in the world, and we have to learn to stop, to sit there and really figure out what's going on. I think people are scared of emotions, especially the difficult ones, and they don't want to sit there and really experience them — but that's why it's so important. To fix anything in your life, you need to know the why — and if you are too scared to sit with it, you don't even get to the why.

When I was a child I knew I was sad. It was an easy word to apply to my situation. But if you unpack that and break it down, it was so much more than sad — I felt worthless and I felt responsible for all the pain. Once you know what's really going on, you can address it. You're not worthless. You're not responsible for this. But kids don't have the language, the toolkit, to deal with such feelings.

On that awful day back when I was a little kid hiding in a bush, facing death and realising I didn't want to die after all, worrying that I would get into trouble for cutting myself, I mostly just felt there was no hope. I'd failed in my escape. I stayed there for a while until I stopped freaking out, then I went back inside the house and cleaned the knife and put it back in the drawer. And no one ever noticed that cut on my wrist.

———

I was lucky that the alcohol and drugs didn't get their hooks into me. I think it was because, for me, doing that stuff was always about wanting to belong, far more than about the substances themselves. So when I found other ways to fit in I didn't need it so much.

That's why I say I got through those years, but I might not have. Also, I reckon that's where my Samoan side really saved me. When I was with my family, I felt like I was on crack already. That's how awesome it was — that was my high. Walking into a room filled with twenty people who all loved me no matter what, no matter that my mum's getting abused, no matter that my dad's an alcoholic and I drink too and I'm only a kid — there was just no judgement and that is so powerful for someone to feel. There are lots of people in this world who say they love you, but it can be full of pretence and without meaning. But my Samoan family *showed* me that they loved me. They showed me with their open arms and with their complete lack of judgement. That really, really helped me, because if I hadn't had that, if I'd truly felt I belonged nowhere, then — who knows? — maybe I would've got lost in the partying thing.

I also think that because I was used to living between two worlds, and had always absorbed and been fascinated by their differences, I was able to see the world of drugs and alcohol in the same way. I could see it as a possible path, and where that path would lead — like, If I do this, if I do the crack, I'll get addicted and I'll end up as the head honcho at a party watching beheadings on YouTube. The drug path could lead to that dark, seedy room, or, like with Hailey, to losing your house and your everything, or like with Meredith, to being covered in vomit, naked in a bath. Dead. Like, that's where this path ends. I had seen it for myself. It was an option, but because of my background, I knew there were always other options, other ways of being.

What is the other path?

I learned really young what I absolutely didn't want — what is *not* love, what is *not* a good relationship, what is *not* the right thing. I wanted to see what the other options were.

RUBY'S TRAINING BAG
If you hit a dead end, you can
always do a U-turn out of it.

9. A real breakdown

Some time in that year when I was eleven, after I'd reached rock-bottom with my suicide attempt, I made a decision. I'd had enough of Canvastown, of living with Rick. I was old enough now to have some choice, and so I told Mum I couldn't put up with it any more. You might be able to, but not me. I told her I would move back to Wellington and live with Dad. I felt bad for leaving her, but we were so poor that I thought, Well, at least Mum won't have to feed me. I can't save her physically, but I can save her a couple of bucks.

I think when I told her it kind of opened her eyes. She hadn't thought it was possible to leave this guy, but with me going she was like, Maybe I can go too. So she and Dane came up to Wellington with me and for a few weeks we stayed with a friend of hers. I enrolled for Year 8 at Evans Bay Intermediate School just a few weeks into the year, and she helped me get my uniform and get settled into school. She said we would get a house and start again. It was cool, but it didn't last. Rick somehow got back into her head, and soon she told me she was going back. She tried to sell me the idea, a picture of it all being different.

I just felt like she was lost in his mind-games. I wasn't going back. I knew I couldn't live in that fear any more. I drew my line in the sand, but she didn't draw hers, and it did upset me because I couldn't protect her any more.

I moved into Grandad's house. So now I had Dad in the basement, Grandad and his new wife Sani in their room, my aunty and uncle from Samoa and their kids in another room — a whole village straight away. I fitted into intermediate, made good friends, I was good at sport, and I was really good at netball. I dreamed of being a Silver Fern.

Even though I shifted around a lot as a kid and had so much else going on, I've been lucky with school. I'm not saying I'm a genius, but even if I didn't try and I didn't care and I fell behind, I could still be average; I could still pass. I feel real lucky and thankful for that because I know it's not like that for everyone. Even in those really horrible times, I still did OK at school and I didn't fall off the edge, like some kids do, like I could so easily have done. It meant I kept my options open. I think that must have been the work Mum did with me when I was little, encouraging me to read, getting me interested in words. And Dad, too, put in some hours teaching me to read when I was younger. It all helped. Dad won't be quiet about a PAT test I did when I was in primary school where I scored quite high. He takes all the credit for that.

So now, I was just gonna try and do the right thing. I had just come out of that phase of being around P and all the drugs at that drug house. I'd seen what had happened to Meredith, and what was still happening for Hailey. Out of school I was spending a lot of time with Dad and Lesh, so drinking was still a big thing, but I also wanted to make my own friends, play my sport and get my own sense of belonging.

———

As that year came to an end, I enrolled to go to Wellington East Girls' College for Year 9, and Mum came up for the first meeting. It was another time she reckoned she was gonna leave Rick and didn't. And then some time after that, just as the next year of school was about to start, she had another go. She pleaded with me to come back down and live with her. It's changed, she insisted. She said I could go to high school in Greymouth.

A major factor for me was Dane. I had always wanted an older sibling and I realised that's what I was to him. He was getting older now and he would need someone to rely on. He didn't have my advantage of my big Samoan family and all my cousins. For him, I was the only sibling, and that's a sacred thing.

OK, I said to Mum, I'll come if you promise to never move. Like if I go to this one high school, you have to promise me that I will only go to that one school. She said yes — so once again I packed my bag and left Wellington.

With her Catholic background, Mum got me into the small Catholic high school in Greymouth, John Paul II High School (student population: 124) and so I enrolled at my sixth and final school, as usual starting several weeks later than everyone else because of all the hoo-ha.

When I got down there Mum and Rick were still looking for a new place to live, so for the first few months I went to live with Mum's brother, my Uncle Neil, and his wife Aunty Karen, at Punakaiki.

RUBY'S TRAINING BAG
I can choose how I want to live.

10. Coast Busters

My mother's side of the family has been in New Zealand for six generations now. Uncle Neil and Aunty Karen live at Punakaiki on the land that's been in our family nearly all that time.

The family originally came from Unst in the Shetland Islands, way up beyond the northern tip of Scotland. The family left in 1868, and like most others who came to Aotearoa, they were looking for new opportunities and a better life. They spent some years in Australia, then Auckland, and then arrived on the West Coast in 1879, when they bought claims on Nine Mile Beach, on the Punakaiki coast. It's wild and cold down there, but they came from northern Scotland and they had their rough attitude and their strength so it was all good.

There are so many parallels between the two sides of my family. The Samoans who came first would have been saying to the people back in Samoa: Bro, come, I know it's a long way and it's scary but you can get a job, and we did it so you can too. On my Scottish side they would have been hearing stories about New Zealand, and about how these other people sailed there and it's all good and if you can just survive the boat trip you could get land. It was the promised land to both sides of my family.

I can imagine my palagi ancestors there at the northernmost tip of Britain, in the middle of the Atlantic, in a place that historically had been swept through by Vikings and was an important resting port on the old trading routes, with all this curiosity to come to the mainland, and then to catch one of those ships that ended up bringing them, at great risk, all the way south, from the top to the bottom of the world. I think people forget that the majority of immigrants didn't know what the heck was going on. Like, you don't really know where the boat's going, you're just hanging on, responding to history, trying to make the best of your life.

I've got lots of Māori friends who can literally name their people all the way back to their ancestor who came from Hawaiki. Historically, New Zealand was the promised land for them as well — we're all just trying to do better for the next generations. But the settlers who came later forgot to respect the ones who were already here. It wasn't right, what happened. Now we hear so much anger and blame on both sides. On a scale of one to ten, a lot of the voices are at level ten — angry, hating Māori; or, on the other hand, thinking that all white people are racist.

But now our roots go deep, too. My mum was born in Westport; I did a lot of my growing up along the Coast. When I say I'm a Coaster, I feel really joined to that land, and it's cool to have that. We have so much history there, and my Uncle Neil still lives on the family land with his wife Karen. They're involved in the tourism industry on the Coast, and run a horse-trekking business.

As a kid I hated going there because there was no cell phone reception, and no friends. But for me now it's this beautiful place that I love going back to, and Uncle Neil is like a father figure to me. He's really good on telling me the family history stuff. Thanks to him, I know where all my people are buried, even the ones who came over on the boat. There are two cemeteries down the West Coast and we go and find the family. There's even a Marion, like my mum, but four generations back.

Neil tells me the stories of how hard we worked. I've always seen my Uncle Neil and Aunty Karen as rich, and obviously my Samoan side sees my white side as real rich, but it was not like that if you go back. It was horrible stuff — people forced into marriages, people drowning on the way here, people dying violently and very young, living off the land. As hard as it was for my Samoan family to leave everything behind and come here, it was just as hard a few generations back for my palagi side. I really appreciate that side of me as well.

I'm pretty proud, especially of my great-grandad on Mum's side. His name was Neil too, and he was in the New Zealand Rugby League team in the 1920s, representing West Coast at a time when league was really big there. He toured to the UK with the team in 1923. He was a huge, physical man, super-athletic. There's a story about him. The family land is at Punakaiki, the Pancake Rocks, and there's these big, beautiful blowholes there, where waves come crashing in. People used to jump in and never come out, but my great-grandad was the first and only person to jump in and swim out alive. He would run over the Croesus Track to Blackball, play a game of league, have a fight and then run back again.

He lived in Punakaiki and farmed the land, and he used to go up the Punakaiki River and Bullet Creek to transport logs from the tall rimu out of the valley. He even lost his life in a work accident. So it was real physical, hard labour, a real tough life.

All this is why I get confused when palagi people say, I don't have any culture. I'm like, I bet you do. I bet your history is rich with stories of adventure and heartbreak and some sort of triumph, because you are standing here today.

———

I've stayed with Uncle Neil and Aunty Karen quite often ever since I was a baby and I never once saw them argue, which, as a kid, I used to find weird because I just wasn't used to that. I'm so grateful to have had their world as a contrast, to know that some things were even possible.

They used to live in a little two-bedroom cottage, but they had vision, and over the years they built not only a beautiful home for themselves, but also five cottages that they rent out to tourists. Uncle Neil was always on a digger, always getting his hands dirty, out there building with the builders. He'd take me out on horse treks, and let me ride bareback and help look after the horses.

To see someone having a vision, working, getting it done, understanding about money; it was so cool to me. I learned that you can go from a two-bedroom shack on a hill with no power to this whole frickin' mini-city.

Uncle Neil always put me to work, like picking up the horse poo or helping drop off hay up the Punakaiki Valley, or changing the sheets in the cottages. On my Samoan side, you always work but you don't get paid, but Neil was like, If you do this we'll count all your hours up and then I'll pay you $8 per hour.

Karen got their tax book out to show me because I had no idea what a tax book was or what that meant. They told me all about tax — like, if you want to actually get $8 an hour, you really need to earn more than that because you have to pay tax. Holy shit. It was mind-blowing for me. They were the first ones to introduce me to these concepts, and to persist with it, and I'm so grateful. And I knew that giving me that attention was their way of showing me they loved me.

I think they felt a little bit sorry for me. One time I took my shoes off and I had on one purple sock and one red sock with rainbow stripes, and my toes were sticking out, and Karen was horrified. What are those? Take them off right now and throw them out! I think they looked at all my clothes and thought, What the heck, and they would buy me socks and other clothes too.

It was a different world Neil and Karen showed me, and it challenged my thinking: Oh true, so you can choose to have odd socks with holes in them, or not. Nowadays, all my socks match and all my white socks are so, so white and when I get a hole in them I throw them out. I look in my sock drawer and it's popping out, and it gives me a little buzz. I love a clean pair of matching socks; they're the most under-rated thing. We train up to three times a day, so that's four pairs of socks a day. Every day I look in my bag at my packs of clean white socks, and it's like looking at stacks of cash. Such a contrast to what I wore as a kid. I still have to pinch myself in those moments because I just feel overwhelmed with gratitude.

Life with Neil and Karen was very structured and diligent. For my first few months of high school I caught the bus into Greymouth from their place, and Neil would be up with me to make my breakfast in time for me to get the 7.30 a.m. bus. I'd get home at 4.30 p.m., and I had to make sure my homework got done. They took homework very seriously. Neil and Karen have a daughter who's a bit older than me, Sahar. She often wasn't there because she went to boarding school, but I remember one time she got home and it turned out she'd been getting Bs and Cs, so she had to sit down and have this tactical conversation about how to improve her grades. Man, I felt for her, and I was chuckling to myself because my parents never cared much about my report cards, not compared to that serious chat.

When she was back in the holidays I would be like, Cuz! I'd follow her everywhere and wanna do everything she was doing. I annoyed the heck out of her. If she went to the computer, all of a sudden I'd want to go on the computer too and she'd be like, Are you kidding me? But I thought that, because she didn't have any siblings, it was really important that we hung out. She was another role model for me. I'm sure she hated it when I was there for weeks at a time in the school holidays, but now as adults we're quite close and I call her cuz and tell her I love her, and she says it back to me. And all that homework and report card chat paid off because she's a lawyer overseas now.

As well as encouraging me to do my homework Karen told me to iron my school-uniform kilt every day. I'd never thought to do that before, and it helped me to take a bit more pride in my appearance. Some people would have hated that, but to me Neil and Karen were giving me attention and I really, really loved it. I loved staying at their house. They taught me how to function in that palagi world.

They taught me my table manners. It was so different to my Samoan family — when they eat, honestly, it's like a show: stuffing down the food, making lots of noise, chewing loudly. But at Uncle Neil's place, you use the proper knives, eat quietly with your mouths closed, and it was always healthy, tasty food, international styles, even vegan meals. Karen had lived in India so her use of spices and vegetables was like nothing I'd ever seen. I had never heard of vegan or gluten-free before. I'd never heard of things like lentils. I sat there confused. Where's the meat? They teased me about that for years. I learned you could have amazing feasts without meat.

When I got home after being at school, or out with Uncle on the horses or quad bike, Karen would always fix me nice things to eat — sandwiches cut nicely, and a whole glass of milk or juice just for me. I didn't have to share it or rush it down my gob and get out of the way because she had other stuff to do. She made food just for me. I felt so spoilt at their house.

They taught me well, and now when I go to important events, like I have with Prince Harry and Meghan Markle, I'm all good, no matter how fancy. I can hold my own. I know what they value, I know how to look good — if I want to. There are some events where you can't just turn up rough, inarticulate, and chew with your mouth open. I'm so thankful for my European side because in this world you need to frickin' know that stuff.

To me, Uncle Neil and Aunty Karen seemed like bazillionaires, because they bought red wine and dark chocolate with their shopping — and things were possible for them that were out of reach for Mum and Dad. As a teenager I got real good at netball, but I was always slipping in the cheap shoes I had, so I'd rather play in bare feet. All the other girls had these high-brand shoes with super gel in them for jumping. I'd seen those shoes in a shop in Greymouth and I knew they cost $300. What in the heck! That's like three grocery shops! I knew there was no way I would ever be able to have those shoes. But then Uncle Neil and Aunty Karen bought them for me as a present. Like, the top of the range. Far out. It meant so much to me, but it wasn't a big deal for them. It was just another world.

———

Neil isn't a loud talker like my grandad. He doesn't really talk more than he has to, and he doesn't say I love you that much, or cry, in the way my Samoan family does. When I talk to him on the phone, I say I love you, and he says Yep, yep, see ya. But I know he does love me. He'll go, Want to go for a drive? And we'll get in the ute and drive for maybe 45 minutes, talking quietly now and then, and we'll end up at a cemetery and we'll walk around and he'll tell me all the stories of our ancestors. Or we'll drive for an hour and then stop and he'll turn to me and say, That's where our family mined coal — just real, out-of-it stories. Some younger people find that boring, but I love it. Older people have the stories, and that's where my family history and culture, and my pride, lies.

On my Samoan side, when we have reunions, we often sit in a circle and talk and talk, everyone shares and there are tears and there's always I love you and hugs and heaps of emotion. But then I go to my uncle's and it's so structured and polite and there's no emotional words, but he gives me time. He showed me his tax book, he took me on the digger, he let me ride bareback with the horses.

We won't talk all day and then he'll be like, Come on Ruby, and he'll get me a pair of boots and find a hat that fits me and one of those big, really expensive but horribly stiff rain jackets that people in the country have, and I'll get on the back of his four-wheeler and we'll drive up the valley and go for a walk. He wants to hang out with me and he wants to tell me things and show me things.

He'll never do the things that are normal on my Samoan side, like saying I love you and crying. But it's still love.

I love both my families for who they are and how they are, just the way they are. I've got the best of both worlds.

I'm just so glad I had those two perspectives offered to me, because I grew up knowing that neither way of doing things is wrong; they are just very different, and they both have their strengths and weaknesses. Now, in my adult life, if I disagree with something I can say to myself, Well, there must be something about this that still holds value. I know there are strengths and weaknesses in everything. I'm very open-minded and optimistic about things, because I know that even when something seems absolute, there will be another way of looking at it.

RUBY'S TRAINING BAG
Even when something seems absolute, there
will be another way of looking at it.

11. Taking refuge

Mum bought a house in Blackball, another tiny little town — this time on the West Coast about 30 kilometres out of Greymouth, and an hour or so away from Uncle Neil's. I could keep going to the same school, as Mum had promised, and now at least we had neighbours not too far away.

Mum said things would be different, but as soon as we moved in Rick was back doing the same old stuff. But I felt a bit safer knowing that other people could hear what was going on.

It surprises me that more people don't show concern for this kind of situation. Some people must have known or had their suspicions. People think, Oh, it's not our business, and they just leave them to it and I hate that.

But behind our house, down the end of a lane, was a honey business, Glasson's Honey, and the man who worked there was real nice. He would make excuses to come over, like to show us a honeycomb and things like that. He'd knock on the back door, and it was pretty clear to me that he did this after there had been a lot of yelling, and I felt like he was checking on Mum, even though I don't think he ever said anything directly about it. He'd sometimes catch my eye in a way that made me feel he knew what was going on. I was thirteen by then and I had a good idea that what was happening wasn't alright, even though no one talked to me about it.

Rick didn't like it. He bailed the honey man up one day, told him to eff off and made him leave the property. But it was still so nice that the honey man tried. Someone's listening. Someone can hear.

When people are brave enough to check up on others — just by making themselves known, like pretending to borrow some sugar or something — it's not like you might save their life then and there, but you plant the seed that the kid's not alone or the mum's not alone, and it's actually really powerful. It can change the game.

While Mum had said things were going to change, to begin with it seemed like they'd changed in the other direction, for the worse. But I wonder now whether Rick knew Mum was changing and he responded to that by becoming even more controlling and furious. It was a make-or-break moment, I think.

Dane was still a little boy, not yet at school. When the shouting started now, I didn't have the big Canvastown property or a sleep-out to hide in, so I just took him into my room and tried to distract him. One day we were hiding in there, but the thumps were getting louder. Way too many thumps and way too many screams from my mum, and there was just something about it that sounded bad. I grabbed Dane's hand and we ran out and Mum was cowering on the floor, her little tiny frame on the floor, the whole lounge upside-down, and Rick was lifting the couch over her.

I screamed his name at him in a horrified way, like, Bro, what the frick are you doing? There was this weird feeling of everything being still suddenly — him there with the couch, Mum on the ground, me and Dane staring. He looked over in our direction and — probably because he saw his little son — it was

like he came to and realised he could really mess Mum up if he
didn't quit it.

Mum, I said. Mum. You've gotta stop. I had no doubt that
if it carried on it was going to get worse. That's the way it goes.
I was still a kid but I knew that. The only end after too many
uncontrollable outbursts with no boundaries is death. I was
scared for my mum's life.

It wasn't long after this that it looked like it was going to
happen again. He was popping off, starting to get into his red
zone, calling Mum names, calling her stupid, and I was thinking,
Oh here we go . . . when I saw some red and blue lights sliding
past the window, down the drive at the side of the house. A police
car. There's no police station in Blackball. How did they . . .? It
stopped, and two large policemen stepped out — big tall guys,
awesome, like angels to me. And Rick was shouting, You will
regret this, you're so effing stupid, you're gonna pay . . . He was
mouthing off, arrogant, patronising. They marched him out the
house and took him away. And I was terrified thinking of what it
would be like when they let him go and he came back.

As they drove away, Mum was suddenly full of urgency.
Pack your stuff, she told us. What the heck? So we rushed around
grabbing all our stuff, and then we got in Mum's car and we left.

Thank God, I thought. Thank God we weren't in Canvastown
where help was so many hours away. But there weren't any cops
in Blackball either, so how had they got here so quickly?

We drove. We headed into Greymouth, and then turned
northwards. The sea heaved below us, and the sky kissed the
horizon but had no limits above us. No one spoke, but then Mum
said, Where we're going, you can't tell anyone where we are.
Don't give the address out to anyone. No one at all. It was like
she'd turned into an FBI agent. After we'd driven for what seemed
like ages we got to Westport, and soon we pulled up outside an
old villa. This is it, Mum said. Our hideaway.

I'd assumed we were going to stay with a friend, but there was no one in the house, although someone came to let us in. I found out this was the Women's Refuge — not a place to live forever, but a place for women and children to stay when they are running away from violent or abusive relationships, while they recover and figure out their next moves. Mum kept saying, Don't tell anyone, not your dad — no one can know where we are.

It felt like a secret society, and I took it very seriously and I told no one where we were. We had the house to ourselves. It seemed massive to me — we each had our own bedroom, and there was a big lounge with lots of toys, so Dane was sweet. It was a perfect little set-up.

Mum rang my school and said I would be away for a bit. She said she felt real bad about doing that, which I found silly because here she was doing the greatest thing she could've done for her kids.

And the days went by. It was peaceful. The absence of threat. It was strangely euphoric. We had Mum to ourselves, and I watched her with awe that she'd done this thing.

Various women stopped by to talk to Mum — they were refuge volunteers making sure we had everything we needed, and a counsellor, and Mum spent ages having real in-depth chats with one who was guiding her on how to completely separate herself from Rick: legally, financially, everything.

I was a bit *wait and see* — I'd seen Mum try and leave Rick before, and she always went back to him once he started begging her. It's just crazy to think you can't break up with someone even when they're violent and controlling, because to me you should be able to, but I've seen how hard it is. It's not just a matter of simple logic for women in my mum's situation. She was burdened with so much — getting the money in, raising the kids, running the house, and Rick was always in her ear. He could have made her believe anything. She was depressed, trapped, ;
there was absolutely no room for thinking straight and stickir
up for herself and doing the right thing. Like most women ir

that situation, she thought it was her fault and after years of being told she was stupid she had lost faith in herself. You blame yourself for getting hit, for all the conflict. You blame yourself for not knowing how to deal with the situation you're in. In what world does that make sense? But the truth is, if you blame yourself you're much more likely to go back.

Blame and fault are dead ends. But switch that over to responsibility and it's easier to move: OK, I get hit, my kid gets hit — but I have a responsibility to be a good mum, and a responsibility to live my own life. In that space, there's a choice to be made. And then the next choice. And Mum had made a choice — still to this day the bravest choice I have ever seen anyone make — and she had taken her first step.

I still felt like I needed to see what would happen once we got back to normal life. But at the same time, this did feel different. There was something different about my mum. She'd planned this. It seemed serious. And it was so cool to see her do something this strong.

After a few weeks we came home to Blackball. Mum had a restraining order against Rick, but I didn't think a piece of paper was going to make any difference really. I was waiting for him to come, but he didn't. He was living somewhere else in Blackball. I think he knew that if he breached the restraining order he would lose his access to Dane, so from then on we didn't really have anything to do with him.

One bad thing, though. When Rick got together with Mum, she owned her own house in Newtown. Over the years she and Rick had been together, it was her money that had bought first the house in Tākaka, then Canvastown, then Blackball. But under New Zealand law, when a couple has lived together for three years, the relationship property is divided equally. Mum and Rick had been together for three years and one week. He came with nothing, didn't have a job during that whole time, but he walked away with half the value of Mum's house. A couple of years later when she eventually sold her Blackball house to move to Greymouth, she couldn't afford to buy a house in the town, so from then on she was renting.

I think in that time after she got rid of Rick, Mum struggled a bit, but what I noticed was that she was way happier. She had more space for other projects and she began doing up the house. She even painted it bright pink with purple windowsills. Oh my. It was a bold choice. She was hanging out with friends more. She and her friend Donna would get together and be really annoying, mocking me and teasing me and giggling. Annoying for me, but really cool for her. Really, it was awesome. I felt free and I decided, Yeah, I'll stay here with you, Mum.

She had come back. It was the first time I'd had a mum since we left Wellington.

———

If you set your foot on a path, and you keep going, it will take you to its destination. As soon as you take step one, step ten is waiting for you. If you're in a situation like a violent relationship, and if you don't have hope and you can't see another way of being, your path is hell. It will get worse. If you're in that hell and you keep conceding, it eats you.

That path will kill you inside, and it might physically kill you.

I saw that with my mum, but thank goodness she got off that path. I also saw it with my friend's mum — and she ended up dead.

I had this friend in Blackball, Falon, who was the same year as me. She'd moved here from the UK and her mum and stepdad used to fight hard out, too, and we kind of vibed because of that. Everyone's parents fought, but not everyone's parents fought like Mum and Rick, and I felt like Falon's stepdad was extra-psycho.

One night we went out together to the home of a friend whose parents Falon's mum and stepdad didn't like. They'll never know, Falon said. But Blackball is a small place and her parents did find out, and they came home to confront us. Her mum was lovely and trying to explain why they felt embarrassed that Falon had gone to these people's place. But her stepdad . . . he was red with anger. He walked over to Falon and grabbed her neck and pushed her up against the wall and it seemed like he was strangling her. I was just standing there watching this happen. I knew what it was like to have this happen in front of a friend; you get real embarrassed. I knew she wouldn't want me there, and then she was gasping to me, Go home, go home.

It was one o'clock in the morning, but Blackball is safe — on the streets if not in the homes — and I walked back to Mum's feeling pretty shaken. Man, I thought, there's gotta be a line. I knew that if it was Mum, she wouldn't mind if she was getting strangled but I think if she saw *me* getting strangled, that would be her line. But Falon's mum had been there and she hadn't stopped him. Maybe she was too scared. But there's gotta be a line.

Next time I saw Falon was on the school bus, and straight away I saw the bruises on her neck. She said she was fine. And I understood how it's too hard to talk about those things.

Don't worry, she kept saying. He'd never actually do anything.

We moved away from Blackball not long after that, but Falon's family stayed — and a couple of years later, when we were seventeen, her stepdad killed her mum. He stabbed her to death. He didn't just stab her once; he stabbed her 26 times, bending and breaking three different knives while he was doing it.

One too many uncontrollable outbursts.

Everyone in the Blackball community was shocked, but I wasn't shocked because I'd seen him with his temper that he couldn't control. I'd seen him when he lost it, and to me the steps are so obvious. What happens next? How bad does it get? That's how bad it gets.

Her stepdad turned himself in and went to jail. Falon went

back to the UK. Her mum was gone. There was nothing left in New Zealand for her.

It was one of those moments where I saw the truth, and it's a truth that applies to everything, to good things as well as bad, and definitely to mental health. Whatever direction you're going in, each step will take you further along the path — but you can get in and change direction, and you can begin with one simple step in a different direction. Falon's mum was such a kind, beautiful woman, but she wasn't able to do that and then it was too late. But Mum changed paths — she took her first step, which was contacting Women's Refuge, and then her new path unfolded with every step she took after that.

We are always one decision away from changing everything.

RUBY'S TRAINING BAG
As soon as you take step one,
step ten is waiting for you.

12. Grey-tful

We stayed living in Blackball for a couple of years after Mum left Rick. I had good mates in Blackball then, girls and guys — there were about fifteen of us who hung around together, at the skatepark, at each other's places, kissing a few boys.

We'd get the school bus into Greymouth in the mornings, pick up the kids from all the other surrounding towns, and bus home again at night, but I was the only one going to John Paul; the others went to Greymouth High School. That meant I was meeting other kids from Greymouth through them. We'd be like, Meet you at the shop after school, so it was a good time for me and I had lots of mates and I felt popular. All I was interested in was hanging out with my mates and going to parties.

Those first two years of high school, when I was thirteen and fourteen and even up to fifteen, they were my rebellious years. I had this mindset where I was just taking the piss all the time. I had this attitude: You don't know what I've been through, where I come from or who I am. I was just really like that, and I was probably trying just a bit too hard to be cool. I didn't have a perspective on it at the time, but I really played up. I didn't need to make any effort to get through the schoolwork, and so I didn't. Instead, I'd be showing off to my mates, taking the piss, being naughty and getting kicked out of class. It was fun getting kicked out of class, making the other kids laugh. Getting away with stuff. There was one teacher, though, Mrs Costello the English teacher, who wouldn't kick me out no matter what I did. She would move me around to different seats away from friends, or closer to the front, but finally she put me in the book room at the back of the classroom. Anything other than kick me out.

Take your book and sit in there. Ruby, I really don't want to kick you out. Please just focus and stop acting up.

But I got on my phone in the book room and went on to a game, really loud so the whole class could hear, and finally that did it. She had no choice. She wrote me a note and off I went to the office. I just laughed because that's what I'd forced her to do and I thought I was cool.

Later on, when I'd changed and stopped behaving like that, I said to her, I can't believe you put up with my behaviour — like, why? By that time I was getting really good marks, and excellences in her English class. I could see the potential, Ruby, she told me. You were so smart and you never tried. You were one of the kids I really wanted in my class, but you just played up so much.

I knew she had really tried. Good teachers like her are such rare, wonderful things. No one pays them extra to try like that. Man, I said, I'm so sorry for being like that.

It was around the fifth form, Year 11, that my mindset changed. I loved being able to choose my own subjects and I did it by picking the teachers that I wanted to go with, and that really helped me.

I chose chemistry because the flamboyant science teacher, Mr McCarthy, was the fellow who helped me with speeches. Calculus, because I loved Mr Wilding. Hard subjects aren't hard if you've got good teachers.

I did Classics because the teacher used to swear and be so real and honest with me. I wished more adults were like that. I thought he was cool.

I did not pick Religious Education. I'd had a problem with RE right from the beginning. Going to a religious school wasn't that big of a deal to me because my family on the Samoan side are so hard out and I had grown up going to their church, which was Presbyterian. But now at this Catholic school I was learning about religious differences. I got confused because I was like, God's God, but they were like, No, our way is right. And I thought, *There's no way these random teachers know more about God than Grandman*. They were so sewn up in their beliefs and immoveable, and I could see why there had been wars over this. The strictness went against everything I'd learned about how to get by, which is that there's always another way to look at things. Maybe if I'd liked the teacher it would have been different, but we weren't a natural fit.

Meanwhile, my little brother Dane had started at St Patrick's, the primary school next to my school. He was such a cute little kid. One time we were playing around outside the school and being silly, and I grabbed his knee and gave him a mean horse bite and he squealed. The principal came running and was like, Ruby, get away from that little boy! I let him finish his scolding and then I was like, Yes, Mr Stone, that's my brother. He got so awkward, because of course he couldn't tell from looking at us, with me being Samoan and Dane being palagi. Me and Dane are so close; he's really important to me. I've been with him his whole life from day dot, I cut his cord, I'm always there. We went through those struggles together. I love my little brother Dane.

————

I think at that time I felt like I was the only Samoan in the whole of Greymouth. I'd had one Samoan mate, but he left town. I had heaps of other mates, and I was happy with them, but being Samoan in such a little town — and even in the South Island in general — was hard.

At some stage in high school I discovered I was good at speeches. I like to think I get that from Grandman, who is the ultimate orator in my eyes. One of my science teachers saw that I could talk well and helped me write a speech for the Bishop Lyons junior speech competition. The teacher helped me practise and I travelled over Arthur's Pass with the other students from John Paul II to compete. It was a pretty cool competition between all of the Catholic schools in the middle of the South Island. It was something outside of sport that I could compete in, so it was a really fun challenge for me.

My teacher came up with the topic and I loved it. It was basically the benefits of having parents of two different nationalities, my mother being of British decent and my father being of Samoan. We wrote about all the role models who are of mixed race, and there were so many in sport, politics and the media. I didn't even think twice about it. We played on the word 'mongrel', saying that there are actually a whole lot of benefits to being of mixed race, like the concept of hybrid vigour, having a more open view on the world, and being able to react better to a bigger range of situations.

Anyway, I nailed it and came away with first prize, which was awesome for our school as we were always the smallest one competing. After I received my trophy at the prizegiving I walked down the back stairs off the stage into the crowd where parents, teachers and other students were all gathered. I came up behind a group of older men, all of European descent, who were chatting and smiling and laughing. As I got closer I heard one of them say aloud, Well, that's the first time a mongrel has ever actually won. He chuckled with the others and, honestly, I genuinely didn't care at first 'cos in my naivety I thought he was just playing on words. But when I made myself visible to the group and I joined in the circle to have a laugh too, they all stopped laughing and straightened up and actually turned away.

I was actually gutted — as a teenager who had just achieved something pretty cool, it felt like it didn't mean anything if I was just the butt of everyone's jokes in the mainly white crowd. I felt like saying, Bro, if you've got something to say just say it to my face. I guess the saving grace was how funny the guy's face-drop was when he saw that I had heard him.

———

When Mum first met her new guy, at the beginning of my fifth-form year when we were still in Blackball, I was a bit stand-offish. I remembered when Dane's dad had first come along and I'd tried to laugh at his jokes but it didn't get me very far. This time I needed proof before I gave the guy anything.

Mum was waitressing at the Blackball Hilton and she got me a job there, too, so I saw when this guy walked in. Have you ever seen your parents flirt? It's so unsettling. This guy didn't look like anything to me — tall, old. But Mum leaned over the bar, and she thought no one could hear but it's a bar so you've got to yell, and she was like, You're a sight for sore eyes . . . I wanted to vomit.

His name was Neil, the same as my mum's brother, and he was respectful. I felt like he did his first steps the right way, and I ended up thinking he was real cool. He turned out to be what you're told a guy should be like — always willing to help Mum out, never yelling, and real handy. Like, he could build a house. He and Mum would just talk, and they laughed and flirted. I'd never been around this healthy relationship stuff.

For me, the coolest thing was that he taught me how to drive. Legit help. I'd never had help from the adults at home, but he was different. It was frickin' unreal, to be honest, and I felt like I had this great life now with Mum. I was still going to parties at fifteen, sixteen. But I wasn't being as much of an idiot any more. I think it is a little bit beyond a coincidence that when things settled down for Mum, I got my head together too.

After a while, around the beginning of my sixth-form year, Mum sold her Blackball house, which also put that chapter away, and we moved to Greymouth and Neil moved in with us. We were just renting, but it was the nicest house I'd lived in. To me, it was so flash — it was all the same colour, you couldn't see the piles from the street, and I felt rich because we were living in the Greymouth suburbs. We even bought one of those pools with the poles and the sack in the middle so there was, like, a big adult paddling pool out the back. We've got a pool! Mates could come and hang at my house now because I had the best location.

I got my licence as soon as I could, and because I'd saved up from my jobs, I bought myself a car — $1400 for a little Honda Civic that Neil helped me buy and do up. You know if you want to have chrome wheels you can just spray-paint them chrome silver? And he taught me how to change tyres and change the oil.

I paid $400 for a brand-new radiator, but on the week of my eighteenth birthday party an American tourist forgot which way to look at an intersection and crashed into me. Luckily I was insured, and the insurance guy came around and had a look and was like, I'll pay you $700. I was real gutted, because how am I going to get another car for $700? Anyway, Neil was there when the guy was assessing the car, and he went over to talk to him. That's a brand-new radiator there, he told him, guy-chatting about cars, and in the end the assessor said, Hey look, I'm going to give you $1000 for it. Man that was cool, and I remember thinking, Is this what it's like to have a decent adult role model? I felt like I was being shown all these little hacks in life. So sure, Neil and Mum bicker sometimes — they're like, Oh you said blah, blah; No I didn't — but they will never smash up a house and fight. I am so grateful that he's there to look after Mum. It meant I could think about leaving home, and I didn't need to worry.

In the weekends me and my friends would sometimes go over

to Christchurch, to the nightclubs. I still had my sister's fake ID, and I always managed to get in. It was all a fun ride. I did love to drink and party with my friends, but I remember noticing that just because you had fun with someone when you were pissed, it didn't mean you had anything to talk about when you were both sober. It could lack substance, and I learned that early on. By the time other kids were excited about pills and alcohol — let's get wasted — I would definitely join in, but I wasn't that excited for it. I was just so over the moon to be having this great life now, and I didn't need to experiment with that stuff to feel cool any more. The whole get-wasted buzz was alright but I was searching for more now. Because I'd seen where that led. Seeing Meredith die, that was powerful in my life and the memory stayed with me. The dead end.

I'm not convinced I've seen everything this life can give me — that was the feeling I had. What else is there?

——

For those last two years of school, I was in a pretty good space. Somewhere I've still got my school tie with all the badges from the sports I represented the school at. Anything and everything: netball, rugby, soccer, squash, hockey, athletics — and speeches. I was also a representative on the school council.

I still got into mischief, of course. One year I made the finals of the Lions Clubs' youth speech competition for the top of the South Island. The night before the comp I went to the school ball, partied all night and had a few drinks, then early the next morning I got in the back of Neil's ute and slept all the way to the event in Nelson. Mum and Neil were giggling as I hopped out of the ute, hungover and still low on sleep. Then we giggled all the way home because I friggin' won.

Another time, I somehow ended up hosting the after-ball party for the biggest school on the West Coast. Don't ask me why — it wasn't even my high school — but the next morning I was desperately trying to clean up all the beer cans before Mum and Neil got home. Then I heard a voice.

Hey, Ruby?

It was the neighbour, Mrs Cain. There she was, this white-haired lady, gripping the fence with one hand and holding out a half-crunched-up can of Double Brown in the other.

I think you missed one.

My stomach dropped. We must have been *so* loud last night. I didn't even think about our elderly neighbours. I hobbled over to the fence like a dog with its tail between its legs, and reached out for the can.

I am *so* sorry, Mrs Cain.

I could've cried from embarrassment, guilt and the heaviest hangover I'd had since I was eleven. I was ready for her to lay into me about how she was going to tell the police and my parents.

But as she handed me the can, a huge cheeky grin spread over her face and she just said, Good night was it?

She chuckled softly and walked off. I couldn't believe it. Say what you will about the small town of Greymouth, but there are some serious good buggers in that town. I'll never forget Mrs Cain.

Over those years of high school I still drank with Dad and Lesh in the holidays, but not as much. I wanted to drink with people my own age for a change. I wanted to sip Mum's wine with my mates and giggle about how naughty it all was. By the time I turned eighteen, just as lots of kids my age were getting into that clubbing lifestyle, I was unimpressed with it because I'd already done it all. I really did think there had to be more to life.

———

As soon as I finished high school I was ready to gap it.

I'd always looked up to Mum for her intelligence and how she'd been to university and polytech. Dad also valued the idea of university and he was always in my ear, like, Go to uni! You need to get a degree! He was always saying that word — degree, degree — but I don't know why and he didn't seem to care what subject it was in; he just wanted me to get the degree. One of the things I loved about my palagi family was how they knew their way around the numbers and the books and how to go to university. So Mum and her partner Neil helped me decide what to do.

Neil was probably the first white guy I'd ever met who was still close with his siblings, kind of like my Samoan cousins were. His brother had started a programme in Rotorua for under-privileged kids to help them figure out what they're good at — you put all your info in, and it spits out all these suggestions of jobs you could do. He got me to do it. I'd wondered if I should be a lawyer because I was good at being witty and trying to outsmart the teachers, but *journalist* came out as a top suggestion and it was like a light-bulb — Oh my gosh, then I could specialise in sports *and* talking.

It's hard to know when you're leaving school what you will end up doing, but my Uncle Neil was so helpful, too. He told me, Even if you don't know for sure, you're not wasting time if you're at uni getting a degree. It's like you have a tool-belt, he said, and you're adding tools to it, so whatever happens it's all good because you're resourcing yourself. You're making yourself a better resource for the world. Give it a crack and see what happens.

All the people I looked up to were saying these things. I had no idea what I wanted to do; all I knew was that it was time to move on from Greymouth and see what else the world had to offer. So I chose a Media and Communications degree, with a second major in English, at the University of Canterbury. And I'm so glad I did because I went to university and that is where I discovered women's rugby.

RUBY'S TRAINING BAG
Keep adding tools to your tool-belt so you can
be a better resource for yourself and the world.

PART TWO

GREATITUDE

Greatitude is one of my values. It's close to gratitude, but with a little bit more punch. Greatitude to me is not simply *saying* I am grateful for something; it is doing great actions that *show* I am grateful. If I am truly grateful for being a professional rugby player you will not just hear me say it, you will *see* it. You will see me studying the game at any spare moment, going over and above our team analysis sessions — that's a great action. You will see me adding extra one-on-one meetings or extra passing sessions when I recognise a need. You will see me visiting schools and giving keynote presentations to grow our game. If you were to spend time with me and watch what I do, I hope you would see what I am grateful for; I would not need to tell you. That is *greatitude*.

Today I am grateful for my freedom. I'm back from tour. We've had weeks of being organised by our managers, getting told to go this way and that way and now do this, and then we're in the plane home, in business class, but still we're in the whirlwind of the schedule.

And then we land and at last I'm home.

I wake up next morning and I'm in my house, and if I want to eat I'll eat, if I want to do the dishes I'll do the dishes, and then I get into my own car and I can change the gears and I can turn the steering wheel and I am in control. I go to the cafe I want to go to, and I buy a toasted bagel with jam and my favourite coconut latte, extra hot, because I can. And then I stroll across the road to the beach and it's a sunny day and I can just take my sweet-ass time, take my shoes off and feel the sand and the sand's warmth. Put my feet in the ocean, and if I wanted to I could jump right in with my clothes on — it's such a beautiful freedom that we have in this country. It's even more powerful if we've just come back from Brazil or Cape Town where we stayed in hotels alongside slums and saw everything wrong with the world. So in these moments of savouring the ordinary things — the car, the coffee, the sand — I remember the good parts of life.

We take so much for granted. To really appreciate my everyday life, my family, my relationship, my career, my everything, I need to practise, to be still and acknowledge all these good things. And I do practise — I press pause, I learn the patience to do that, and it serves me so well in all facets of my life.

I find myself a nice spot on the sand and I sit and I close my eyes and I let my ears settle in to the moment. I can hear people chatting, laughing, at the cafe — it's all the way across the street and I can only hear it if I tune in. There's a dog barking. Cars at the intersection nearby slow down, take off. A couple of seagulls are arguing about a crab somewhere. And there's an ever-so-slight sound of the breeze against my eardrums. Five things. This is a game I like to play, really a mindfulness exercise.

I'm lost in the sounds, letting them gently anchor me, but then I open my eyes and the light and colour floods in. The visuals are different now, more striking. Four things. I see the whole horizon from Maketu to The Mount. Three container ships are way out there, tiny toys, coming into the Tauranga harbour. What else can I see? Jellyfish washed up on the sand. A mum playing with two kids.

I close my eyes again. What can I feel? My bra strap is a little bit tight on my left side — funny, I hadn't noticed it before. A little sand hopper by my left foot. The wind whispering on my skin. That's three.

With my eyes still closed, I am on to smell, and I find two things. I notice this slight stench, what is it, either seaweed or a dead fish? — maybe that's why the birds are going so crazy. No, it's not that unpleasant, so I decide it's seaweed drying. And then behind that, what is that . . . it must be the ocean, the salty, salty ocean.

And finally, taste. I swallow a few times, move my tongue around, and it's the coffee I have just enjoyed. Five, four, three, two, one. And that leads me to feel this warmth, the warmth of gratitude, because I love coffee, and I love this moment that I have found myself in.

There are so many things I need to do this morning — vacuum my house, take care of business, call people because I'm back in the country and it's been weeks. I will do these things. I want to chase success, to embrace my amazing opportunities. I love my competitiveness, my hard work, my *Let's go, let's go*. This is greatitude — how hard I will work for my career, for my team — anyone can look at my work and my life and know how grateful I am.

But these quiet moments of mindfulness are pure pleasure. The mindfulness of really being in that moment on the beach, being present, and the gratitude that is manifested in that moment, is such a sensuous, visceral experience for me.

I am a professional rugby player and shit gets crazy. I find myself in crazy storms of pressure in China, Dubai, France, all over. But if things get tough in the whirlpool, I can picture myself on the beach, alive to all my senses; and wherever I am, I get this overwhelming feeling of calm. I feel the positivity and the warmth. I carry it with me. I can be on this beach wherever I am in the world.

2010

13. This rugby thing

Oh jeez, Mum said. That's a lot. She was looking at the cost of me staying in University Hall for my first year away from home. She looked worried. It was a lot, well over $2000. Inside, I was begging her — please! I've done everything else myself, bought my own first car, but there's no way I could afford that much all at once.

Dad had always helped me out whenever he could, but at such short notice it was just too much.

I know, I said, and it's not even the flash part of the hostel, it's the cheap side. The students even called this side the 'ghetto' and the other side the 'Ritz'.

But Mum came through for me. You've got to live somewhere, Mum said, and the legend put it all on her credit card, and so I was all set. I packed up my car and drove myself over to Christchurch and moved into my room in the hostel, all set for the year. I was so pumped.

So it was a pretty big surprise, two or three months later, when I got an invoice for staying at Uni Hall. No, no, no, I told them. My parents paid — it's all done. And that's when they explained that the two and a half grand was just for one quarter, and now the next payment was due, with two more after that.

My heart sank. There was no way I could ask Mum again. She'd already given me everything she had.

I was distraught. I'm going to have to move out! I'd been so proud of myself for leaving home and getting into this whole new world. Come on, this can't end like this. Yet I could see that it could end like this — other students around me were moving out, unable to afford any further payments. Bugger this.

I went to talk to the people in the office. I can't afford to pay, I explained, but what if I work and I try to pay it myself? They were rolling their eyes, like they'd heard this before, and it was obvious they didn't believe I could do it. But to their credit they gave me a chance — I had till the end of the quarter. End of June. Come and see us again then, and you'll need to have the money with you. OK sweet, I said, thank you. But inside I was like, Oh shit, oh shit. Where am I gonna get that money from?

I was lucky that Dad's cousins, Aunty Nette and Uncle Sa, had a niece that worked at the main campus bar, the Foundry Bar, and they got me a job there, every Thursday, Friday, Saturday night till 3 a.m. First-year students normally never got those jobs because everyone knew they just got wasted, but I promised myself there would be no getting wasted on the job and I would always turn up to every shift. I was going to work my ass off, I would never complain and I would sell more drinks than anyone else. I was desperate for the money, and also I had my family's word on the line — I definitely couldn't let them down.

But it wasn't enough, so I looked on the Student Job Search website and took any odd job I could get, weeding an old lady's garden, helping out with demo work, picking up dog poo. I can't even tell you how many jobs I did in that first year at uni.

One job, I was working with two men, one of them little and old with white hair, the other huge and strong with tattoos and not quite as old, and our job was to crawl under an old house and smash up the concrete around its piles. It was so tight under there that the big guy, who would have been strong enough to smash the concrete, couldn't fit; and the little guy, who would've been in his fifties or sixties, could fit but he wasn't strong enough to smash it. Which left me, athletic enough to move around in that tiny space, and strong enough to smash the concrete into pieces. I was under that house for days, and even skipped some lectures so I could do that work, carrying the concrete down to a skip so it could be taken to the dump. And on the last day the hirer gets all this cash out and pays us all the same, even though I'd done most of the work, and he goes, I trust you all to do your own tax. The guys chuckled and took the money. I was confused 'cos even if I was going to do that, I had no idea how. Everything Uncle Neil had taught me about tax seemed a bit meaningless in this desperate world of cashies I was now in.

Slowly, slowly the pile I was saving under my bed was growing. But when the day rolled around when I needed to go into the office to pay, I didn't have enough. I got out every single coin that I had, every note, counted it again and again, but it only added up to about $1800. I took it to the office and I pushed it across the desk.

I know this is not enough, I told the woman. But I give you my word I worked every moment I could outside of study. Please don't kick me out. And I waited for her to shake her head and say, Ruby, you're $600 short. I remember her face as she looked at the money — it was either real bad or real good, I couldn't tell.

Finally she looked at me and she said, I can't believe you actually did what you said. Ruby, this is amazing. The kids who come through here, like you did, they never come back. But you've almost got $2000 here. Of course you can stay. She took all my money, and I was so happy. I didn't cry, but as I walked out of the office my eyes welled up. I could stay. I was so proud of myself.

So all that year I carried on working, and every quarter I took my money to the office, and it was never quite enough, but they always let me stay.

———

Through my whole childhood, it was sport that pulled me through. It was the one constant, and it always brought me happiness. It's where I found friends, a sense of belonging, and it always gave me something to look forward to each week. I'd play anything to get those good feelings — netball, soccer, rugby, squash. At John Paul II High I represented the school at pretty much everything, and I always gave my everything to every sport, even if I wasn't great at it all. But my absolute focus and love was netball, and my dream was to play for the Silver Ferns.

In my high-school years I'd spend all day at the courts if I could, reffing, jumping into other games. The only person from my school who was there more than me was Jess Kersten (now Jess Coll). Jess was one of my best mates at high school and I think it was our talent at sports that made us so close. We both played for our school club CSC, Catholic Schools Combined. She was the only person I'll ever admit was way better than me at netball — she would effortlessly leap and glide across the sky, and net after net would rack up our points. I would be at the other end, the defensive circle, watching how the mid-courters moved, reading the plays like a book, and if I read it right — boom! Intercept so I could send right back down to Jess. Damn we had some fun: Club netball, Canterbury Netball Academy, even a trip to Australia to play in our first overseas netball competition!

Jess made every team she ever trialled for and had fun doing it. She was a year ahead of me in school, and at one point she moved to Christchurch to pursue her netball career. But the world of high-performance sport is intense, and to succeed you have to be committed and selfish with your time and schedule. Jess had had enough, and she wanted to be with the people she loved in Greymouth. She wanted to build a family — and that's exactly what she did. She's now happily married with two beautiful children, Brin and Andie (my god-daughter). She inspires me every day to remember what's truly important in this world.

But anyway, a year later, I too made it over the Alps to Christchurch and set out to pursue my Silver Ferns dream. And I came up against some of the same problems. It was hard.

I felt like I was a good player, and I had assumed I'd make it straight into a premier team, who play indoors. But I missed out on that and found myself playing normal club outside on the concrete at Hagley Park, fighting to make the premier grade next time. So it wasn't what I thought, but I was focused on the effort, and on making it.

But it wasn't just that. Everything was hard. The shoes — oh, they're so expensive! Catching the bus all the time was expensive too, so I struggled to get to practice, and it was hard finding my way around Christchurch by myself. I had to bring all my food with me, because there's no way I could afford to buy food while I was out, but that was hard to organise as I was living in the hostel. Going to trials, I didn't know anyone. I still backed myself. I was still going to give it a good crack, but I missed the support of Jess and I didn't find anyone else to help me get into the swing of things.

Those things made it harder for me to follow the netball path, but weren't enough in themselves to turn me away from it. I still wanted to do it. But that day, early in my first year at Canterbury University, when a uni hall mate invited me to come down to the Ilam fields right next to our accommodation and check out the rugby players . . . well let's just say that it didn't help my netball dreams.

————

Strike hard, go forward. Not a bad philosophy either for a rugby match, or for life.

My rugby life began in March 2010 when I joined the University Rugby Football Club, one of 45 clubs within the

Canterbury rugby framework. Our coach was Ernie Goodhue, who'd coached sevens and fifteens for both men and women and, along with his wife Kay, who was a manager with the Canterbury Rugby Union and managed the Sydenham club team, lived and breathed the game. Plenty of his players developed into Black Ferns. Astonishingly, four of the women down at the field that day — Kendra Cocksedge, Kimberly Smith, Anika Tiplady and Olivia Coady — were in the Black Ferns squad. Later that year, Kendra Cocksedge was selected for the Women's Rugby World Cup squad. I tried not to stare.

Have you ever played rugby before? Ernie asked me.

Yeah, I said.

For who?

So I told him about the school side, but I didn't mention about playing in netball shoes, or that we only played one day a year. I could see him thinking, Well, we'll see what she's like.

It was almost unbelievable to me that I could just walk into the middle of this world, this Women's Rugby world. To put it bluntly, I was completely starstruck as I floundered around in my $20 boots that I had picked up off Trade Me.

Side note: it is actually so hard to buy yourself rugby boots when you literally have no idea what you're looking for. I bought these huge wide-sprig boots designed for front-rowers. I was a winger. But these women, you could just tell they were good.

These tall, toned women came out of their cars at practice and they had these sports leggings on and their rugby socks came up over the leggings, and they had the New Zealand Black Ferns shorts over the leggings and these state-of-the-art Adidas rugby boots (they looked a lot faster than mine) that they tied up nice and tight in a way that told you they're good at what they do. They had special Adidas windbreaker rugby jackets, Black Ferns caps, their hair was tied back tight, and they just looked like they were about to do something impressive.

My mind was blowing that I had the chance to play alongside

the very best. Like the best in the world. This is so cool! I knew I was in the perfect situation for my own enjoyment of life, because, to me, getting better means I get more happiness, and how could I not get better when I was surrounded by people who were so good. And they were all so friendly. I made friends on that first day that I've still got today.

Ernie got us playing touch, and later he said, Well, you've got speed. And good ball skills. But you pass like a netballer. The other women, these brutal battlers, were laughing at me for that, too. I don't blame them. Honestly, you should have seen me. I wanted to be good at this, but that oval ball is the hardest thing to pass. Ernie showed me how to spiral the egg, and from then on I always had a ball in my hand. I took one back to my room in the uni hall and any spare moment I'd throw it up, throw it up, throw it up, trying to make it do the right thing, spin the right way. My passes slowly got better. They still weren't great, but because I was so bad the immediate level of improvement was quite good, and I think Ernie and the others appreciated that. Mere Baker, who first entered my life at the end of that year, still tells me to this day that my passing is the worst thing she's ever seen. But by the end of that first season I could pretty much get it where I wanted it to go, even if it didn't look pretty.

As that first season went on, I was getting what felt like real extreme coaching from the New Zealand players, as well as the coach. I was always at Ernie, asking him questions, and every time we trained I had a Black Fern in my ear going, *Don't step in . . . run there . . . run right around . . .* and everything they said, I did it and it worked. I was getting this constant, instant, trustworthy feedback so I was improving all the time.

——

I didn't make the decision immediately, and for a while that year I kept my relationship going with both sports — I'd play rugby on

Saturday, then netball on Sunday. Choosing one, letting go of the other, was a huge decision for me, and I talked about it endlessly with my friends. *I don't know what to do.* Netball was so familiar, and it was a goal I'd had what seemed like my whole life. But this rugby . . . even though I thought I was so bad at it, I was getting lots of positive reinforcement from my team-mates — *You're really good at this, Ruby* — far more than I was getting from the netball world. Maybe I could just take a break from netball and see what I could do in rugby for a year?

The deciding factor wasn't that netball was terrible, or that I didn't think I could make it, or that I couldn't afford it. In the end, the deciding factor was simply that I fell in love with rugby — the game itself, the culture around it. And I could afford to play it, because the practice fields were so close I could see them out my hostel window, and anyway, in rugby people were always saying things like, *Need a ride? I'll give you a ride* or *There's a massive feed on after the game* — it was such a tight-knit community in the overwhelming big smoke of Christchurch. So I had this sense of togetherness that I just wasn't getting in netball. Or anywhere else for that matter.

Rugby was the whole package, everything I enjoyed: connection, travel, fun, laughing and winning. By the time a couple of months had ticked by, it was clear that rugby offered me, as a person, more than I was getting from netball. So in the end, it was an easy choice.

On 26 May 2010 I made it official. I posted my decision on Facebook: 'I've actually hung up the netty boots to try out this rugby thing.'

This rugby thing. Let's do this!

RUBY'S TRAINING BAG
If I'm surrounded by the very best
people, I will get better myself.

14. Black Ferns are actually real

I thought our team was cool because we had Black Ferns but, oh my gosh, we weren't the only ones. Sydenham were the reigning champions in the Canterbury Women's club competition, and they had Black Ferns too. The very first time we played them was when I was still quite new.

I watch them as we get ready. They're huge! I feel sick. I don't know if I want to play. One of them in particular is massive. With red hair, she looks as if she could pick up a sheep with one hand. I don't know it yet but this is Casey Robertson, the Black Ferns No. 8 who is about to head to the UK for the Women's Rugby World Cup. She will be my first rugby idol, but right at this moment I have no idea who she is. We're not that different in height — I'm 1.77, she's 1.74 — but she is almost 30 kg heavier than me. As time goes on I will get a lot more muscly, but on this early day I'm not much more than 60 kg to her 90 kg.

It's lucky I don't know who she is before we start playing or I'd be too scared to tackle her. The game has hardly started before she comes off the scrum, taking the ball with her, and it's like she's grabbing women by their throats, picking them up, throwing them on to the ground, one after the other. I'm the winger so I'm the last out on the edge and it seems like she's going through the whole team and then, oh my gosh, it's my turn . . . and all I can think is what I've been taught: Just get them to the ground. *Get her down.*

Usually I grab a leg and they fall over, but I hold her leg and she doesn't fall, and I grab wildly at anything and she kind of falls sideways on top of me. And for a while that's how it goes — she throws this player away, then the next away and then it's me. Bodies like skittles all over the ground, and she's the bowling ball, and now she's coming for me. And then I get it: *I can't grab one leg; I better get two*, and boom — I drop her, and I do it a couple more times and I'm pretty pleased because it's not common for a winger to tackle a No. 8; almost always someone else will get her before she gets to me.

And as if things can't get any better, I score in that game too. I catch the ball and there's nothing to do but run — my team is yelling Go Ruby, go Ruby, and I'm scared because there are three massive Black Ferns running at me, but I'm quick and I have no choice. In rugby you just have to back yourself, and if you don't run fast there's no point you being on the field. Like, hurry up! And the line is there and the three Black Ferns are almost on me and I close my eyes and I try to reach out and *boom*, I'm smoked. The three Black Ferns crash into me and it feels like they fold me in half over myself and I hit the ground and now I'm lying in this heap with these three six-foot titans on top of me, and I'm way over the touch line. I don't know if I put the ball down before or after I let it go. It happened so fast. Damn! But my team is running towards me and I'm going what the hell, and they're celebrating, and they go, Look! Look! And there's the ball resting perfectly about a metre inside the touch line. I had actually placed the ball just before I got smoked out but I couldn't even tell!

They're all hugging me, and I'm thinking, This is so fuckin' cool. In netball when you shoot a goal or you get an intercept your team can't come and celebrate with you; that game is non-stop, and you just keep playing. But these girls, I hardly even know them, but they're jumping all over me, high-fiving. This is awesome.

We beat Sydenham that game, the only team to beat them that whole year, and afterwards in the changing room people were drinking and smoking, getting the party started, which was so weird to me, because in netball that just wouldn't happen.

Olivia Coady came over and sat next to me. She was already a Black Fern — she'd been selected two years previously when she was just eighteen, the youngest in the squad — and I looked up to her. She was No. 7 so her tackling was outstanding.

Ruby, she said, how did you tackle Casey Robertson?

Which one was Casey Robertson?

That huge red-haired chick that was fending people in the throat, said Coady, acting out everyone getting choked and thrown to the ground.

Oh, so *that* was Casey Robertson.

She's like the starting No. 8 Black Fern, Coady said. She's been to more World Cups than anyone in the whole of Canterbury.

Holy shit, I said. I'm glad I didn't know that.

I just couldn't believe how cool this all was. It was like playing club netball with Silver Ferns legend Casey Kopua on my team, except that would never happen. So this was incredible — how could I not grow when I was playing next to New Zealand players? Being the worst in the room is actually super-useful. I knew I could only stay there if I got better. *So I had better get better*. And that thought was pure excitement to me.

Later on, when rugby became my career and I found myself within the New Zealand training structure, I had the opportunity to talk to the sports psychologist David Galbraith, who over the years has helped me massively in understanding the Ruby–rugby–Ruby relationship. He's talked to me about courage and cowardice, and the spirals each one can take you on. If you are a coward, you feel embarrassed, you feel shame, you have self-hate, so you're a coward again. But if you're courageous you do the good actions that bring you pride, which means you have self-love, which gives you confidence and enthusiasm and you want to take on more so you do another act of courage.

So it's like, *woohoo!* For me, tackling Casey Robertson definitely took courage, and I felt pride about that. So I know the truth of that — it could be anything that's a challenge, but if you take even one courageous step it will set you on your path.

We would go on to play Sydenham in the final. It was a huge occasion for us. And we beat them! It was the first time our club had won for years.

I'll never forget winning my first club final with a women's rugby team. No one parties like club rugby players. We took over the whole rugby club — all of us women dressed in the colours of our mini-teams, our teams-within-a team, purple, green, whatever, the bar all to ourselves. If the world was the Ilam Field clubrooms, it felt like we ran the world. The music blasting, ladies standing on tables and on chairs, stomping, yelling the words to the songs, drinking from the club championship trophy. It was my first year but you could tell these ladies had been after this win for a long time, and I was so happy to be able to help them get it. My cheeks hurt from smiling.

And at that celebration, I won one of my favourite trophies ever — the trophy for the Best First Year player. I felt so welcome, and so appreciated. I keep it still, displayed on my wooden bookshelf at home in Tauranga — it's the only trophy displayed there, and it's alongside a photo of my maternal grandma, Sue, and a photo of my paternal grandad, grandma and their children in Samoa before they left for the land of opportunity.

———

One of the things I loved about rugby was the honesty of the game. I remembered back to a prem-grade netball game in Greymouth where I was goal keep. The other side's shooter was much taller than me — I'm 177 centimetres, she was nine or ten centimetres taller. Netball is supposedly a 'non-contact' sport, but in reality there's contact all the time — players get real good at not showing they're contacting, but meanwhile they're constantly jabbing you with their hips and elbows. My problem was that I was never very good at hiding when I contacted.

But rugby, this new game I'd discovered, was unashamedly a contact sport. We literally ran head-first at each other, and you wouldn't be on the field if you didn't want to be contacted. There was no lying, no deception, just: boom, and you got a high-five if you contacted really well. It made so much more sense to me.

———

In early September 2010, New Zealand made it through to the final of the Women's Rugby World Cup, being played that year in England. They would play for the cup against England at the Stoop stadium, across the road from the larger Twickenham, in London, in front of more than 13,000 people. From never having seen the Black Ferns play, all of a sudden I was hanging out with a whole bunch of women who were like, get the popcorn, get the beer, setting themselves up in front of the TV like it was an All Blacks game.

We all got together and watched it in a place called the Skank — a flat a couple of the girls lived in, and it was definitely the cool house, the cool club. Some of them had jobs so there was money for drinks. It wasn't just our team, but players from Sydenham were there too, everyone watching and talking about the Black Ferns 'cos they were all mates with them. I was real quiet, but super-aware of how incredible this was, losing it on my inside. Because there they were on the screen in front of us, that ghost team I'd heard about but never seen. They were right there and they were friggin' awesome.

There on the TV was Kendra Cocksedge — I'd just played my first season with her, and been part of the same winning team that had just won the club championship. And the chick who was the youngest — just two years older than me — and scored the most points, including the winning penalty kick, Kelly Brazier. I didn't know it then, but she would be my team-mate for ten years in the New Zealand Sevens Rugby Team.

I can honestly say that watching the Black Ferns, seeing them on the screen, seeing that they were *real*, changed my life. The memory came back to me of Canvastown, the dark Wakamarina River, the unhappiness, the screaming that went on all the time. How I played rugby there because there was nothing else, no netball, no hockey, so the three of us girls played just for something to frickin' do. How they'd always say to the boys, You can be an All Black and they'd all love it and then they'd say to me, You can be a Black Fern, and the anger I felt. My frustration when they said that because, bro, what does that even mean? Are they even real? What do they look like? And if they are real they obviously don't count for much because they've never been on TV.

That was when I was eleven, and then fast-forward to eighteen and I was sitting *here* and I could see them as they beat England 13–10 in that final, their fourth World Cup win in a row. *That's* what they look like. That's their names, that's their faces. They exist. They are real. Frick, I thought, and my next thought was as real as these awesome women sitting next to me. *I* can be a Black Fern.

———

The club championship finished mid-year, and then that year I made the Canterbury team — that's like the next step up, and to make the team I had to compete against players from all the

Canterbury clubs. I admit I was lucky — the Black Ferns were still away, so I definitely got opportunities I mightn't otherwise have had. But I sure as heck was going to make the most of them.

But even though it was a World Cup year — and even though the Black Ferns had proved themselves yet again by winning against all the other nations — the fact was that 2010 was a really hard year for women's rugby. Normally, the regional women's teams from all round the country competed in the National Provincial Competition, the NPC (now known as the Farah Palmer Cup or FPC), but back in January, New Zealand Rugby, which administers the sport in New Zealand, announced it was cancelling the women's NPC. This meant that as well as there being no national competition for female players to aim for, the top players went into the World Cup with no meaningful top-level competition. There was limited money for women's rugby anyway, but this was a savage blow and there had been an outcry, with some famous Black Ferns very critical of the move, and some commentators saying it would be the death of the women's game.

The upshot was, there was no money to support the women's competition that year. If we wanted to play, we had to do it all ourselves. So the Canterbury coach had to ring up the Wellington coach and ask if they had a team, did they want to play — and if they did they might have to fund-raise a bit or gather sponsors. It was a throw-together year.

But, as a rookie, nothing could spoil it for me. I honestly felt like I had found this new drug, and I just couldn't get enough. There I was, my first year, in the starting line-up of the Canterbury team. And something that was so crucial to me was that I was standing next to Amiria Rule (née Marsh) — Mids, who is one of the greatest New Zealand players ever. She'd been in the Black Ferns squads that won the 2002 and 2006 world cups, and she should have been over in England at the 2010 World Cup, but she'd had a knee injury. So it probably sucked for her but it was pivotal for my career.

In the club games I played on the wing, but in the Canterbury side I was playing centre and Mids was alongside me at 10, and for me she was like this one-woman masterclass on how to read a rugby game.

Like a lot of the old-school heroes, Mids was a very scary player sometimes, with a short attitude and she didn't give you much. I've seen her make people cry while we were playing with like one sentence without even meaning to. If you made a mistake, a lot of the women would be like, Oh well, next time . . . but she'd be like Oh, fuck, and she'd just walk off. The reality was she was too good for the competition that year, and she was frustrated. But I didn't give a shit if she was angry at me or she swore at me or whatever, because the stuff I was getting off her was just too good. If you could learn not to take stuff personally off her, she could teach you how to read rugby like it was a book.

Thanks to her, I learned about running holes and manipulating defences. She would almost pass the ball where someone was *supposed* to be, so if I didn't run in the right place I wouldn't get the ball but if I did, I would run through the defence like a hot knife through butter. It was amazing. She made me feel like I had the answers to an exam or something, so I just hung around her all the time. I was just always at her — Hi Mids! — and it probably annoyed her, to be honest. But for me, the chance to play with her was just such an incredible opportunity.

For the next couple of years making the Canterbury team was harder. The top players had come back from the World Cup, and I just couldn't get into the starting team. So that one little chance, in that strange 2010 year, was crucial for my development.

Still, in 2011 when the Canterbury rep side travelled up to Wellington, I was in the team. Dad and Lesh came along to watch, bringing Lesh's two boys, my nephews Jack and Daley. That day I learned all about what a 'stinger' is in rugby.

I was on the wing again, so usually I'm defending the fullback coming into the line or my opposition winger. But this

game, there was this centre that could not be stopped. She would
have two players outside her and still not pass because she would
simply run over the top of players. By this stage in my career
I had become quite good at tackling because I was fearless in this
new-found love of mine. So when this particular centre ran over
our flanker, our first five-eighth and then her opposite centre,
I had to come in to tackle her. I didn't understand why my team
wasn't just going low on her. So I came in, dipped to tackle with
my right shoulder and wrapped my arms tight. I tackled her,
don't worry. But upon contact I felt an electric shock go from the
top of my shoulder at the point of contact all the way down my
arm to my fingers. And then when I got up, my whole right arm
wouldn't move.

The physio ran on to assess my dangling limb mid-play: Can
you move it?

Nah, it's numb! I said, keeping an eye on the play. She moved
my arm — Does this hurt?

Not at all, I just can't lift it.

She tried a couple more things and then nodded, You've got
a stinger.

Will the feeling come back? I asked.

Yes. Do you want to come off so I can check it properly?

That was all I needed to hear. I took off back into the action
and just waited for the feeling in my arm to come back, hoping it
would be before that centre came crashing back on to my side of
the field. I got two more stingers that game from that centre. The
centre's name was Shakira Baker and she would become one of
my closest team-mates for ten years in the New Zealand Sevens
team.

I played on, and the feeling came back, and after all that
kerfuffle I still managed to score a try — right in front of my
family on the right wing. It was so cool to have something to unite
my family with, even if my nephew Daley was more concerned
with the sandpit than his aunty battling away on the field. Dad

was super stoked. It's cool to give your parents something to be happy about in this life.

Back at the end of the 2010 season, though, with summer beginning, some of the others were like, Oh, Rubes you going to play sevens? I didn't want to lose what I had so I was like, Yeah, sweet, I'll follow the team.

RUBY'S TRAINING BAG
When I do something courageous I am
proud of myself, and that increases
my self-love and my confidence.

15. Sevens heaven

My old netball mate from Greymouth, Jess, pulled out some old clippings from our school yearbook recently, and we couldn't stop laughing. It was us playing sevens with the other Westland high schools — just a day of fun. Sometimes we had boots, sometimes we just had our netball shoes, or not even that. It wasn't anything like the real game — we didn't do scrums and lineouts, for instance.

Our school was the smallest on the Coast but we won several years in a row. The on-field chemistry between Jess and me was captured in the school newsletter:

The best play of the day came from a bit of Jess and Ruby brilliance during the Westland High game. Ruby won the ball in a cross field direction, taking the defence with her, before flicking the ball behind her back to Jess, who took possession and ran half the field to score under the posts.

If I had even half an inkling that sevens was an actual thing, or that it was worth playing rugby seriously, I would've pushed Jess and myself to pursue it way back then. But all we knew was it was just a day out of school. As fun as it was to have a go at it once a year, we simply did not see a future in it.

But now, at the end of 2010, I found the game that was made for me.

In fifteens, my 62 kg frame had not been an advantage. I was always getting pummelled by groups of much bigger women because even though I was fast I wasn't fit enough to get away. In fifteens I could get caught out if I wasn't careful, and I wasn't yet strong enough to sustain the impact. But suddenly, in sevens, being smaller and quicker was a game-changer. I'm a prop in sevens, something I could not be in fifteens, where those women are often over 100 kg. But in sevens, no matter the position, you need to have all the skill-sets, which means whatever your position you need to be fast, skilful and agile.

Sevens is quick. Same size field as fifteens, pretty much the same rules, but half the number of people. So all of a sudden you've got twice the amount of space to cover, and you have to run twice as fast. In fifteens, if you miss a tackle it's not the end of the world because there'll be a flanker, or someone to help you out and grab the one you missed. But in sevens, honestly, if you miss a tackle that person will probably get a try. So sevens is super exciting. And to be a good sevens player, you have to be the ultimate athlete.

In fifteens when you have a scrum, there's a pause and you can stand there for a bit. In fifteens, you've got a minute and a half to kick a conversion, and again the rest of the team can breathe. In sevens, you've got 15 seconds for a scrum and 30 seconds to make that kick. It's bang, bang, bang. It's just 14 minutes, but it's crazy fast. Exhausting. You know how you might do one sprint and then you're puffed and buggered and you need a rest? That's what sevens is but constant, constant, constant — and you're not just sprinting but you're tackling and hitting a ruck and getting up at the same time as you're sprinting. If you need a rest you're screwed — like, you *will* get scored on.

And you've got to do that six times in two days — that's the way the tournaments are structured, for maximum entertainment. What it requires, physically and mentally, is huge. There is no let-up, and it's a battle of who can last the longest in that extremely high exhaustion rate.

So for me, what it meant was that all of a sudden the other, bigger players couldn't gang up on me three to one — with fewer players, if they did that they would simply create space somewhere else. And if I could find space I could take advantage of it. I could get the upper hand. *Wow, this is different.* Even though I wasn't super-fit I never cared that I was tired. I would just keep going.

So that summer I played for the university sevens team in the club championship and, without knowing it of course, took my first step towards what was to be my career for the next twelve years. Not that there was any indication of that at the time. I was the worst in the team, and the least fit, but they had to pick me because I was literally the only one who would get to every single training. I wouldn't dream of missing out, no matter what else was going on. It also did help that I lived right next-door to the fields.

There's a saying that there are three key attributes to being a good employee, and it applies to team sport as well: skill, reliability and being good to be around. Well, you can, for free, turn up when you say you're going to turn up, and I always turned up early (mainly because I would rather run around than sit in my room and do more study). I was OK to be around because I was just so happy to be there. And while I don't think I had the competency, I did everything the coaches said and so I kept growing. I used to think being bad or average at a certain skill was a put-off, but all that means is my growth will occur at a higher and faster rate than someone who's better at me. I love growth.

I have diligence for all the important things, and that's something anyone can do for free.

We won the club sevens that first year, and after that I thought Ernie, the club coach, looked at me a bit different.

And then it was the end of the uni year, and I headed back to Greymouth.

———

I'd worked hard all year getting the money so I could stay in the uni hall accommodation, but I never quite made enough. By the end of the year I was still maybe $500 short overall, and I said to the woman in the office: I'm going to go home to work for the summer, and I will bring you the money the first day of the next semester when I come back. Because of my diligence throughout the year, she trusted my word and we said goodbye with a smile.

By this stage Mum and Neil had left the Coast, so I boarded in Greymouth with a friend from a job I had at the swimming pool and paid him a hundred bucks a week, meals included. I set about working myself to the bone. I had three jobs that summer. In the morning I was a postie — got up at 4 a.m. and began my routine of a heap of Weetbix (I grew up with the ads telling me this would make me a good rugby player so why not), an instant coffee and a Berocca (I had also seen on TV that this helped). I was tired and barely functioning but there was no way I was turning down $17.50 an hour! That was more than double my first wage. Sometimes I would just do mornings, but when I had to cover the big shifts I was doing the full day's run. Most posties are so good they can do the morning run then have a four-hour break in the middle of the day, then quickly finish off their pick-ups. They had their rhythm down. Every single morning they would be in and out faster than Portia Woodman on a rugby field. But not me, I would still be sorting long after the sun was in the sky, then it felt like my run was always so slow and I would be lucky to get 20 minutes to snooze or eat. Most days I was non-stop packing, sorting, running into houses, running back, zooming the van around, dodging dogs, back and forth, hurling packages out. I'm so sorry if anyone reading this sent a 'fragile' package in the summer of 2010 in or out of Greymouth.

Or, if I'd just done the morning postie shift, I'd work through the afternoon at the pool as a lifeguard. Whichever daytime job it was, I'd be done just in time to quickly heat up my dinner back at my boarding house, then head down to the most popular bar in town to start my late night shift at 6.30 p.m.

At the beginning of my shift at the Railway Hotel, the Razza, there were always a few old codgers in the bar, lining up their shrapnel for their 70 c 6 oz beers that we would just keep refilling. They were nice, some of them extremely nice — I got a small bunch of picked flowers from one of them.

Then at night-time it became a different place, lights off, music blasting, the only place in town that was open past midnight so all the young-uns, riff-raff and noise headed straight for us every Thursday through Saturday nights. DJs, league players, artists or NZ celebs looking for fun — anyone that came to Grey all came through the doors of the Raz.

Work, work, work. All together, I was doing 80-hour weeks plus. I needed the money and all I knew was that the way to get the money was to do the work.

This was the end of my first year playing rugby, and I was super-focused on my ambition, my new dream of becoming a Black Fern, so any gap I had I'd go for a run, or go to the gym, or find a playground and do a bodyweight session. Every single hour, I was busy working, sleeping, eating or training, and I took pride in what I was achieving. But you can't sustain that kind of effort. Working late, up at 4 a.m. — one night at the bar I got such a bad migraine because of my lack of sleep that I lost my vision. I wanted to keep working, but I couldn't see people's faces when they were ordering to lip-read over the music. I had to call it a night and walk home, head throbbing. I was so pissed at myself.

One day working at the pool I found out one of the other lifeguards had actually represented New Zealand at the Commonwealth Games, in track running of all things. I managed

to convince her to take me for a session on how to run faster.
We went down to the athletics track in Greymouth where I had
always come second to Jess in the 100-metre sprints at high
school — it's a grass track but it has the lanes.

Your hands need to be controlled but still light, she told me.
Imagine you're holding a blade of grass between your thumb and
your index fingers. You need to keep hold of the grass but without
squeezing it.

She plucked a piece of grass and showed me.

I still think of that today when I do speed-training now.

She was a great teacher, and we did a few reps, but as I walked
back to the starting line a sudden nausea took over my body.
I fell to my knees and vomited. My body was making it clear it
had reached its limits. She asked me about my schedule, and
I explained I was training every day around my 80 hours of work.
She quickly concluded the session and told me it was too much.
She was right. I wasn't giving myself time to recover. I learned
heaps that summer about how much you can work, and how
much you can't.

I earned about $7000 over that holiday break. I bought a new
car — a cool little two-door 1998 Mitsubishi Mirage — through
a friend of Aunty Nette. It was navy blue, and after a mate put
in a stereo with aux cord capability it was officially the flashest
and coolest car I'd ever been able to call mine. In Christchurch
I went straight to the accommodation office and slid over the
exact amount I owed and thanked them for believing in me. And
that's when they offered me a job.

Ruby, the woman said, you've paid your debt in full. We are
so impressed with your diligence. We want to offer you a spot as
a Residential Assistant in our accommodation . . . Far out! That's
free accommodation and free meals for the whole year. Even
though I had to turn them down, because I had already sorted
out a flat for myself, it was still massive for me to be offered a job
when for a while there it looked like I might get kicked out.

It was hard in its way, working like I did in those years of uni, but I learned that if I want something I've got to work for it, and get it for myself. Mum and Dad couldn't afford to help any more. That was the simple fact. I was growing up and I only had me to rely on. I also learned the importance of keeping your word. The office lady trusted me to come back because I did time and time again. It even got me a job offer! I kept my word to people and I kept it to myself. I learned that I could rely on myself, and all that knowledge is such a gift.

Also, hard as it was, it wasn't hard compared with how I felt when I was nine, ten and eleven. That was hard. I would rather work myself to the bone so I could study and train — exhaust myself with working — than be in a house where someone is getting abused in the next room. I'm not dead, I'm not OD-ing on drugs. This is fine; I can do this.

But mostly, for me, university was this big fun place where I made friends, found rugby and worked hard to make a living.

I stayed on top of my academic work. Uni isn't that hard if you can handle high school, until the third year when I definitely had to put my head down. I didn't really apply myself, not like I would learn to do later, but I applied myself enough, and after three years I came out with a Bachelor of Communications with a second major in English. I'd happily have become a sports journalist — that was the reason I embarked on that degree in the first place. That could have been my purpose, but I fell in love with rugby and I found my purpose in my team. And by the time I finished my undergrad degree, at the end of 2012, I'd already played my debut for the New Zealand Sevens, at the Oceania World Series in Fiji.

RUBY'S TRAINING BAG
If I want something I've got to work
for it. I can rely on myself.

2011

16. An underground world

found sevens at just the right time. It was hard enough in those earlier days playing women's rugby fifteens, but if you played women's sevens, good luck. It had been treated like nothing by the rugby establishment, even though the women who actually played it had won many international championships over the years. Those women who kept the game going, and the men who supported them, were almost completely unsanctioned and unfunded. They're not recognised in any official history, yet they carried the game for nearly ten years. They deserve accolades and admiration.

The Hong Kong Sevens tournament was established in 1997 and, while NZR (or NZRFU as it was then) wouldn't send an official team, New Zealand was unofficially represented by an invitation team made up of Black Ferns and other upcoming players. It was awkward for the other countries because it wasn't actually an official New Zealand team. They called themselves Wild Ducks, and they won the tournament in 1997 and 1999, but because it wasn't a national team those games don't appear as official internationals.

In 2000 and 2001 an official New Zealand team did go to the

tournament, and won, but after that the women's sevens team lost funding again.

However, one of the organisers of the Hong Kong tournament, United States coach Emil Signes, was desperate to keep New Zealand in the competition. He was worried that sevens would fall off the map without New Zealand there. He went to Bay of Plenty coach Peter Joseph, who since 2000 had coached the Aotearoa Māori Sevens, and invited him to bring that team over to Hong Kong. But because it wasn't an official national team, Joseph couldn't get funding, so that's when he and his wife Shelly mortgaged their house and put in just over $64,000 to get the team to Hong Kong.

It's such an awesome story of commitment and resilience, and so crucial in the history of our game. Aotearoa Māori Sevens — which started out as a Māori team, but after the first year players of other ethnicities were also included — won the tournament that year and also the following five years; and also won three Rome Sevens Championships from 2010 to 2012. In 2012, Aotearoa Māori was in the final playing another unofficial New Zealand team, the KUSA team set up by Mere Baker, largely based in the South Island, to give more opportunity for our female players.

All those titles, but never officially recognised, and not even a mention on the NZR website. It was like it was nothing. It was an underground world.

The change started happening in 2011 when the International Olympic Committee voted to include sevens in the Olympics, with the debut to be at Rio in 2016, and that had an impact around the globe, with lots of countries finally putting decent resources into growing women's rugby in the hope of winning gold at the Olympics. The official World Rugby Women's Sevens Series, which began in December 2012, was a sanctioned tournament and a direct result of that heightened interest in women's sevens (of course, the men's sevens had had their World Series since 1999).

In New Zealand there was a big campaign with lots of pressure coming from people like Jonah Lomu, and the official attitude changed from thinking *These pesky women's sevens* to *Oh my gosh, a possible Olympic medal!* Work began at the national level to create a national women's sevens team under the auspices of NZR. Building a team from scratch was how it was reported in the media, which must have been a kick in the guts for the women who'd been playing it, and winning, all this time.

I didn't know anything about all this background at the time, not until the end of 2011 when NZR started looking for players for the new national sevens team. I didn't know that my own career was going to exactly mirror the new era of the game.

———

My second year of rugby, 2011, I focused on saying yes to every single opportunity I could find to train and play, and after another year of playing NPC fifteens for Canterbury, Ernie asked me to come along for a different kind of sevens trial. Real sevens, he said. This was the KUSA team, coached by Mere Baker as another option alongside Aotearoa Māori, totally under the radar of New Zealand's mainstream rugby structure, and yet with players who had played all round the world.

Because it was unofficial you had to know someone, and thanks to Ernie I got my ticket in. Which was so cool because in KUSA they were playing international tournaments — only of course there was no funding: you had to pay to register your team, pay to get yourself there, pay for your accommodation. For each player I think it added up to $3000. So much money. If only I could've worked 160 hours a week during summer!

Now we had to fund-raise. The team organised quiz nights, car washes, sausage sizzles. Baker bought tiger tails (foam massage sticks) for $10 and told me to go sell them for $20. Everything we could think of. I was sure there was no way I could ever get that much money, but slowly, slowly we got there. Some women could pay their $3000 in cash, so then we could split our fund-raising between the ones who couldn't pay. I made sure I turned up to every single fund-raiser I could. I would stand in the sun outside the Mitre 10 Mega in Sumner selling sausages and dreaming about playing sevens around the world.

I wasn't selected for the June tournament in Rome where they came second, beaten in the final by Aotearoa Māori, the other New Zealand team that included Sarah Goss (Gossy; now Sarah Hirini), who in a few years' time was to captain our Black Ferns Sevens team. So Aotearoa Māori got the prize money and my team had to go back to ground zero and start fund-raising again.

I wasn't selected for the Byron Bay tournament in October, which KUSA won. To be honest, I still felt pretty out of my depth. But around that time was when I had that breakthrough training moment with Baker, when she told me that if I caught that next group she'd make me the best sevens player in the world, thus showing me the power of my mind over my body. And not long after that, November 2011, I made the KUSA team travelling to Queensland to the Gold Coast Sevens. My first-ever overseas international rugby competition, going against teams from Australia, Tonga, Fiji. I felt like I had really made it.

Unfortunately we bombed out in the quarter-finals. Tonga played a tactical game; we made bad calls, and it was so disappointing, and no one was more disappointed than Baker. She was losing it on the sideline, kicking bottles, absolutely spewing. At one point she even threw her clipboard across the sideline.

A couple of times she pulled me out for not coming across to cover the space quick enough. You were just watching, she told me. You've got to keep moving. You can't stand and watch, or walk and watch, you've got to run and watch and scan everything that's happening. The time you stop running is the time that space will open up for the other team.

I paid attention and even though I wasn't fit enough I did my best to get up and go, get up and go. To never stop.

I was angry with myself the whole time that I couldn't play better. But then Baker put me on to start ahead of some more experienced players, and she didn't sub me off. *What does that mean?* And after the tournament, even though the team had done so badly, she came up to me in her Baker way, not really looking at me, seeming totally disinterested, and she was just like, A couple of people asked who you were, eh. And I was like, Oh cool. Thinking again, like, *What does that mean?* And then she was like, Yeah, I reckon you can make the New Zealand team. Of course at that time there wasn't a New Zealand team, but there had begun to be whispers about one being established. So that was huge for me coming from her, but I just acted real nonchalant. Oh yeah, cool, as if I didn't think anything of it. But when she said it she made it real. It was my fire, and now it was burning inside me.

And everyone's pissed that when we get home we have to start fund-raising again.

———

Bombing out, like we did in Australia that first tournament, showed me something really important.

You can train till the cows come home, but it's not enough. You need that pressure. Those KUSA trainings were some of the hardest I've ever done but they didn't have the pressure like that quarter-final did. Because as we saw at that tournament, people do weird things under pressure in rugby, just like they do in life. In one of the games we were actually winning, but then the other side scored a try and we hadn't been expecting it, and we started going oh my gosh, oh my gosh, and then little things happened like Tonga broke the rules and we were unsettled because the ref didn't see. And it all started snowballing and we

Top left My dad, Vaki, was a superhero to me when I was a little girl. Here he is guiding me around the dance floor.

Top right Me and my beautiful mum, Marion.

Bottom Dad teaching me how to do a haka. Little did we know that years later I would be performing it in front of international audiences before big games.

Top left Me at about three years old, dressed up in some rugby gear at the Pōneke club in Wellington.

Top right Happy times with some of my cousins before they left New Zealand. Clockwise from top left: Sammie, me, Hemi James, Joseph and Rachel (with her arm around Joseph).

Bottom Performing the siva, a traditional Samoan dance, with my cousin Oriana. My cousins were my world when I was growing up — I just wanted to be like them and copy everything they did.

Top One of the clippings my friend Jess dug out recently, showing our high-school sevens team. I'm in front, lying on the ground, and Jess is kneeling directly behind me.

Bottom Mum and me at my eighteenth birthday party.

Top A family reunion in Samoa in 2018. We're standing in front of the fale that Grandad built.

Bottom In hospital on the Sunshine Coast after getting the mumps while in training camp, April 2018. I was forced to miss the Commonwealth Games.

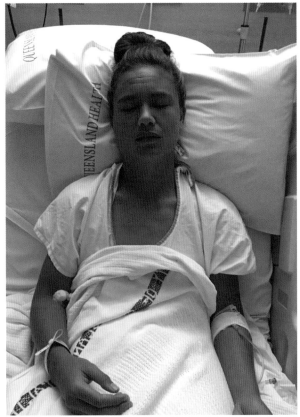

Top Posing with my trophy after being named Rugby Sevens
Player of the Year at the World Rugby Awards in Tokyo, November
2019. *Photo by Matt Roberts/World Rugby via Getty Images*

Bottom Getting my game face on ahead of a match at the Sydney
Sevens, 2020. *Photo by Rachael Whareaitu/NZR*

Top Bleeding from a head wound after the match against Fiji at the Oceania tournament in 2021. I wear my scars with pride. *Photo by Rachael Whareaitu/NZR*

Bottom Sharing a moment with Fiji's Reapi Ulunisau after we beat Fiji in the semi-final at the Tokyo Olympics 2020 (held in 2021). I know how she feels. *Photo by Mike Lee/KLC Fotos for World Rugby*

Top The agony and the ecstasy. On the left, a flashback to the Rio Olympics in 2016: consoling my good friend and team-mate Portia Woodman after we lost the sevens final. *Photo by Mark Kolbe/Getty Images.* On the right, me and Portia celebrating winning Olympic gold in Tokyo. *Photo by Mike Lee/KLC Fotos for World Rugby*

Bottom Me and Risi (Risaleaana Pouri-Lane) proudly wearing our gold medals at the Tokyo Olympics. *Photo by Mike Lee/KLC Fotos for World Rugby*

Top Catching up with my friend Jess's kids after returning from the Tokyo Olympics. Brin is modelling my gold medal and I'm holding little Andie, my god-daughter.

Bottom Me and my partner, Dani, celebrating Christmas 2021.

didn't know what to do. We weren't prepared and we freaked out.

In those days we just didn't get the time to train properly, what with all the day jobs, life outside of rugby, and fund-raising, and mentally we weren't prepared. But now, all these years down the track and in the professional era, the Black Ferns Sevens treat the training with the same intensity as if it's a game. Even in training we are so intensely competitive. The coach will yell, *There's 30 seconds left and you're losing 5–nil.* It's a must-score play, and we have a choice. We can go, Oh whatever, Coach, we're just at training . . . or we can go, We're scoring. And that's the mindset we have. We'll do anything to get that try in those 30 seconds.

One time my team was hot on attack 10 metres out from scoring a try. Gossy was penalised and she knew if we quick-tapped we would win because her and her team-mate were still on the ground. I went to grab the ball because I knew it too. As I tried to pick it up she fell right on top of the ball, acting like she couldn't get up. I tried to reach under to grab the ball but she leaned her body into me so I couldn't grab it. I was wild. I shoved her, she shoved me back. We started to swing wildly before the rest of the team came in between us. I was so pissed 'cos the moment was gone and she had won by rarking me up because I could no longer score the quick try. After I had calmed down it just made me respect her even more as a player.

Obviously getting physical with each other is extremely rare, but it just shows how much we care and the different places we push ourselves to get into mentally. When we lose at training it genuinely feels like a loss to me and it hurts. Even at training I'm aware of the score, I ask the ref the time, I treat it the same as a game.

To some people it looks a little bit aggressive or intense at training, but you watch us when we're in those same moments on the international stage and it's not even a thing. Who cares if we're down by one try and there's 30 seconds to go. We've been here before, we know exactly what to do.

On the other hand, it's hard to understand why we do it or even how to train like that unless you've been under that pressure in a real game. Girls are always scared to come off the bench into those big games, but I'm like, You need to jump in. Who cares if you lose, who cares if you drop the ball. It's scary, but you will learn and you will never make those mistakes again. And no matter what happens on that field, if you give your all and still lose, you will always grow. You will always remember what happened and learn for next time.

A metaphor. That's what rugby is — a living, breathing metaphor.

You've got to take all your opportunities, give everything 100 per cent, so that when it really matters, you're ready. Tackle all life's got to give. Straight up the guts.

RUBY'S TRAINING BAG
You've got to take all your opportunities,
give everything 100 per cent, so that
when it really matters, you're ready.

2012

17. Debut-iful

Hey Ruby, look at this. It was March 2012, and the Archibald twins from the Burnside club, one of them in gumboots against the early autumn mud, were handing out pamphlets and I took one and had a look. 'Go 4 Gold trials', 'Sevens in the Olympics' . . .

The Olympics?! To start with, I couldn't relate to it. No way. Surely that's for other people! I didn't have anything like the self-belief I'd need to see myself as an Olympic contender. But I read down the bullet points, and right at the bottom it said, 'Potentially fourteen Sevens contracts up for grabs!' And that was what hooked me. Contracts means getting paid. Imagine that! Imagine if all these amazing women I had met through rugby, who had jobs that meant they couldn't get to practice on time, could get paid. Imagine if I could be part of the generation that secured that. I could help. I could be a part of this massive change that brought pay to women's rugby.

Frick, I'm in, bro! What do I do? So I got straight on the website and registered for this thing called Sevens Academy.

All the old-school sevens players, the ones who'd fund-raised, organised, played, won all over the world for ten years with no support from NZR, were like, What the frick is this? Who are these people? Nobody knows sevens like we do. But I was young, naive, keen and I just saw an opportunity for all of us.

———

Go 4 Gold was designed as a high-performance screening programme to select athletes from all over New Zealand, even luring them away from other sports such as netball and hockey, and train them to participate in the global expansion of sevens, in particular aiming for the Olympics. Trials were held throughout the country, attracting more than 1000 women. I went to the Canterbury one at Burnham in early 2012. Gradually, the number was whittled down to 60, and I was still in there and they took that group to a training camp at Waiouru, the Army camp in the rugged, alpine desert in the middle of the North Island. It was intense, but it was still fun and we were all so new so I took it as an opportunity.

There were lots of testings and trainings and running and press-ups. And on the last day we finally got to do the dreaded 'confidence course'.

We form into threes to try and complete this course on the last day, and I'm with Michaela Blyde, who we now call Mini, and Selica Winiata, who we call Shorty. Mini is only sixteen, still at school, and Shorty is already a police officer and has been in the Black Ferns since 2008. We don't know each other at all, but we quickly form our bond as a team. I'm like, Are you keen to really get after this? Like, I'm not here just to participate; I'm going to try and catch the first place . . . And they're like, Hell yeah. I've only met them this weekend but after they agree so quickly to compete I learn in those few words that they are both extremely fit and hard workers. I like it. I now know them both really well and of course they were going to come with me — they're both absolute beasts to train with.

I take off as fast as I can go, sprinting up a hill with the other two just behind me. I go, Shorty are you there? Yeah. Mini are you there? Yeah. I run the whole time, over the jumps up the hill, without looking back, just listening for their voices, just checking to make sure we're all still together. Shorty? Yeah. Mini? Yeah. Into the freezing water, under these huge poles, up slippery banks, over a wall. It's no walk in the park, but we pass a team, we pass two more. No one else has even passed one. Shorty, you there? Yup! Mini? Yes!

And they're right there with me, and we're passing even people I really look up to like Huriana Manuel who we all call Huri, and Carla Hohepa who I'd watched in the 2010 World Cup become the IRB Player of the Year. Our fight is our own.

No one else notices particularly — they're all busy with their own challenge — but us three . . . I think we're pretty good. And we must be, because we pass almost every team and we finish together.

We don't know it but we'll be team-mates for years. Me and Mini in particular will both win World Rugby Sevens Player of the Year, her for two years running. We'll both win gold medals at the Tokyo Olympics. But that was the first camp. That was the very beginning.

I saw so many women in those early camps who had amazing talent, but some had perhaps not yet had that Baker moment as I had — that moment when the purpose and the path become startlingly clear — and so the numbers were whittled away.

I took it all so seriously. At my first camp I began keeping a diary. In breaks, or at the end of the day, I'd write up into my diary everything I'd learned that day, drawing all the moves so I could understand them. It might have been basic stuff for some players but for me everything was new. It's a habit I've never lost. I've got a pile of notebooks, well over twenty of them stretching back over my entire career, and in there, along with the prosaic business of rugby plays or the records of training schedules and fitness programmes, are all my hopes and dreams, my mantras, my gratitude.

Through 2012 I took every opportunity there was. I played tag in Christchurch to help with my rugby skills, and everyone I looked up to in sevens was playing that too. I even played in a Te Waipounamu Māori Rugby tournament. I kept telling them I wasn't Māori but the older aunties in the team would tell me to hush because I was fit, fast and a decent player. I'm actually glad because I had so much fun and learned heaps.

By the next camp we were down to about 30 women. I felt like I made my mark not so much by scoring tries as by tackling. I wasn't scared to tackle, and the selectors would have seen that.

In my journal from that June 2012 camp, I recorded the plan:

2012: Learn
2013: Build
2014: Challenge
2015: Perfect
2016: We are an Olympic team of gold.

What could possibly go wrong?

Soon after that, the team got named for the 2012 Oceania Women's Sevens Championship, to be played in Fiji that August. This was the first team to be named since sevens was officially chosen to be in the Olympics. Twelve women were picked from the whole entire screening of New Zealand. I got the call. I'd made the Fiji tournament team. *What?* They picked me, even over and above some of those incredible Black Ferns? I couldn't believe it. I didn't really understand, or fully know what that meant, and it wasn't until we were in the aeroplane with New Zealand disappearing behind us, and the Pacific Ocean opening out, that it hit me. Oh my gosh, I'm going to play for New Zealand!

———

The fields we got to train on in Lautoka were very overgrown, and we had random locals laughing at us and trying to grab our balls — it was very different to the kind of treatment we get nowadays. But we didn't care. There were only two of us, Huri and Linda Itunu (Bindy), who'd played in the last World Cup, and the rest of us were all new. We were wide-eyed and green and just hanging on for the ride. Everything was new to us, and when everything is new nothing is really bad, like, it's just new, and we all were on this cool buzz.

We were excited and lucky — the twelve who made it out of the 1000 and then out of the 60 in the final cut. We didn't really know each other that well, but we were having the time of our lives, doing pool aerobics together, sharing our hotel rooms, laughing a lot. There was no expectation because we were all brand-new; but it felt like the beginning of something pretty special, and we all felt that. We were these young, keen pioneers, and we were like, I wonder what's gonna happen next. That's what it felt like: Let's just do our best and see what's gonna happen next.

Hold on and don't let go.

We trained for a week before the first game, and those sessions were really hard back then. There were no GPS monitors to limit things like there are now, and I got nervous before every training session because they were always full of fitness and I definitely wasn't a fit professional athlete or anything (yet). I hadn't felt any nerves about the actual games yet because it was all such a rush — until we got to the changing room at the beginning of the tournament. Nothing had prepared me for how I'd feel then.

I was already feeling overwhelmed because of what happened the night before the tournament began. In an international tournament, you really don't know until training is over — until right before the competition starts — if you're actually going to be in it. Anything can happen, injury or any other kind of catastrophe. It's chasing, chasing, chasing, right up to the last minute, and people jump in and out all the time. For instance, one time during a World Series tournament, just before we flew out from New Zealand we all had our completely routine ECG screening of our hearts and it was discovered that one of the girls had a friggin' heart condition. It was actually dangerous for her to play and she needed a pacemaker inserted into her heart asap, and so boom, she's not coming with us.

So, making it through the final training is huge — and that night before the games started, we had my first-ever jersey presentation. The presentation of the black jersey. One by one we were called in to see the coach, and he gave each of us our jersey — mine was No. 4 — and what he said is a blur to me, but it was something like, Well done, you've worked hard, you've stuck out of the crowd, congratulations. And I finally got it in my hands, and it was a moment of realisation: I'm playing. Oh my gosh, I'm gonna play. My life took another turn in that moment, in terms of the absolute seriousness — the gravity — of what I was doing.

I'd never before played for New Zealand. Getting that black jersey, I felt like I'd done something with my life.

It's unusual that the coach did it like that. Jersey presentations are really symbolic, so usually it's a team thing, a big event, and sometimes they might get a celebrity in or some sort of motivational speaker. You shake their hand and then you get your jersey — but whatever the setting, it's always that same feeling that melts its way into your body and is special every time. *Far out, I've made it.* It's like joining a club, the club you always wanted to be part of. It's like a prizegiving, before you even go on the field. Finally you have the *right* to play.

And then next morning we get to the changing room. The changing room, just before you run out, is a sacred space and, far out, my stomach is in my throat. I look around at the others, like a trapped animal, trying to copy someone, trying to figure out what to do. No one can help me. They're all going through the same thing. The room itself is like an old cinder-block shed, almost scary in its gloominess and dilapidation, old hooks driven into the walls, paint peeling away from the concrete walls. My heart is pounding fast. Some of the women are praying. Others are sitting silent.

I grab my jersey off the hook. Someone's got a boombox and that song by Black Men United, 'U Will Know', blasts into the room. They're singing about dreams that aren't easy and sticking to the plan. This song will become like our anthem even though it's about men. We are actually trying to inspire guys as much as girls; it's our whole nation we play for, and often it's the guys we need to inspire and grow the most.

I'm about to run out for New Zealand for the first time and I can't even breathe.

And then somehow we are on the field and there's the Tongan team and the whistle goes. The ball kicks off and I'm in, I'm sprinting up, I'm sprinting back, I'm smashing someone, I'm upside down, I'm trying to get out and then all of a sudden I'm catching and I'm passing. It's a washing machine, and I'm in it. Any normal person would be in pain from even one of these tackles, but there is no pain because it's all a rush, all a blur. For that seven minutes, then that 14 minutes, I hardly know where I am or what I'm doing or what I should do next. And I can hardly remember anything about any of it. It's just like we practised; it's nothing like we practised.

Don't muck up.

We win that game, 54–0. We play Cook Islands and we win 27–0. Then we face Fiji, getting to the business end. The stadium here is not big — the spectators are a couple of hundred people, if that — but they're all yelling for Fiji.

It's kick-off, and the ball just has to go past the 10-metre line, and then they can play it. I'm at the front, and I've started way too deep. I sprint up to the 10-metre line to make sure I'm there when it goes over. I'm waiting, waiting, waiting to make sure the ball rolls over that line before I touch it, but the Fijian girl, she doesn't wait. The ball is close to borderline, definitely not at the 10-metre line, but she reaches forward and picks it up. So confident. *But she's not meant to* . . . I look at the ref. *Bro!* And he doesn't say or do anything. *Shit.* I know I look real bad because it was right in front of me, and I could've grabbed it if I wasn't waiting. The lesson is instant: you can't sit there, waiting to follow the rules; you have to friggin' assert yourself on this field. Also: you cannot live by the letter of the law, because it doesn't mean anything if the ref doesn't bloody care. There's literally no way a ref can get 100 per cent of the calls right, anyway.

This moment, of standing there watching someone get that ball that I should've got, is my big takeaway from that tournament: If you don't step up and take the opportunity, you end up looking like a fool. Ever since that day I will never, ever let anybody touch the ball before it rolls over the 10-metre line. Even if it's nine and a half, I'll play it early. If you're confident, which the Fiji player was, and you just pick up and run off, the ref's not gonna pull it back. In that moment I also learned that in the games you make mistakes you can learn the biggest lessons.

This is the big-time now and no one waits for anyone.

Fiji are an amazing sevens team, one of the best and I will never forget that first time I played them. That Fiji game, I was in the mixer again tackling, getting up, tackling, getting up. I even tackled people I wasn't supposed to — that's how keen I was. I was just so keen. That was probably my craziest game.

———

The build-up to that first selection was so big, there was so much talk about the awesome black jersey and the history, and in the back of my mind there's all these women I look up to who have been there for ten years playing for no money, so I was full of the feeling of *I want to do them proud*. But the reality of that is, it's not easy actually living such powerful words and statements. It takes time to know what that means, and it starts way before you find yourself on the field, playing for your country.

By the time we got to Fiji I'd played sevens for a couple of summers and had a great time, but because of all that legacy, and also the feeling you get at high levels of sport of being under the spotlight, it was inevitable that when I got to a game where I was actually wearing the black jersey, I would pack the pressure on to myself. It just felt different. I felt like, if I don't get that ball, I let down everyone who trialled and didn't make it, I let down everyone who's ever played. I took all those feelings on to the field with me, and found myself in this washing machine. And yet, in some ways the pressure doesn't even really exist — not in a way that should affect the way you play. I now remind myself often — it's the same-size field, it's the same-size ball.

Is there a difference between training and playing, between playing a normal game and playing a game where you're wearing the black jersey? Yes, in the obvious sense; but in a more fundamental sense, no, not at all. It all comes down to preparation — to picking apart every single thing that happens inside that washing machine, and preparing properly. There in Fiji, I didn't have the nous to be in control of that space. Learning to do my prep and break down the pressure into smaller steps that are easier to focus on would be a huge part of my development as a player.

When the pressure comes in hot, the questioning starts coming for your deepest insecurities — Have I done enough? Am I fit enough? Did I really train as hard as I could have in every session? Did I study the plays well enough? What do I do at a left-hand scrum again? I have now learned as a player to go hard in every training session I can, to do the extra passing, to analyse all the plays far more than just what the coaches tell you, so when that pressure comes bearing down on me asking me if I have really done enough, I can take one breath and answer: Fuck yes I have. Watch this.

But even before I learned all that back in Fiji we ended up beating the host nation 19–7 and ended up in the final against Australia, which we also won, 35–24.

We won! And my first tournament cap for the New Zealand Women's Sevens Team. Wow. I couldn't wipe the smile off my face. Far out . . . so what do we do now? Nowadays, we do our haka, which is such a purposeful, meaningful celebration, but that first time we didn't have anything like that. But the Fijians, who love a party, especially for sevens, have got music coming over the loudspeakers, so me and Bindy shouted out and got the music guys to put on 'Azonto', which was a very in song at the time, and we bowed to the crowd and we started dancing, and the others joined in. There were no cameras in those days, no TV. This was a moment that was just for that moment. Boogying together. Pure happiness.

Throughout that whole tournament, I watched my team-mates — Huriana Manuel, our captain, who had so much experience; Sarah Goss, a debutant with me who did a couple of really awesome runs and seemed so calm and collected for someone even younger than me; Portia Woodman, this up-and-coming netball star from the Northern Mystics who was scoring these amazing tries, even though it turned out her shoulder was broken — and I was full of the feeling of *Wow*. They were such cool people . . . I was just like, This is where I wanna be. After all my searching, and my childhood of feeling lost and like I didn't fit in perfectly anywhere, here I felt like I was in this amazing circle. I felt like the worst in the circle but I was still there. And when I say I was the worst — I definitely thought I was a great person and an asset, and I knew I'd trained my butt off to be there, but skills-wise, tactics-wise, understanding-the-game-wise, there was no way I was good enough yet. I had so much to learn. If I'm allowed to stay, I'm gonna get better.

What happens now? What's next? I felt like this team could go on forever.

At the end, the assistant coach, Allan Bunting, came up to me. We really like your energy, he said, and we want that energy in Rio. He was the first one to drop the huge seed of the huge dream. Rio. The 2016 Olympics. Four years away. Not long after that, the great flatwater canoeist Lisa Carrington came along to a New Zealand sevens camp and I got to hold the gold medal she won at the London Olympics. The first one I'd ever seen and touched. I wouldn't dare to put it on, though, because I knew I would have my own around my neck one day.

In those days, with the lack of funds for women's rugby, we didn't get paid but we got $2000 for a tournament like the one we'd just won. So, my first annual income from rugby was $2000 and I thought it was awesome. I truly felt like I had cracked it when I saw all that money in my account. Of course, though, I spent it straight away. As soon as I got back to Christchurch I went straight to the mall and bought two iPhones. In those days, iPhones were the flash things that rich people had, and buying one for me and one for my friend was the coolest moment ever.

RUBY'S TRAINING BAG
It all comes down to preparation.

18. Weighting game

But then I didn't get selected for the next Sevens World Series Tournament, or the one after that.

It was a massive year for women's sevens — the inaugural year of the World Rugby Women's Sevens Series, part of that explosion of women's sevens that followed its inclusion in the Olympics. The first series comprised four tournaments on four different continents, with Dubai in December being the very first tournament, followed by Houston, then Guangzhou, China in March, and Amsterdam, The Netherlands in May. Over the years things have changed a bit — it's grown to five then six tournaments, sometimes eight or nine in a year if there are other events on top and the countries change, but it has always kicked off in Dubai in December, and the games go on until around the middle of the next year. Over the nine years it's been running, New Zealand has won six times.

After we got back to New Zealand following Fiji, we had more camps and we all had our hopes pinned on being selected for Dubai — obviously, a huge, huge moment, the first tournament of this brand-new series.

When I got the call to say I didn't make the team it hurt bad.

I'm not good enough to be in that circle. And it was an extra kick in the guts because to make the final travelling team of twelve you had to attend the trial camp during the week leading up to travelling, and I couldn't even attend that. I couldn't even trial to show them I was training and improving. It was a tough pill for me to swallow.

I was still studying and now I needed to motivate myself to keep training, even as the others were heading overseas. That Baker moment was so important to me at that time — thanks to her, I knew exactly what I had to do to keep focused on my big goal. I had to keep doing my best at every step, even though I was training by myself. I was training at six in the morning, and again at six at night.

I felt like maybe the reason I didn't get looked at much was because I was too small. I was skinny and had no muscle. Obviously I was going to the gym, but I didn't have a good enough understanding of what I was trying to achieve, and I didn't yet understand nutrition properly either, so I wasn't getting the gains I wanted.

I need to get bigger, I need to get stronger. But how?

Through an old Coast mate, Jean, I got a summer job at a sawmill. The workers there were different than what I was used to but they were nice-as. And the manager guy running the place didn't seem to care about what was on your CV (or your criminal record) as long as you turned up when you said you would and did the work.

I thought, if I lift heavy-ass pieces of wood all day every day I'll get bigger. But the sawmill manager took one look at me and he was like, Hmm, and he sent me out to the far corner of the car park to weed the garden and pull out old shrubs. Come and find me when you're finished, he said. Here I was thinking I'd be with the men in the mill, hefting logs around. But then I was like, Whatever. I'll do my best here, try and get something out of this, after all small steps lead to big goals, right?

It took me maybe three or four hours. I went all-in, sweating, face dirty . . . I ripped everything out and then I went back to the office and told him I was done. He stared at me. What the hell! He later told me he'd thought it would take me a week.

He found me another little job and then another little job, and I just kept turning up and smashing it, and then eventually he gave up. I got put in with the boys, on the heavy stuff. Some of the timber was 20-metre-long planks, huge as, and I couldn't even lift them. But of course I didn't want to lose my job so I quickly learned how to manoeuvre them, and combined with some gym sessions my body had definitely changed by the end of that summer.

At the beginning, I had boobs and a little bit of weight around my hips; by the end of summer my tits had got smaller, which I was slightly gutted about, but I had abs with the cool V-shape at the bottom and I had deltoids. Holy shit. It actually worked.

———

Rugby is always called New Zealand's national sport, but for a long time, like more than a century, it was treated as if it was only the men's national sport. If rugby's our national sport but only the boys are shown playing it, that doesn't make any sense to me. There have always been women playing the game in clubs around the country, although those women never appeared in the history books, never got any recognition, their games weren't sanctioned by the rugby authorities and they were never recorded in those almanacs that record all the official games.

Not only that, but rugby itself was what the sports historian Jennifer Curtin has described as hyper-masculinised — that is, totally tied up in a particular image of manliness — physically tough, and what All-Black-turned-mental-health-advocate John Kirwan called the harden-up culture. This meant that when women did play it, they were considered morally abhorrent. Unwomanly.

On the other side of the equation, the stereotype of what women *should* be was all about fragility and politeness, which meant some people were shocked at the idea of strong, muscly women playing a sport that was all about smashing into each other. *Chicks are being manly* — even I had a bit of that feeling when I was still on the outside. Rugby represented the antithesis of everything the dominant New Zealand culture believed women should be.

And women's rugby wasn't taken seriously. Even as recently as 2017, when the Black Ferns played Wales in the opening game in the Rugby World Cup and beat them 44–12, that incredible success only rated a tiny mention in one of New Zealand's leading newspapers, well after stories about much less significant male games, treated as less important even than a feature about South African (male) rugby. That kind of treatment, of course, was a common theme of women's sport in general, but with rugby it was especially marked as footy is our national sport. The Black Ferns won that World Cup, as they have won five out of the past six Women's Rugby World Cups. You'd think the media in 2017 would have been more interested in women's rugby, given that in 2016 at the Rio Olympics, the Black Ferns Sevens brought home a silver (the men's sevens placed fifth in that Olympics so didn't bring any medals home).

But coverage had been even worse in earlier decades, which was why when my coach told me, when I was eleven years old, You could be a Black Fern, it meant nothing to me, in fact it angered me, because I'd never heard about them, didn't have any idea what they looked like. I had never been given the opportunity to be inspired by them.

And yet down through the decades, many women did play rugby. Little girls hung out on the side of the rugby fields, just like little boys did, watching their dad, and then maybe their mum played a bit too, and those little girls were like, Why can't I play? I wanna play . . . So when the Black Ferns was founded in 1990, in the run-up to the first Women's Rugby World Cup in 1991, the women players did not come from nowhere. They might have been invisible to most of us, but they had been there. And those women who played in that early time were amazing. Courageous, amazing women who busted stereotypes and didn't care and just played because they loved it.

I think that all of us women who play rugby, in both fifteens and sevens, have helped to change the way our sport is seen by the public and by the media, and even — or perhaps especially — by rugby administrators. All the financial and professional support we now get, all the coverage in the media — all of that is a result of our successes, and by *our*, I mean all the women who have represented New Zealand both officially and unofficially for decades.

The women are playing it and the women are winning. Our winning percentage rate is one of the best in the world, of any sport. Looking at NZR's most recent figures, from 2016 to 2019 (2020 and 2021 are considered incomplete because of Covid), you can see that rugby participation of girls and women has increased by 40 per cent while male numbers have dropped 3.9 per cent. Former head of Women's Rugby Development at NZR, Cate Sexton, has said that the growth of women's rugby in New Zealand is because of the success of the Black Ferns and Black Ferns Sevens and the example we set to little girls now. And I agree with her because I used to be one of those little girls.

I'm so proud of that. I never get tired of visiting schools and talking to girls about my career. And I know we're helping to create new ways of looking at women's bodies — that women's bodies are about strength and confidence, and that beauty lies in strength.

Here's a small thing you can do. If you're a New Zealander or a fan of rugby in New Zealand and you own an All Blacks top, maybe you should go out and buy a Black Ferns top and wear that instead, so that girls learn it's something to aspire to, and it's real. And you can even ask your friends which team has won more world cups out of the two. Every boy wants to be an All Black. Why shouldn't every girl aspire to be a Black Fern?

————

I've already said that Casey Robertson, who debuted in the Black Ferns in 2002, was my first rugby idol, and she was so punishing with her powerfulness and strength. Like many of the women who played in the early Black Ferns teams she was a farmer, tough as, rough and rugged, super-capable on the rugby field and in life. Oh my gosh, I thought when I watched her and the other older Black Ferns. You wouldn't mess with them. Even the way they walked just said they knew their place on the earth. To me it was scary, but also exciting.

When I first started, I was a little bit caught up in that tension between society's attitude towards how a woman should look, and the sport I loved — worried I might get too manly, too bulky. Now, with it being official that sevens was going to the Olympics, we players gained access to High Performance Sport NZ and my journey to understanding mental health began when I met the psychologists attached to professional rugby. This means that over the years I've been able to challenge those insecure thoughts.

Going deeply into identity with my psychologist, I have had to answer important questions. What do I want? Do I want to look great? Do I want to look like a model? Because I know I can, I scrub up real good. Or do I want to be the greatest sevens player I can be? It was a choice about what I want in life, and my answer was: I want to take on the world. I want to be part of the best team in the world — and because I chose that, I had to go to the gym, I had to bulk up. I had to eat all the right food, drink my protein.

And instead of seeing my body as *Yuck, muscles,* I see my body as a result of my decision and my goal.

Now, I look at my muscles and I'm like, That's what you call hard work. I don't need to tell nobody that I work hard; they can see it. I'm a walking metaphor for hard work. Being muscly boosts my confidence and my ability. I look great, but it's a different definition of great. As a young adult trying to build my body at the sawmill, I laugh now that I got upset about my breasts getting smaller, 'cos now when I look at my body and how muscular I am it excites me so much and makes me so happy. We are all made up differently genetically, but being solid enough has been hard work for me. I've always been generally smaller than other rugby players, some of my New Zealand team-mates have incredible muscle mass just from doing the team programmes and I admire them very much. But for me, I have to stay and do extra sessions just to build and maintain my muscle size that others don't even think twice about. I now look at my body and all I see is all the hours, sweat and extra work I do. It makes me so proud to look at the shape and size of my body. And I also understand that my body won't look this strong forever so I am so grateful for this time. My body gives me so much happiness.

And then there's the effects on the field of all the extra work in the gym I do.

Early on in my club days we were playing against Sydenham. The huge women of Sydenham, so much bigger and stronger than me. I tried to steal a ball and I got dumped, landed on my right shoulder and damaged my AC (acromioclavicular) joint on the top of my shoulder. As a result of trying to play on with that injury I got dumped again and ended up with a concussion, seeing stars, spewing. My shoulder is still crooked to this day.

Fast-forward to years after I'd started all that work getting stronger . . . I was on the field and there was this solid-as chick, she had at least 30 kg on me, and we were both going for this loose ball rolling along the ground. I was slightly quicker so I landed on it first, I had it tucked under my shoulder on the ground but a split-second later here she came, and I knew her whole weight was going to land right on my shoulder. *This is it, I'm done, this is going to be my AC again.* Sure enough, boom, all her weight crashed on to my shoulder and with the ball stuck underneath I had no chance to protect it. The ball was eventually cleared, she went away after the ball again and I got up. I was clutching my shoulder, so scared to move it. Carefully, I moved my arm. No pain?! Moved it a bit more. No damage whatsoever. So that's when I learned, Oh shucks, man, you can't muck around in this game. You can't just not train and think you will be sweet. You have to get stronger. Your muscles will protect you.

This is the kind of thing that male athletes don't even have to talk about. Guys love being bulky. It's part of the definition of looking great for guys, anyway. But society would have women fragile and vulnerable, so the way women athletes look is definitely something that some young women struggle with, sadly, and I empathise with them.

But after I'd done all the work I needed to do to play the way I wanted to — after I'd taken my skinny body to work in the sawmill, and later learned to use the gym properly — I gained 10 kg of straight muscle and my whole attitude changed. When I looked at my body now, I knew that every muscle I had was a direct result of all the hard work I'd put in. I was ripped, and I felt strong. I was fitter. I was faster. I felt really good. Man, I never thought my body could be like this.

Some people train to look like this, but I didn't; I just trained to be the best rugby player I could, and this is what it looks like. And so I turned it all around in my head. I loved it. It sounds weird to say it, but I love my body, how it is, because it's a physical reminder every day of how hard I work.

It's not easy to take the hits rugby dishes out, and to keep sprinting and running non-stop for an entire game. The only way you can, is if you look like *this*. My muscly body is like a badge of honour. It's a confidence boost.

So this is what I think about my muscles: I look like a frickin' athlete. I look extremely diligent. I just look frickin' awesome. I jump on a ball and the biggest attacking player I know lands right on top of my shoulder and I walk away like it didn't even happen.

It comes back to greatitude. This is the great action I take out of my gratitude. I eat heaps, I sleep, and I do all the extras to build my strength. It takes me triple the amount of bicep curls to get the same arms as some of the girls, just the way genes work. I know this incredible strength of mine is not forever. I've seen people that were really intimidating on the field and then three years later I see them with no gym training and they look like pip-squeaks and I find that real confronting. So I am always doing the little extras because I know these muscles, this body, are gifts. Temporary gifts. Understanding all of this has truly been life-changing for me.

RUBY'S TRAINING BAG
I love my body. I trained to be the best rugby player I could, and this is what it looks like.

19. Seeing red

I n January 2013, the New Zealand National Rugby Sevens women's tournament was reinstituted, after a break of ten years (even though the men's tournament had been going all that time). It's a tournament for all the provincial teams, and I was playing for Canterbury, with Ernie as our coach. There was a lot of excitement, with all the 60 girls from those selection camps on fire, representing their regions. Frickin' cool, and I was loving every minute as we settled in to our hotel.

I was looking pretty sharp, pretty eye-catching because I'd done something I always wanted to do and dyed my hair red. I would love to have dyed it all red, but I couldn't afford that so I got this bright red streak in the side of my hair, which I loved, and when I tied my hair up I was unmissable.

Maybe it worked too well, because the night before we played Ernie called me into his room and he said, I'm going to name you team captain tomorrow.

I wanted to sink to the floor. I had just turned 21, the youngest and the smallest in our team. All these other girls in the Canterbury team had been playing for New Zealand for years. All I had done was made that one tournament. I hadn't even been selected for the Dubai tournament the month before. How could they possibly respect me enough to let me lead them? Are you kidding me, bro? And then I thought: Oh my God. Mids! How could I ever expect to lead *her*? I was sure they'd all roll their eyes, even laugh, maybe. My mind would always go to the negative perspectives of things.

But he wasn't asking me. He was telling me.

I didn't sleep that night, and then the next day he told everyone, and I just kept thinking that the ones from Sydenham were thinking he only did that because he was my coach in the varsity team and I couldn't help but agree.

But then we started playing and I began to relax a bit, because the one thing I could do was play sevens. I'd got really fit and strong, I was quick, and I'd always been keen. I felt I was earning the girls' respect because I was everywhere, playing every minute, and I was doing a real good job.

It hit me — the thing that Ernie probably wanted me to learn — that a captain doesn't have to be top-down, because there was no way I could be top-down with these women. A captain doesn't even have to be the best in the team; the captain can just be really good at whatever it is they're good at, and I was really good at just putting my head down and going to work — picking players up, encouraging them, pushing them to go harder, leading by example. I didn't try to talk down to anyone, I didn't even try to talk really; I stepped aside and let the old girls talk out of their experience, and I stepped in at a moment when we were having a rough time. That was my moment.

It came after a game where we hadn't done too well. We were in our huddle, and I remembered something that had been said to us at camp that seemed so relevant in this moment, something like, You don't have to do too much, you just have to do your one job. So I said that to them — Girls, all you've got to do is your job, just one job at a time. And then we were breaking from the huddle, and Mids turned around and looked at me, and she goes, Well said, Rubes, and I was just like, Bro. To me, that was like

getting a frickin' law degree. This was Mids, the hardest chick
in rugby, who would never give out a compliment to a young-un
unless it was absolutely deserving. Well said, Rubes. In front of
everyone. It meant heaps to me.

We made it to the semi where we played Auckland, who had
two of the fastest women in New Zealand — Portia Woodman,
who I'd debuted with in Fiji and who is such a big star now, as
well as one of my best mates in rugby; and Kayla McAlister,
who I also debuted with in Fiji and who later that year would
be named IRB (now known as World Rugby) Women's Sevens
Player of the Year, the first New Zealand woman to be named.
Ernie put me on the wing opposite Portia. I got the ball in our
own half and she came running at me . . . after playing with her
I knew she was new at tackling and I saw that she came in high
on me. I pushed out my palm as strong as I could and aimed for
the middle of her chest. I fended her off as she fumbled slightly,
her arms reaching out to no avail. I almost couldn't believe it
and took off, sprinting around her outside. I was busting my gut,
just all-out . . . past halfway, past the opposite 22, almost to the
five, c'mon, Rubes, you can do this! But the whole way
I could hear these crazy fast steps following me, much faster
than mine — Kayla McAlister. And on top of that, Porsh didn't
stop chasing me after her slight stumble so she had caught up
again already. So just as I got to the five-metre line just before
the try line, they took care of me in a covering tackle and
bundled me into touch. I was so pissed. I remember thinking
if that try line was a little closer or it was bloody well not those
two of all people, I could've got that winning try. Ernie could see
I had gone so hard in that play so he subbed me. I didn't want
to, but I came off the field. There were cameras everywhere, but
I found an empty tent and went behind it and spewed my guts
out. I'd given everything. I was vomiting, vomiting. No one saw,
and then I came back out to the bench and Ernie said, Are you
ready to go back on? And I was like, Yeah, bro, all good.

We gave everything, but lost that semi 12–17. Mids even came up to me after the game and said, You've always gotta beat the fast ones twice ay — she was spot-on with her feedback. Even in those moments when you feel like you just lost the whole game for your team, there's always a lesson and thanks to Mids I learned a goodie.

That day helped me understand more about leadership, and I was so grateful that Ernie saw me in that light. I hadn't thought that I was ready for it, but it was cool that he believed I was ready. It was very cementing for me in my career.

I learned so much from Ernie. He always said, It's all about performance. It's not about just going out and thrashing people for the sake of thrashing them. It's about doing what you've trained to do. If we won a game by 80 points he could still be pissed off if we were blowing tries, and that's right because the next week we might come out and play a better team where we need all our skills and training. He was always like, Do the processes, get the performance, enjoy yourself. He and his wife Kay have been massive influences on so many young players in Canterbury.

We made top four in that national tournament, and I felt like we did Canterbury proud. And for me, I was the youngest player there, I was captain, I'd had the approval from Mids, and I felt like I could play with the big girls. I learned the magic of being 'the worst in the room'. I hadn't thought I was any good but I was in such a good team that I definitely felt the growth. If you think you are the worst in a team, that is actually an awesome gift because then growth is inevitable. And if you think you might be the best in the room — it might be time to find a new room.

———

I got invited to a couple of New Zealand camps again after that, and it truly felt like I had found my room. It meant so much to find somewhere, after everything I had been through . . .

I felt like I belonged and it was full of amazing people I looked up to. I honestly can see why people join gangs because if I hadn't found sport I would've wanted a group where I felt like I belonged.

In one of my diaries is a passage that I wrote straight from my heart about this at the camp I went to in February 2013. The psychologist, David Galbraith, came in for a session, and he set us a question to think about: Why am I here?

I was 21; I had so far to go, but there's no question I knew exactly why I was there. I stood up and read out what I'd written:

Ever since I accomplished the monkey bars at primary school (before anyone else my age could do it, that's what Mum used to tell me), I've been searching for a family and a place to show that it's not your skin colour, your salary or any of that stuff that makes you great; it's your fight, it's your work ethic, it's every day not leaving until you're done, not going to sleep till you've filled out your IPP [Individual Performance Plan], not just going to the pub and have three jugs too many and a social smoke.

And it doesn't matter what happened at home, it doesn't matter I love a girl, it doesn't matter I'm not even Māori, it's what you put into your training — it's all those lies you never told, it's that time you did a hundred push-ups when she only did 85 'cos you counted. It's when you slipped up and ate two blocks of chocolate but the next day you did eighteen 40s [40-metre sprints] when it said to do 10. It's honesty, 'cos on the field there's no option to lie. Your tackle is the truth or it's a lie, your pass is either real perfect or fake practice. And to imagine that there's a place where all these other great women who train like that, who play like that, who pass like that, no lies, no slack fake-pass bullshit.

My whole life I looked and I found my family. It's a long road but we have time. The tunnel is long but the huge,

bright gold light is visible for generations. I don't care.
I found that in me, and my heart ain't going anywhere.

Looking back at that young Ruby, I feel real proud I stayed on my path. And it must have been soon after that camp that I got the call — not the 'sorry' call, but the right kind. I'd made it into the team to play the next World Series tournament, in Guangzhou, China, at the end of March.

RUBY'S TRAINING BAG
It's not your skin colour, your salary or
any of that stuff that makes you great;
it's your fight, it's your work ethic.

20. Black in the room

It was a shock, landing at Guangzhou airport and sensing the scale of the place. I'd never seen that many people in my life. I thought I'd seen a queue before at Pak'nSave, but here the queues stretched for honestly about a kilometre. Then we got in the bus and I stared out at the massive infrastructure of this place — buildings a zillion stories high, motorways 50 metres into the air, and everything murky with thick yellow-grey haze so that it didn't even feel like we were on Earth. It was mind boggling. The size of the world hit me. Fiji was fun and frivolous, but China was *Holy shit, I'm away from everything and anyone I know and it's really serious now.*

While New Zealand's newest rugby team had won Dubai Sevens, they lost at Houston so now the pressure was on. And when your superiors feel the pressure, that comes down to you. The underlying reality of this great new adventure, this fun dream was: If we don't do well, we don't get the money or the support and the dream is over. So a different feeling was in the air.

But still I couldn't have been happier. All my childhood I knew what I *didn't* want to do. I didn't want to be in a place where there was yelling and violence and abuse; I didn't want to be scared and feel alone; I didn't want to die from drugs and drinking. But since discovering rugby I had had an equal feeling of certainty about what I *did* want to do. I just wanted to be in the room. It gutted me to not make Dubai and Houston. I'd definitely had moments of doubt in myself, and I felt like maybe I wasn't going to make any more tournaments. Did I screw something up?

It was a rocky beginning, but it's good that people know the road can be rocky, because when you see a team succeed on the field, and you see the photos with the medals and the hugs, you assume everyone has a right to be there, and that the road getting there was inevitable. But there's no such thing as inevitable. I had plenty of times of questioning: Am I going to be able to do it? Am I good enough? And now here I was in China. Back in the room. Nothing — no pressure, no stressed coaches — was going to dampen my joy.

We played in this huge stadium that had hardly any people in the stands, and the pollution was so bad I was thinking, *How can you even breathe . . .* I was a world away from Greymouth where you could always see green trees and there's not even a set of traffic lights let alone sky-scrapers and smog. And on top of that, the weather was next-level — it didn't just rain, it stormed, and a couple of our games got pushed back a few hours. We just had to adapt and focus in on the tournament.

But I wasn't in the starting line-up, of course. It was one thing to make the trial camp and get into the travelling twelve, but it was another whole thing to be in the starting line-up. I was sitting there on the bench waiting for my opportunity and knowing it might only be a couple of minutes each game. I didn't care if I didn't get a whole heap of game time, though — I was in the room. I'd even figured out a way to be mentally present with the game even when I wasn't on the field, by paying close attention to the person in my team who started in my position, being really conscious of what she was doing. I'd watch her go into a ball, but then I'd keep watching her after the ball went. *Oh yep, she just reloads. Yep, I can do that, I can totally do that, that's easy . . .* and so I found ways to not just sit there like a nervous wreck, but apply myself in a more logical sense, not getting carried away with all the emotion but putting my mentality into the game before my body went on the field. It helped me narrow in and focus, so when I came on it was an easier transition. Already, this was an advance on the washing machine I'd put myself in in Fiji.

Anyway, we made it through to the final, against England, and it was tight, 7–5 with us barely in front, so we needed to score. Honey Hireme, who was starting in front of me, rolled her ankle and as she limped off, that's when the coach took a risk: he told me to get up and sent me on. His confidence in me must have built through the tournament, but it's still a risk to put a new player on at such a crucial time. Coaches want to blood players, but of course they also want to win. It's not unheard of for new players to get 20 seconds at the end when victory is assured.

Almost straight away, something incredible happens. Kayla McAlister, the fastest player I've ever played with, is on the left wing, and England are all coming over trying to mark her. She steps about three players like they're children, then gets an offload out and then in a flash it's all coming back towards my side. Gossy is outside me. No one knows who I am. They know who Kayla is, they know who Gossy is and they are marking up on them hard. Katy McLean, the amazing English player, is marking me, but I catch the ball and Katy doesn't even look at me. Instead, she goes to push out to Goss, expecting me to pass, and as she does that, it flashes in my mind: Bro, I'm quick; if you're not gonna mark me, why would I pass it?

And in that instant, time stops. It's like I've pushed pause on everyone but myself. I look around, I see everything, I assess it all, I'm taking my time. And it's like the friggin' Red Sea opening for Moses. So much space, right there. This huge hole in the defence, it looks like a highway for me to run down. Is it this easy? I wonder to myself. The game plan is that I send it wide to the wing, but I don't care. I could have self-doubt and just follow the game plan but I don't because I know I can get through. I accelerate a little bit but not too much, and I coast through. Because Kayla has stepped so many people on the other side, there's no sweeper anywhere close and I float effortlessly over the line.

Not really. I watch it later, and I'm sprinting, and nothing slows and it all happens so fast. There is no pause. I run under and put the ball down. I'm so shocked I don't even celebrate the try. I'm confused at what just happened because it was like time stopped and I'm remembering Fiji and how it was like being in a washing machine, but *this*, this was like a slow-motion scene in a movie. The ball goes down and I run back. I'm not even smiling, and then one of the girls, Bindy, smacks into me going Ruby! And then another team-mate, Huds, is running at me, hugging me, celebrating. And I'm like, Oh yeah, I just scored! Every time someone gets their first try on the World Series I always run over and say congrats because it is a big achievement and I know what it's like — you can sometimes forget to even celebrate!

That try was crucial in the game, and defining in my career. Sevens is a sport that's on the edge the whole time, but then occasionally there are moments where you go, Oh yeah, we're gonna win, and that was one of them, and then the rest of the game was sweet as, we never felt under pressure from that moment. Kelly Brazier crossed again for another try. And we did win, 19–5, and I knew I'd contributed to the win, and ever since that game the coach had a different attitude towards me. I'd built the trust, and he knew he could rely on me.

It's hard as a new player when the coach doesn't trust you. And it's not because they can't ever trust you, they just haven't put themselves in a position yet where you could show them that trust. He had to put me on in a tight game, in a final, and I scored a try. But if you get put on for two minutes and you drop the ball — *everyone* drops the ball, but if *you* drop the ball — you might not get on again.

I'd learned so much over the past eight months since Fiji. I had built my mental and physical resilience and I felt like I really deserved to be there and I was there for a reason.

The experience I had on that field in Guangzhou was the first time in my life I experienced a state of 'flow'. Now it's like that most of the time, and if I don't experience it during a game, it's weird. It's not really an individual thing, but usually to do with how the whole team is functioning. Which isn't to say I can't have my own moments of it even if other people in the team are not doing their job; but the ultimate for me is when everyone's doing their job, and then you can simply focus on yourself and do what you need to do. And that's what happened that first time. I wasn't worrying about anyone else — they were all doing an amazing job — so all I had to do was my own work. And *whoosh* . . .

Sometimes I feel like I stop, press pause on the game, and have full-on conversations with a team-mate about what we're going to do. Are you going to chase? Are you friggin' kidding me, you're closer. I don't want to take your role though . . . Will there be a try in it? Stop being silly, you just go. No words, but just looking at each other, exchanging our thoughts, as clear as a bell, that's what it feels like. A kind of telepathy, full of questions and answers and decisions. After one of those telepathic conversations between me and Portia, I went up to her afterwards and was like When I looked at you, did you understand what I meant about you chasing but then you telling me to just chase? Did you understand me? Yes, she said, and it was just so cool we could do that.

I believe in my heart it's something that arises from the culture we've built in our team — our hard work at building our relationships off the field so we can have that ability on the field.

But you watch it and it's like fingers snapping. There's been no pause at all.

———

Something else happened at a tournament that was like a lightning bolt for me. We'd played USA, and the ref had made a call against me that puzzled me. So when I went up to the bar afterwards to get a (non-alcoholic) drink, and the ref was there being friendly to me, I thought I'd ask.

Hey, how come you pinged me for not rolling away today? You know I was trying to get out of it and I wasn't affecting the play . . .

He laughed. Oh, come on, Rubes, you know how it is. You're New Zealand! They're the USA. I have to ref you guys harder. You were wasting them! No hard feelings, eh, mate.

He chuckled as he walked off with his drink.

My heart sank. I couldn't believe it. I was penalised five metres off our line, a huge momentum-shifter in the game. My spot in this team was far, far from assured and I felt like it was a massive X against my name, and now I hear the ref say he just *had* to go extra hard on us. Rugby is business. He didn't care or know about my personal situation within the team.

That was the day I learned that it ain't about the rules, it's about how the rules are refereed. If I don't understand what the refs are looking for or thinking, it doesn't matter if I can recite the whole rule book word for word.

So from then on I always try to ask refs how they see the rules, even at nationals level. At lineouts, for example, the rules say you must throw the ball in 'without delay'. To me that means anything from tying your shoe laces to wiping the ball with a towel, but it doesn't matter what *I* think it means. So if I ask the ref and they say shoe laces and towels are OK but if they see the player with the ball talking to their players too long then *that* is a delay, then the words I use during the game will change. Instead of me saying, Ref, laces are a delay, I'll say, Ref, they're talking a lot? It sounds minuscule but the subtle word change is huge in an Olympic semi-final with a tie-break scoreline.

———

It's so early in the morning it's still pitch-dark, but I can hear someone moving around in our apartment. We're back in Tauranga before a World Series Tournament. I look out my bedroom door and see it's Honey Hireme. Just going to work on my pass, she tells me. I check the time and it's 5.30 a.m. Sweet, sis, I say. I really need to do that too.

She texts Bunts — Allan Bunting — at that time an assistant coach, and we meet him across the road from our hotel, on the main beachfront down by Mount Maunganui. The sweeping curve of sand and sea, the first hints of light only making the world seem darker. There's a street light, and we stand under it and with three of us we get heaps of reps in, working our passes from the middle, taking turns running back and forth while the two on the outside stand there catching and passing.

That was Bunts, even way back then. He didn't care what time, day or night, he was always there for us. It helped everything. Whenever I doubted my pass I could remind myself I didn't need to because we'd worked so hard in those early mornings, right up to when we left for the next tournament in Amsterdam.

RUBY'S TRAINING BAG
There's no such thing as inevitable.

21. Knee-ded that

I am very fortunate that I started my sevens career at nineteen and twenty. As I write this book, I'm turning 30. That's a solid ten years, a real good crack, at a time when the game's gone from amateur or even underground to professional with the biggest stars in the world; the game has changed and grown, and I've grown along with it.

I always fought for and wanted to be a professional rugby player, but I never relied on it. And that's not just because I had that rocky, uncertain beginning; it was because at the beginning, we couldn't. We always knew we had to have other options to earn our living and, personally, I'm grateful for that. We see it happen all the time, especially with the guys who get to the end of being an All Black and go bankrupt, get depression, lose their meaning and are left with nothing. It's like sometimes when a young person falls in love, they don't think it will ever end and it's so wonderful and beautiful — and it is, but it does end. It's happening to female sportspeople now too. How do you tell an eighteen-year-old star, coming in fresh to the professional game, who's getting everything paid for and is completely looked after, that they should prepare for the end of all that?

But me, I never relied on just being a Black Fern.

It sounds weird, but I think one of my saving graces happened when I was 21. At the time it was a disaster, but it taught me so much. And I think other players who unfortunately have to go through one of these experiences will agree about how much it can teach you.

After excelling in China, I got picked for the next tournament, which was in Amsterdam in May, and then we were to go on to Russia for the Rugby World Cup Sevens in late June. I felt like I had finally made it. Not only was I in the room but I had started to find my place in the room.

In Amsterdam we pumped our music while we were doing our warm-ups. We noticed the other teams were giving us the stink-eye, like, Are these guys even taking this seriously? But why be serious when the whole culture around sevens is to just have fun? Audiences dress up in fancy costumes, they're real family events, so why should we be all serious just because we're pro? Even at home in New Zealand, club rugby sevens competitions are just a big weekend of fun. Anyway, it wasn't long before the other teams all caught on — fast-forward eighteen months and every single team has a speaker. It's like a speaker-off in the changing rooms, and everyone enjoys it, dancing, getting amongst the party. It will become part of the sevens experience, to hear what all the other teams are playing. There's nothing like hearing the England team blast the Spice Girls. Tell me what you want . . . I just love it, eh. And blasting te reo hits in the Dubai desert straight up just makes you feel like you're back in Aotearoa.

As long as you can learn to bring that focus in and channel all that energy when you pass that white line . . . sweet as, we're here to have fun.

But here we are in Amsterdam in 2013, pumped, getting ready to play China, just our second pool game of the tournament, and it happens for me. The big one you don't forget.

———

I rush up on their first-five, and she does this little in-and-out footwork move on me. She's quite a bit shorter than me and she kind of sneaks under me, and I go to step with her, moving my body to mimic her fast movement to the right, but my knee gets caught and doesn't come, it stays facing the left. There's this horrible noise, an awful pop that is so loud to me it shakes my ears, and I fall. When I go to get up, I can't. I can't stand straight up. And then the pain. What the heck. I've never felt anything like it and I'm trying to walk but I am almost fainting from the rush of this new pain. The physio runs over and puts my arm over her shoulder. I say to her I can walk off the field. But I actually can't. I put weight on the leg and it gives out, like cooked spaghetti, like I've never walked before. Usually I can just jog this stuff off. It's so sudden, so intense, and I feel the strangeness of being here, on the other side of the world, in this moment of confusion. I don't even yet know what a catastrophe this is.

Usually the physio would be saying, You'll be fine. I want her to say it, but she doesn't. At the side of the field she looks at it, does a couple of tests, and her face . . . I'll never forget her face. She just looks down and keeps attending to my leg. Then the tournament doctor comes over and does the same test, holding my thigh and gently pulling my shin up to check on the knee stability — ideally the anterior cruciate ligament, the ACL, which connects the thighbone to the shinbone, will hold your knee and stop your shin from moving, but mine doesn't. There's another horrible sound, a kind of liquid graunching. There is nothing holding my leg in place. Still, no one says anything.

They help me inside a tent and stand outside talking. I'll never forget . . . even one of the NZR support staff who was a bit of a top dog was with us and I didn't know him too well at the time, but he leans down and grabs my hand and tells me everything is going to be OK. He hadn't talked to me that much this tour so I thought something must be serious if he's whispering stuff like that to me.

They get me back to the hotel, and the physio sits down with me and she says, Ruby, you've torn your ACL and you need to have surgery . . . and that's all I hear. Her voice goes on talking but I'm lost. I don't know what that means exactly but we all know about players who have done this, and we all know how serious it is.

The next day I'm back on the side of the field to watch the next game. I'm now on crutches, full of codeine, in pain. A journalist comes and sits next to me and starts asking, What have you done? Are you going to play again? She doesn't read my body language, or she doesn't care, I don't know. But I know I'm struggling. Her questions are about things I can't talk about, can't even think about. I'm still in shock. I don't have any tools for this. What the fuck do I even say?

I am full of fear. Sadness is filling me up. Fear-riddled thoughts flood my head.

I am going to miss the World Cup.

I am going to lose my place in the room.

This might be the end of my rugby career. There are so many amazing players; I know there's no guarantee I will get back in the squad.

I was in so much pain every time I moved my leg, so it was organised that I was to fly home in business class so I could keep my leg elevated, which was a really nice gesture. Sometimes our team would score a couple of upgrades and we would pull names out of a hat to see who would get them and it was so cool to experience. You would take the stairs up to the top floor of the big Emirates Airbus and walk down to your own little cubby-hole seat with a table to the side and drinks in little compartments waiting for you with accessories like eye masks and ear plugs, and you got given this huge bathroom bag, that was way bigger than my own personal one, with Bvlgari perfume and Colgate toothpaste in it. The service and food was ridiculous, flasher than the flashest restaurants I had been to in my life. And at the back of the top floor was a bar. Like a full-on bar that wrapped around, where you could hang out and sit and talk. There were even little snacks on the bar. It was just the coolest thing.

But not this time. I was in a wheelchair at the airport, then I had to hop up the stairs, alone. We flew from Amsterdam to Dubai and then Dubai to Auckland. The direct flight from Dubai to Auckland was seventeen hours and at that time it was the longest direct flight you could do in the world. I was heartbroken and alone and I was literally on the longest flight in the world. And it felt like it. It was one of the first times in my life that I remember looking around, in my big business class seat with all the bells and whistles, and realising that this material stuff can't make you happy if you're not good in your heart. My heart was so heavy from the news about my leg and my future, and I had no one to talk me through what it meant. I was so young and felt so alone. To be honest, even if someone had been there with me I wouldn't have known what to say. I just put my HumidiFlyer on (these special, intense-looking face masks we wear on planes to decrease dehydration and jetlag), I pulled my beanie down over my eyes, I pulled my flash business class blanket up over me, and I just cried and cried. And cried. At times I was heaving because I was weeping so hard.

A couple of times I had to go through the frustratingly difficult task of using the bathroom. It was a hobble down to the end of the plane, into the bar, and one time all the toilets were full so I had to wait. As I waited, a middle-aged Indian-looking guy chilling at the bar with his flash-looking top-shelf drink in a flash glass kindly asked me if I was OK. I said, Yeah I'm fine. He then asked if I had asthma. I just looked at him, puzzled. He said he was a doctor and noticed I was having a semi asthma attack before. He thought I was wearing a breathing tool for asthma, but it was my HumidiFlyer, and he thought I was having an asthma attack, but I was just having a breakdown. I just nodded and smiled weakly and hobbled off as quickly as I could to take the next available restroom.

When I get off the plane and we meet all the cameras and families at the international arrivals, I act brave and smile for all the photos and tell everyone, I'm all good. I've never told a single soul how hard that flight was emotionally.

Eventually I land back in Christchurch and I have to get my ACL reconstructed, go under the knife. But it takes ages to get the surgery because the women's programme isn't funded properly yet so I sit on a waiting list for a few months.

———

That first week I'm high on codeine and the pain is bad, and the weeks after that I'm just sad. I'm sitting on the couch and I want a glass of water, but I'm overwhelmed at the effort and pain it would require to get up and do that one simple thing. I have never had a big injury before, and now I can't even get a glass of water. I sit there on the couch and I cry.

As well as everything else, I am embarrassed. Humiliated. Ashamed, because wasn't it my fault? I must have done something wrong. Humiliated because without sport, what use am I? I am nothing. Humiliated because I had those big dreams and look at me now. I see it on people's faces when they hear the news — they go *Oh*, and I know they mean, *Are you sure your career's not over?*

I feel frustrated, too, as no one can give me a date or an answer as to why it's taking so long. Lucky for me the physio is batting for me, and finally, three months later, I get the call. These days, you'd be in the next day. I'm so grateful our programme has grown because those months in limbo made everything more confusing and added to the identity crisis.

I'm terrified to go into surgery for the first time in my life, but I'm even more afraid of never getting back into that team. So in I go.

People told me not to worry, but I didn't tell anyone just how scared I was. I thought my concerns were realistic — somebody now had the opportunity to outplay me, and there might not be a place for me any more. I wasn't as confident in myself as I am now and it shook my life.

I need to do something. I had nothing to be positive about, so I had to find something. I had finished my degree the previous year, but now I enrolled in the Certificate of Sports and Fitness at Aoraki Polytech (now called Ara). I'd cruised my way through school, and even with my degree I'd mostly had that easy, happy-go-lucky attitude, but now I decided I was going to go hard. I couldn't even walk, but I got mates to pick me up and drop me off, and I'd hobble into class on my crutches. It was such a mission that once I was there I just stayed all day. Other people would leave, but I'd just sit there studying.

I read all the books, I learned all the anatomical words, I knew every bone in the body and every muscle that was taught in the class. I asked questions, I stayed late, I was competitive, I was into it. I went hammer and tongs, and at the end when we had our exams I knew all the answers. I'd never had that feeling before, like being real smart, and then I thought, It's because I put myself fully into it. I graduated top of the class. And I said to myself, OK, if I don't get back in the team I can be a personal trainer, or a rugby commentator. I was going to try my best to get back in the Black Ferns Sevens but I was not going to rely on it. My identity had to expand or I knew I was in serious trouble. I'll never forget how unhappy I felt on that plane and I was sitting in the flashest business class seat ever. I knew the world was cut-throat; I'd seen how things can change in an instant; I had to arm myself.

One of the scary things about that time was not just missing out on rugby, but losing my identity as a physical person. An athlete. Now, anything I tried to do, it hurt. Everything hurt, everything was hard, and I felt so useless. My physical ability, I realised, is even more part of my identity than rugby. Being good physically was who I was. All through my whole life it was everything to me — I could run around, do that sport, join that team. It was easy for me, and it was always how I found my sense of belonging. In my darkest days, I wondered if that would now change.

———

Sometimes when people have these kinds of experiences, they say they're glad it happened. I probably wouldn't go that far, but it definitely changed me as an athlete. First of all, it gave me an understanding of holistic personal development, and why you do it.

Before the injury, my whole world was about making the team. That was everything, and then all of a sudden it wasn't even a possibility and I had to find other things to focus on. Making the team still meant a lot, but I learned I could go and do other things, and somehow that worked to give me a bit of freedom in my mind.

Secondly, it taught me to take responsibility for my body. Up till then, I'd never put much focus on warming up. I did the prep because they told me to, but without really considering what I was doing. Now, I'm proactive about it. I know, absolutely fundamentally, that you never know what's going to happen in a game, and it's up to nobody else but me to make sure that everything — all the muscles, the tendons, the joints, all the things I now knew so much about — is as good as it can be. This prep requires specific attention. That kind of care will not be hand-fed to me; I've got to go to the physio, talk about it, create a plan and do it. This stuff is optional, and you can totally get through in the team without doing it; but for me, I had learned the value of extras.

At the end of 2013, still not able to play but determined, I made the decision to move from Christchurch to Tauranga. I had become concerned that if I stayed put I might get forgotten — KUSA had ended, and the Canterbury Sevens Academy was dwindling. I was often the only person turning up for trainings now. Also, there was talk of sevens becoming centralised at some point, and I knew that would mean Tauranga would be the base (this actually happened in October 2018). Older women couldn't move — they had houses, families, jobs — but I was still without commitments, and I was used to being a poor student. So I put everything that would fit into my car and drove up the country. My first stop was a cottage that the coach had offered me to stay in if I needed. He was married to our physio, so that meant I would be close by her too. Another player was living there, Kelly Brazier, a good friend of mine, which made me feel better about the big move. But I still remember getting there after the drive thinking *What am I doing?* I quickly found a flat in Mount Maunganui and even though the only room I could afford was so small you couldn't open the door fully without hitting the single bed, it was still super close to the beach, which I loved. I set about exploring my new home. I enrolled in a business paper at the Bay of Plenty Polytech — gotta keep working on my toolkit — and devoted myself to getting back in form.

———

At the end of January 2014, while I was still recovering from my injury, a massive development happened within women's rugby. For the first time ever, there was to be a semi-professionally contracted squad. There would be at least four 'tier one' contracts of $30,000; at least four 'tier two' of $25,000; and others on $20,000 and $15,000.

This was still far, far less than the men (whose worst-off players got the same as our best-paid), and only applied to women's sevens rugby and not to fifteens, but it was nevertheless revolutionary.

Despite my injury, I got offered a tier two contract of $25,000. Working my butt off over summer at uni I had still only made around $17,000, so to me I just got an $8000 pay rise. *And* I didn't have to work all those odd jobs. I was ecstatic. Our head coach showed real belief in me by contracting me as an injured player. That was a huge moment for me, to be included in that pivotal moment for women's rugby — the first-ever women to sign rugby contracts in New Zealand.

Already, in the span of my career, that was incredible: I'd gone from getting $2000 for my first year playing to $25,000 in 2014. It seemed an incredible amount to me. Getting paid to play rugby was a dream come true.

Up until then, many of the women had had to work full-time, juggling jobs, studies, families with their sporting commitments. Not only that but, because there was no regular squad, when it came to selection for tournaments women were given only a week's notice, then had to take a week or two off from work, leaving their kids behind to attend the trials, with no certainty they would be selected. And because under the old system the only payment was in tournament fees, you could take the week off, do the trials, and then not make the tournament and so get no money at all. So this new development, while obviously not enough for most of the women, would make a difference to all of us.

———

It took me sixteen months to get back in the squad. I missed the entire 2013–14 World Series. I thought I was ready exactly a year after my injury, when I set my goal to get in the squad to play Amsterdam, the last tournament of the 2014 series, in the same city where I'd had my injury. I played hard out during the selection process and thought I was all good, until they finished up with some tough honey-badger training sessions and after two and a half hours I got a bit of a limp. My leg just wasn't used to the load and I couldn't even tell I was doing it.

I could tell the coach wanted me, but the physio was shaking her head.

That was incredibly disappointing. However, by the time I got selected for the Oceania in September — the same tournament I'd debuted in back in 2012, only this time it was in Noosa, Australia — I was beyond ready. I played awesome, I was fast, nothing hurt. So, in hindsight, it was probably good I didn't make Amsterdam. I no longer needed to even think about my leg. What bloody leg?

And then I made the squad for the first game of the 2014–15 World Series, in Dubai. I was ready for everything.

RUBY'S TRAINING BAG
You never know what's going to happen
in a game, and it's up to nobody else
but me to get my body ready.

22. Culture shock

After I recovered from my ACL injury, I didn't really look back. The precariousness of 2012–13 disappeared. The roller-coaster of not getting picked for tournament squads was largely over, and my position in the squad solidified through to 2015 when I made every tournament except for one when I injured my PCL and missed playing the fourth tournament of that year's World Series, in Canada. Not only was I now in the core group of players, but I was where I had dreamed of being — in the starting seven. Every tournament I played for New Zealand up to then, we won. We were now a year out from the Rio Olympics and our goal of winning gold. Everything we talked about was around winning gold, Go 4 Gold, gold in Rio, gold this, gold that.

But then we began losing. Even though we were the overall champions of the 2014–15 World Series, we actually lost the final two tournaments in London and Amsterdam, coming third in London and fifth in Amsterdam. And heading into the 2015–16 World Series, we just couldn't stop losing. We didn't win in Dubai, Brazil, Atlanta, Canada, and even France, barely two months before the Olympics. We came second to Australia in that World

Series, getting there on overall points but failing to win a single tournament. It felt so weird.

But every time we lost, the coach would say, Don't worry, we're going to win gold at Rio. Nothing matters except for Rio.

It was confusing. What he was saying didn't align with what was happening.

We'd lost our way. It was like we no longer knew how to win.

———

Our head coach from 2012 up until the end of the Olympics campaign in 2016 had a background in coaching men's fifteens. He had led the Go 4 Gold programme, and he was so passionate about rugby and about getting us all to the top of the podium.

He's the guy who gave me a shot, who believed in me — even before I recovered from my ACL injury, he got me on a contract as an injured player while I fully recovered. He certainly didn't have to. His passion for the game was his great strength, and he was a real technical coach — we'd spend hours working on the little, tiny things — and he knew enough to lean on his coaching team who had more experience than he did of sevens tactics. So, thanks to him we got better as a team and were so excited about this big new experience in sevens. And for a while it worked.

But as much as we grew under him, there were times when he didn't know how to relate to all of the players, and not all of the players saw things the same way he did. This unfortunately happens sometimes in sports teams, and our team became divided.

We had a variety of players with strong personalities and lots of experience. Some just wanted to go to the Olympics so had jumped over to sevens, some had hardly any sevens rugby experience and none of us had ever been professional before. It was all new, and some people thrived and some people didn't. I had always dreamed about being a contracted player, but with contracts comes a dynamic I had not anticipated, where everyone is after a contract and people become secretive about whether they have one or how much they are on. Some were saying the coach told them one thing about a contract but someone else would say he said something completely different, and whenever I asked him it would be different again. That season of the Olympics, players were getting pulled in left, right and centre who had never been around before. The coach also decided to change captains, which was a massive decision that split the team too. I could see he was trying to take the team forward but he needed more guidance and help on how to go about it. There were already so many tensions in the team.

So while I saw the coach's strengths and was grateful to him, I also saw how his coaching style did not create the culture I desperately wanted. I honestly thought that winning and playing for New Zealand was everything I had ever wanted, but suddenly I didn't want to be a part of the new culture.

Team culture is not everything. I don't want anyone to think winning is just about culture. Obviously, you have to match it with hard work as well. And every team works hard. Everyone's doing fitness, everyone's doing skills, everyone's doing extras. But the culture is the secret layer, and at that time our team culture was not enjoyable and I believe that contributed directly to our sudden lack of success.

Because of the whole leadership conundrum, and the split that caused, we didn't know which direction to look — was it our new, young, exciting captain or was it our older, experienced captain? Was it the head coach or the assistant coach? We had a leadership group — the players who met with the coaches — which is a system that's proven great for the All Blacks, but we had no consistency within that group. People were in, then they were out. So when the shit hit the fan, it wasn't clear whose responsibility it was to stand up. All this affected us on the field.

I made the starting seven under that coach. Under him, I became part of that first-ever professional squad. I was there,

I was where I had always wanted to be, having an awesome time, loving my team, winning. But when it turned into *not* an awesome time, I got turned off. I was like, Oh *this* is not what I wanted. Nothing made sense to me.

Loss after loss, I realised I wasn't happy even there in the starting seven — not because we were losing, but because of the tensions within the team.

Everyone was unhappy. I was unhappy. All my partner at the time was hearing at night was how unhappy I was. I was tired.

I decided I'd leave the team after the Olympics.

In the meantime, I was determined to be honest with the coach and to speak my mind, and so we clashed sometimes — but I couldn't stand how some of the girls were feeling in the team. That's just me. If I don't feel something is right, I have to say it. It gets me in trouble sometimes but I'd rather be in trouble than be quiet and unhappy.

I knew I had to reach inside myself to deal with this situation in a way that was honest and true to myself. I didn't want to lose *me* in all the carnage. I intuitively knew that if I just stayed true to who I was, I would survive this crazy storm.

If I'm living with my heart and I am speaking from my heart and I'm always acting from love, no one can take that from me, and I can't go wrong. I don't mean I don't make mistakes — obviously I make mistakes — but if I can look back on a terrible week, or a really difficult situation, and know that I was always respectful to people, I was always honest, and if someone pissed me off I responded in a respectful way, then I'm OK with myself.

Every time I talked to the team, and to the coach, I was honest; I didn't act one way in front of one person and a different way in front of someone else, which in that divided situation I felt some people got caught in the trap of doing. I didn't waver from my values. I was just trying to have a decent relationship with everyone because they were all decent.

———

Objectively, it was a difficult time even apart from any coaching or team issues. We were in transition from no money to becoming professional, and we were right in a difficult stage where the middle ground was moving.

The 2014 contracts were such an important step but it was always apparent that they weren't enough. Even if $25,000 was like a super pay rise for me, it was peanuts for the women who had children and mortgages to pay and were walking away from jobs where they were on $70,000 to $90,000. They still didn't bring in enough money to live off and so we still had the situation where most of the players were under enormous stress balancing their paid jobs with the need to train to a professional level — and where they could sacrifice their precious time only to be dropped at any moment.

When everybody was on no money, sweet, it was all just fun, exciting, *Do your mahi before and after work, let's all fund-raise together*. We were all doing the same thing. Now, all these years later, we're all professional, this is how we live, this is our paid job, sweet. And eighteen-, nineteen-, twenty-year-olds can come in, straight out of school, get paid, grow and by the time they hit 25 they should be the best in the world. But that bit in between, which happened to coincide with all the bad feeling within the team, was so difficult and so variable. In fact, it wasn't sustainable. Women were still juggling work, families and sport against massive uncertainty.

By 2015, with the help of the NZRPA, the New Zealand Rugby Players Association, we assembled a whole lot of information to present to NZR: every day we were assembled in camps, every day we played in tournaments, and we compared it with the men's sevens, and we found that even though we had fewer tournaments we were actually assembled for more days of the year than the men. So, we were expected to leave our jobs, leave our lives, everything, for longer than the guys, and we weren't getting paid even half — yet we were both expected to win gold at the Olympics!

It didn't make any kind of sense. I was real pissed off because I remembered back to when I got that first Go 4 Gold pamphlet with its promise of contracts and payment, and we still had no real system. The pay wasn't equalling the expectations. It was not sustainable.

Then everything — the coach and culture and the pay — all came to a head. There was a meeting where some of the top guys from NZR flew down to meet with a group of us players from the team — me, Carla, Huri, Honey, Gossy, Kayla, a couple of others were in the room too. Three top dogs from NZR — I didn't even know them all by name but I knew they were important — sat us down. The room was tense. I assumed because of all the background work we had been doing with the NZRPA that this was finally our shot to chat face-to-face about contracts. I was nervous and a bit on edge because we didn't have any help with representation in the room, but I was ready to stand and speak up for our contracts. There are moments in life when you get an opportunity to speak out and if you miss it, it might not come again. I was all ready to fight for our case — a full-time contract, and $40,000. To me, 40K was so much money, a full-time wage. I'll work 365 days for 40K. I was like, Let's go, let's get this across the line.

But the first thing they said to open this meeting was, Is your coach really the man for the job?

They had come all this way and finally given us time only to see if we wanted to organise some secret coup against the coach. All of a sudden my nervous emotions evaporated, and they were replaced with rage. Are you frickin' kidding me? Firstly, to me, no matter what kind of issues I or any of us had with the coach, going behind his back with NZR was not the way to do it. We had no representation in the room, most of us players didn't know the men standing in front of us very well at all, and we hadn't chatted as a players group about this. I cannot speak for any other player in that room that day and how they felt. But for me, I was completely caught off guard. If I was going to review the coach I would want the process to be open and honest and fair, and to me it was important to align as players first — not like this.

Secondly I was ropable because I thought they had finally taken time to fly down and talk about contracts for women, for the first time ever in this country. I thought this was a special occasion to celebrate all that. I now know I was naive to think that. I also now know to try to prepare for these kinds of meetings — ask what it is about, ask if there is any information available so you can prepare some good responses and not just waste time.

To me, the issue with the coaching was so small compared with the overarching reality of what *we* needed, which was clarity on what our role was and sustainable contract conditions. They didn't seem to have any understanding of the real pressure most of our players were under.

Oh, I was so mad. I couldn't help myself. I stood up and my speech went a little bit like this: How can we sit here and act like the most important thing is the coach when we're here scraping dollars? I've got mothers sitting here scraping their dollars together for this frickin' dream!

I told them I felt like they were taking the piss if they expected us to achieve the demands they'd just put in front of us for the Olympic year, and they weren't even willing to pay us.

We deserve contracts! I was getting emotional as I was talking, like I was holding back tears because this moment meant so much to me. And then the worst thing was, one of the men who had a clipboard and was taking notes, when I started to get emotional, honestly, he didn't quite roll his eyes but he looked at the other guys like, *Urgh. Just another woman crying about pay* — whether he meant to do that or not, that's what it felt like.

I gathered myself and finished my statement. I'm here trying to do the right thing for women's rugby, bro. We're here to create a better future for this programme. This coach, us players, we're nothing if we don't fix what's actually going on.

I sat down, and he was just like writing, and in a minute he looked up and he said, in this bored kind of voice, You're gonna get paid, OK? We've got the contracts all sorted out. Then he carried on talking, but I didn't hear anything else.

And that's how I found out that we were going on to full-time contracts. After all our years of arguing and providing our case, this was how I found out — in a meeting that was really supposed to be about something else.

It was huge news for us. From now on we'd be on full contracts, the top players earning $40,000 a year. Shamefully, we were way ahead of the Black Ferns fifteens — who would get part-time contracts in 2018, with more comprehensive contracts in 2022 — but a million miles behind any of the comparable men's teams.

And yet it was strangely dampening because of the way it happened. I learned that day not to expect anyone to coddle you or hold your hand or celebrate your huge steps in this world. You've just got to do it your damn self, and make sure your relationships right here in front of you are good.

Being in that meeting had the effect of clarifying my focus as we headed to the Olympics. Screw all this stupid surface nonsense that everyone is back and forth about. We're all good people, we all want to be here, and we've actually all just changed history. Let's frickin' go. Straight up.

RUBY'S TRAINING BAG
If I can look back on a difficult situation and know that I was always respectful to people, I was always honest, and if someone pissed me off I responded in a respectful way, then I'm OK with myself.

23. Honey Badger, I'm home

In pre-professional days, at the beginning of camps we'd do these things called honey badger sessions. The honey badger is a metaphor — it's actually a scrawny little rodent-like animal which really doesn't look like much, but this little critter is notorious for never backing down. There are videos of this little creature taking on animals much bigger than them, like leopards or even six lions at once. It is known as the fearsome animal who does not die.

The honey badger sessions lasted up to three hours. These sessions were relentless and they were such hard work that I swear you weren't even fully conscious for some of it. One time we were on the beach, running through the water while carrying these heavy tyres over our heads, and as we jogged to the next activity I kind of passed out. I saw a bright white light, and when I came to I was still on my feet, still jogging, at the back of the group, and I turned to Bindy next to me and told her, Sis, I think I just saw God.

It was always like that in those sessions — you ran and ran, you retched and retched, but you all got up and kept running, again and again. So much carnage. After ten years of training for sevens we probably could've handled the sessions a bit easier, but all of us being amateur and just turning up for a week at a time in between our normal jobs, they seemed almost unbearable. By the time we got to a game, the game wouldn't even come close in what it demanded of us. Get through one or two of those sessions together and you've got a bond for life.

———

So there was no doubt the coach knew how to push us to our limits mentally and physically, and through all the background issues, of course we kept training. Training hard for Rio.

In 2015 he took us to Fiji for a training camp, these hideous fitness sessions, twice a day every day in the stinking heat, basically trying to break us. Unless you're spewing, you think you're tired but you're not, he told us.

So I took that as, Here we go, let's push the body, you're not working unless you're spewing.

We were doing triangle sprints — there's three of you and you all run these 50 by 50 by 50-metre triangles as fast as you can, and you just keep going, like there's no end. And most of the 'rest time' was spent in the plank position. There in Fiji it would have been around 30 degrees, and very humid. We'd been going an hour and a half, maybe two hours, and I don't know if I lost consciousness but one minute I was running those interminable triangles, and the next I was in a foetal position, and Kate the physio came over and went, Are you OK? But I was already projectile vomiting, and they decided I had sunstroke, and not only did they pull me off the field but the coach pulled me from the next training.

I was so pissed off! And confused. I thought I was just following instructions . . .

After Fiji, the next camp was back at Waiouru where we'd been on my first-ever training camp. I had fond memories from our first camp — it was where I met everyone — but this time the coach told the army to have us. This time it was different. And even with reeling shin splints so I couldn't do all the running, it was one of the hardest things I've ever done. I usually find the training camps really motivating, because I know we'll be playing rugby for parts of them, but this one was really tough for me and I didn't find it motivating at all, I think traumatic is a better word.

It wasn't just the 2 a.m. air-horns that dragged us out of bed into the light dusting of snow-covered ground to complete our 1200 burpees. It wasn't just the three hours spent exhausted in a huge, deep cold pool trying to erect a canvas army tent underwater and being told that if we got caught under it we would drown (a few of the girls were weeping before we even got in). It wasn't just the daily 5 a.m. multiple circuits that if your team lost you didn't get breakfast . . . I remember trying to sneak Gayle Broughton a cardboard sausage at about 6 a.m. as her team had to sit there and watch the rest of us eat and I just couldn't stand my team-mates going hungry. Of course we got told off for trying to share. It wasn't just how the army kept pretending that their Mogs were broken down and we had to push them for kilometres and then chase behind as they sped up. It was the whole thing — a blur of hell. I actually couldn't even tell you how many days we were there, they just all blurred together.

Tempers were lost in the extreme tiredness and hunger and freezing cold. And we were yelled at all the time, which I felt missed the mark and seemed a bit ridiculous. But I was determined to make the most of it, and to just try my hardest every minute.

One of the most memorable days we were given a pack each, a big army backpack, and we had to learn how to fit a sleeping bag into it, a small sheet of camo material and this little shovel, they called it an 'e-tool' or 'entrenching tool'. I remember the grin that the army people had when we asked what the shovel was for — You'll find out. I assumed we might have to dig a toilet or something, and kept packing. Suddenly, a few hours or days later, I couldn't tell, we were instructed to grab our pack and get on the Mog, the big army truck. By then the girls had been pushing this truck for kilometres, pushing and pushing. Management was told by the head coach to stop trying to help push the truck, so there was a bit of a divide created between management and the players.

We drove for a couple hours and pulled up to a place somewhere in the middle of the North Island. Then we walked with our packs for what seemed like hours. There was nothing in every direction, like a vast cold desert of tussock grass. It was freezing. We stopped when we finally found the army instructor waiting for us. But then behind him, we saw to our terror a grave-like hole, 2 metres long by 1 metre wide by half a metre deep, which had been pre-dug to show us what we were to dig. *What's the hole for?* He showed us how to attach our piece of camo material over the top to cover us from the wind, saying if we weren't out of the wind we would catch hypothermia with a very real chance of freezing to death. Snow had been falling on the army base.

I still didn't understand what the hole was actually for. But he cleared that up real quick when at the end of his demonstration he announced, This is where you will sleep for the night. You have 30 minutes to dig your hole before the sun sets — Go! We all took off but I couldn't help but think, Bro, is this guy all good or does he have screws loose? A few of us had to laugh at the stuff this guy was making us do, it was the only way to cope.

The army people led us all to individual spots so that we were far enough apart from each other to feel all alone all night. The whole time it was getting darker and darker. Laughing really pissed the main army guy off — he thought we weren't concentrating. But how hilarious is it being told to dig a grave somewhere out near the Desert Road, in the middle of winter with snow falling, by yourself and then go lie down and sleep in it? Straight up, the whole thing sounds like a joke. We were hungry, delirious, so laughing seemed appropriate.

As we ran off the army guy yelled out, Oh, and remember to sleep on top of your army boots or they will freeze!

Jordan (Jordy) Webber was to my left digging her hole, Shiray Kaka (née Tane) was somewhere close, and Carla Hohepa was just up a bit from us, maybe 20 metres up the slightly slanted hill of nothingness. Jordy had a really good flow going with her bloody e-tool but I was struggling, and it was getting darker. But next thing we heard Carla scream. I tried to see what was wrong but she was flailing her arms and just kept screaming. Jordy, Ray and I all ran over. She couldn't stop screaming, then when we arrived we saw why. Carla had accidently dug down directly into a huge spider's nest. I spotted the spider, no exaggeration it was the same size as a tarantula, just not hairy. It had huge, thick, shiny black legs. It was a species I had never seen. I googled it when I got home and found out it was a funnel-web spider, a poisonous species only thought to be found in Australia. Well I can tell you now, you can find them in the middle of the North Island of New Zealand somewhere near the Desert Road.

After our last activities for the day, which seemed to never end, we had to go and 'sleep' in our grave holes we had dug ourselves. I didn't sleep at all, I just kept fighting in my mind the thought of all the baby funnel-web spiders crawling all around me. Some of the other girls cried their way through the night. It was Kayla McAlister's birthday that day . . . I'll never forget how it was probably the worst birthday she ever had. I was so happy to hear the angry army dude yelling at us to wake up and giving us five minutes to sprint and get back on that damn Mog or we were getting left behind. You didn't have to tell us twice.

On the last day of this horrific experience I found myself back on the confidence course I had run so ferociously with Mini and Shorty at that first camp all those years ago. Except this time it had been snowing, storming, and we had been pushed to our physical limits all week. After our blurry first attempt, I'll never forget the army guy looking at the other army people and making the 'cut it' gesture with his hand across his throat. Too many of the girls had been pulled from the confidence course with onset hypothermia and even lost control of their bowels and had to be rushed to a medical room. It was becoming medically dangerous for our team, so he had to pull the pin.

———

After any dream I'd had to ever be in the army was completely destroyed, the head coach took us back to Fiji in June 2016 and that's where we had our final trial for the Olympics squad. I may have been starting, but to me the big hitters that were in front of me still had every chance. As the 2015 season went on, in my personal opinion Kiwi Ferns league immortal Honey Hireme and women's rugby legend Carla Hohepa were absolutely in front of me. Honey unfortunately got injured and stopped coming to the camps. I was confused by her disappearance and quite sad, to me she was the in-form striking prop for New Zealand sevens and she had been working really hard on her pass to change it from a league throw to a rugby spiral. We had been up together for those early mornings in 2013, and she had been flicking off defenders like they were insects for years. Then in Fiji I thought for sure that Carla would be named in the team. The first trial game against Fiji, she caught the ball and lined up half a gap and went for it . . . I was so excited to see her do her thing again. I was on the other side of the field watching from a distance, but I swear I still heard the crack. Her first touch, her first carry, she snapped and broke her arm. What the heck, I thought, this shit is serious.

Partway through the selection process the coach separated the team. He got seven of us to sit over there, and the rest had to keep going with all the physical stuff while we just sat there. I was one of the seven. And that's how I found out I was in the starting line-up for the Olympics. I didn't like how he separated us out. It definitely felt like yet again there were unnecessary divisions being created.

After that, the team was announced — it was official now that I had made the Olympic team. It was a weird experience, as so many legends that had been in the team for years, who I had absolute certainty would make the team, did not — Carla, Honey, Hazel Tubic, Jordy Webber, to name a few. The selection announcement is definitely the worst part of making a team. The players who have made it are so happy, of course, but on the other side it's heartbreaking. I was so sad, but nothing was said; they just stopped being invited to camps.

So we kept going, going for Gold. We went to Tampa, Florida to train in the heat, preparing for Rio where we knew we'd be playing in temperatures over 30 degrees. In Tampa it was getting north of 40 degrees some days and there was one training session where a few of us were doing our running extras that we always did. It got so hot that our trainer made us stop. That had never happened before.

We were in a new era.

In the earlier days, before we went on to full-time contracts, we were just turning up for two weeks, smashing ourselves, and then going home till the next time. Now we're professional and we turn up every day to do physical exertion, so it's really important that we keep an eye on it. We now have GPS systems built into our uniforms to track our distance, average speed, top speed, contacts, even heart-rate monitors when returning from sickness so we can measure everything about our performance. There's a weekly limit that people are allowed to hit and if we go over it the trainers will call the session.

It's good, it keeps us safe. It ain't smart to train full-time, twelve months a year. But sometimes I think that to get to the really hard state mentally and physically, you need to be in that zone where you've pushed past everything you think you're capable of. The majority of the time we need to listen to those limits, but sometimes, straight up, I reckon you just need to get chucked in the wringer and see who can cope. When you're in overtime in a final, nobody is going to stop the game and say, Hey everyone, that's too many high metres.

So I struggled with the training getting pulled. I didn't like it. I wanted that extremity. I knew this was our last chance to get to the right fitness level. And I figured I was mentally tough enough to handle whatever the circumstances.

———

There is a massive mental factor in peak fitness. I'll never forget how Tenika Willison, then one of the newcomers in our team, watched me training just after we'd got off a long-haul flight to Paris. I didn't want to stop, even when everyone else was heading to the hotel, and out of nowhere she was just like, How are you so mentally tough?

That was such a shock to me. What the heck? I didn't even think in those terms. To her, I'd just travelled 34 hours and I wanted to do extras . . . I wasn't letting the mentality of being fatigued from travel get to me. But to me it was just planning. I've learned how to set myself up.

At one stage, years ago, I wrote myself a commitment that I'd have the ball in my hand every single day of the year. I used to piss off my partner at the time because I'd be like, Where's the ball, where's the ball, I need to touch it every day. It sounds weird, but it's actually hard to do every day of your life. But then, still playing with this idea, sometimes I'd starve myself of it. Maybe for a week I wasn't allowed to touch the ball, and then when I finally got it in my hand I'd be like, *Aaah*, and I'd just love it.

That's what I'd done before we flew to France. I'd had a little starving period, we landed, we got to training, and I was like,

Whooo! The ball! I'd done it on purpose and I was just loving it and enjoying it. So I didn't see it as mental toughness, just as part of my life. This is how I roll. Tenika probably thought it looked like discipline and motivation, but really I've just set myself up to find joy in the littlest of things, like touching a rugby ball for the first time in a week.

But it was cool she said that, because afterwards I was like, Shit, am I mentally tough? It was an insight for me.

I remembered how when I first started out in rugby I was so bad that I needed to find something that would get me ahead of these great rugby women I was suddenly playing with. One of the things that happens during training is that when people are absolutely buggered, they rush to the water bottles as soon as they can. So in my very early days I made a rule for myself: I am never going to be the first one to let the water touch my lips.

It sounds easy, but for some reason there's always drills where you're right next to the water, and oh man, you want to squirt it all over your face and feel it running down your throat. But I'd wait, and stare at it, wait for that person to stop tying their laces and reach for the bottle, and honestly it was so excruciating. But to me it was this huge deal. In the early days I couldn't get ahead of anyone, I couldn't beat them in speed or fitness, but I could beat them in the mental. I was going to be mentally stronger. Of course, no one even knew I was having this huge battle with them.

Finally I made it into a New Zealand camp, and I brought my water discipline with me. I was proud of myself. I'd got used to not drinking. But in camp we had to do hydration tests every morning. I didn't know how to read the scores yet so I just wrote down what the hydration pee stick said every morning, and that's when the physio pulled me up. Ruby, you've been clinically dehydrated every day of this camp, if you were in hospital you would be on a drip. You need to drink more! And she made me buddy up with someone and every time they drank, I had to drink. So much for my rule. But it had served its purpose. I'd challenged myself, succeeded, built my confidence that I could win at other things.

And now here I was in Florida training for the Olympics in 40-degree heat, and I'm demonstrating another example that some people might call mental toughness, although others have definitely called weird.

It began in São Paulo, Brazil, in February 2015. I came down with flu before game day. I felt like shit but I couldn't tell anyone because I was desperate to play. I was still so scared that if I dropped out someone would come along and take my spot. Because I was feverish I was freezing cold, so in between every game I crammed on my beanie, hoodie, jacket, pants, socks — everything I could find. It was Brazil, it was hot — around 30 degrees, so of course everyone in my team was like, What the hell are you doing?

They just thought I was mental, and maybe I was, but then I remembered how I'd lived in Canterbury for years playing club rugby in a singlet and shorts even when it was literally freezing, and I couldn't do that now. In other words, I knew I could get used to any temperature if I trained myself. And I thought, the Rio Olympics is my goal; it's a hot country, I'd better acclimatise myself to frickin' hot. And so every hot tournament from then on I was in track pants, hoodie, beanie, all the time. The hotter the better, I thought.

Players from all the teams hated to see me like that. They'd be going, Oh my gosh, I'm so hot, I'm so hot. I was reminding them how hot they were, but I'd be saying to myself, Ruby, you're fine, you're absolutely fine.

It was very hot down on the field in Hamilton in late January when we hosted the first-ever New Zealand leg of the Women's World Series in 2020, and I was there in my beanie, hoodie, pants, etc. The other teams were all wearing ice vests and talking about how they were training for Tokyo. But then the next week we

were all in Sydney for the tournament there and it was heading
over 45 degrees and their ice vests all melted, and I was sitting
there with my beanie going, I'm all good. I had 100 per cent
trained my body.

I know that sensation of it being 40 degrees and I'm putting
on a hoodie, a jacket, pants, socks and a beanie. The immediate
feeling is almost unbearable, but I know it's only temporary
because I've done it so many times. So even when I walk out
on to the field and it's like walking into an oven, I already know
it's temporary. This passes — and it always does. Your body is
incredible and you can change what it's capable of. Plus, showing
those other teams a Black Ferns Sevens player in a beanie is
a little bit of a competitive mind-game.

Those kinds of personal tests, like the water rule, like the
beanie, work well for me. The sports psychologist who worked with
our team in the earlier years, David Galbraith — DG — calls them
'mind-gyms'. We push our physical bodies at the gym, or when we
go for a run — but what exercises are we doing in the gym upstairs?
We can work on our minds like we work on our muscles.

When we're aiming to play sevens at the Olympics in
the hottest of hot countries, of course as a team we do heat-
acclimation work that year, but for me that mental work starts
years before. To me, *now* is the time to start living like you're
going to make it.

So when I think about Tenika using those words, *mentally
tough*, I'm like, Faar, true — I am a little bit weird.

———

Meanwhile, as we got closer to Rio, our team was more divided
than ever. The differences between us had become like a chasm,
and misunderstanding was everywhere.

When shit hits the fan, whose responsibility is it to stand up?

I had no official title in the team. I wasn't the captain,

I wasn't even in the leadership group — but even my captain was a little lost and unable to fully unite us because of the weird circumstances. I was hurting for her and for the other players. Maybe it was audacious, but I thought perhaps I could help my captain and the team. I took it upon myself to find ways to bring us together, to be the catalyst for better communication and connection, to find a way to remind us we are on the same side. I believed that finding that sense of unity was the key, because when we're out there on the field, all we have is each other. No one's holding our hand. Whether you're the teacher's pet or you hate the coach, as long as when we're on the field we can see eye to eye, it will be OK.

I needed to find ways to show how important each and every one of us was. I made videos of the girls, of all of us, with downloaded clips from YouTube and inspirational quotes. I went on GarageBand and made a song, changed the lyrics to make a tribute for every single person in the team, to highlight that no one's better than anyone else. In here, we all get the same air-time. These days personalised videos are common, but back then this was quite impressive and effective.

I brought us all together when we got to the Olympic Village and we played the videos. Then I got them doing fun things like playing spin the bottle where whoever it landed on had to tell the group why they were here, and what it meant to be here. And sure enough, whoever's turn it was would get all emotional and immediately everybody could connect with them because, like it or not, everybody has emotions. Everybody's really proud to be here; whether it's for our mum, for ourself, for our teacher. We're all human.

And in case you're wondering, my 'why' — which I wrote in my journal so I'll never forget — is Mum, Dad, Lesh, Dane and Nikki; Grandman, Grandma, aunties, uncles, cousins; for a better life, for knowing my worth; for making my family and friends proud.

In this team we're all on the same side. I knew that if I could get that across, we could knit ourselves back together.

But the whole time I just kept thinking, It's not enough. It's not enough. I'm too late.

RUBY'S TRAINING BAG
Now is the time to start living like
you're going to make it.

24. Golden dreams

So at last, in early August 2016, we had made it to Rio. Rio, the city of golden dreams. It was hot. Hot and crazy. I'd never seen so much security, so many guns, and we knew the country was in turmoil, although we were shielded from the reality of it. It made me sad to think of those contrasts, because as Olympic athletes we were so elevated — everything was provided for us on such a grand scale. In fact, it was like a fantasy land.

I get off the bus and my mouth is open in awe instantly. We walk through security, and all around us the buildings seem ginormous, covered in patriotic flags and signs announcing which countries are in which towers. I'm almost dizzy from looking up and all around. We can walk into a McDonald's and not have to pay for anything. Vending machines — we flash our Olympian pass and the frickin' door opens and you just take everything you want for free. On arrival we're each given a little bag and it's got a brand-new top-of-the-line phone and all sorts of other things. Funny, I guess I didn't need to spend this year's pay cheque on a new phone or two then. There's an on-site athlete's dentist hub and I get this flash mouthguard, for free. The food hall is like something you'd see in a movie, and as I'm walking out Michael Phelps, the most decorated swimmer of all time, is walking in. He's safe in the middle of a group so he won't get accosted, and I make eye-contact with him, me wide-eyed in awe, and he must be thinking, Another bloody fan. And we walk into the gym and there's weight-lifters the size of hulks to my left, and little petite Chinese gymnasts stretching to my right and their legs are up *here*. I can hardly do my own training for looking around at this other world. On the training track that loops around the whole village there are people walking faster than we are running, and others doing three-minute kilometres. *Zoom!* It's hilarious.

I'm thinking, Man, these people are so intense! Like, what is this, the Olympics?

I feel like I'm flying.

Even just attending an Olympics as a spectator would be a bucket-list thing, but to frickin' be involved in it, to walk into that village, that's a whole other level. I feel the momentum, and just feeling that makes me understand like I've never understood before: how the Olympics raises any sport, how it's a huge catalyst for any kind of dream or hope. Until I got here, I just didn't realise the magnitude. Before this, I would probably have said the World Cup was the big one, but now I know: it's the Olympics. You want to be in the Olympics; everything is focused on the Olympics.

And here we are, little us. Celebrities, free stuff . . . it's all absolutely surreal.

A big part of our training is sleep, and we've been lectured about it for years, all the crazy benefits. I've always been a really good sleeper, trying to get 10 hours a night, I'm extremely diligent with my sleep. But the night before our first game, me and Gossy sit up talking. We are each supposed to be in a room by ourselves, but my whole thinking around the Olympics is trying to be more together and I love Gossy a lot, I want her to know I've got her back out there. So I was like, Nah, I need to be with the girls, and we spent ages manipulating my bed through the apartment into Gossy's room. We've each been given a little card packet with pictures of our family and legendary players on the cards, and notes from our loved ones, and we are all so emotionally in awe and excited. Gossy and I debuted together in Fiji, and now we're like, Faar, I can't believe we made it, we're here, all the things we've done to get here . . .

And then we look at the clock and start laughing because after years of being so diligent with our sleep, it's one o'clock in the morning and we have to get up at six to get ready to play Kenya. Bro, are you kidding? I just did three years of sleep prep and I didn't even use it!

Later, I read somewhere that athletes should leave no regrets behind them at the Olympics, but I do feel that because of my youth and my inexperience, I got just a little bit caught up in the excitement. It was like I was in Fiji — I hadn't yet mastered being present with the pressure of a pinnacle event. Because I'd missed the World Cup, this was the first huge sporting event I was part of and, far out, I really didn't know how to deal with it.

———

The next morning I ran on to the field of my very first Olympic game off the bench, got the ball, Kenya got a penalty, I flicked the ball down — it was hardly anything, but I got a yellow card and sat back down. So: ran on, yellow-carded, sent off. That was my Olympic debut. After five hours of sleep and that whole emotional night, I was just like, Oh my goodness, I may as well not have played.

The Olympic sevens tournament was played over three days, two games a day, in the newly built Deodoro stadium, with a capacity of 15,000 spectators, although with the sevens being brand new at this Olympics the stands were not quite full.

Nevertheless, it was intense. We made it through the pool games and into the quarter-final.

That quarter-final against the USA, I don't know how we won. It was just some sort of blessing from above. It was ridiculously tense from beginning to end. USA did a couple of things that they will never forget, and we got two yellow cards and were playing with just five players for some of it. How the heck we managed to beat them I don't know, but we did: 7–5, thanks to Portia Woodman scoring a try and Tyla Nathan-Wong converting it. And somehow here we were in medal contention. And I let myself think: Maybe we can do this. Maybe we can do this after all.

Then again in the semi-final, Great Britain didn't play well at all. They definitely had a better performance within them but they were making mistakes. There was a bounce ball, I jumped up to get it and one of them grabbed me and tipped me up, and I knocked my head on the ground. She was instantly yellow-carded, and they kind of fell apart from there.

I'd already got a good try in that game, but with that knock on the head a funny thing happened. I was sitting there on the grass holding my head, feeling foggy. As I got picked up, into my field of vision swam a really good-looking, familiar face. Am I unconscious? Am I out of it? Have I died? Because there right in front of me was the Hollywood actor Matthew McConaughey. I'm definitely out of it, I decided, as I got supported off the field. But then a bit later Gossy came running up and goes, Guess who's watching our rugby game? And we were like, who? Matthew McConaughey!

We won that game, but in reality I felt like Great Britain lost it. We definitely weren't playing our best. But then, miraculously, we were on to the final, against Australia.

———

Gold, gold, gold, gold. For nearly four years, that had been the magic word. Go 4 Gold. That programme wasn't named that for nothing. From the very beginning, we were going for gold. Gold medals at the Olympics. That was our focus, our purpose, literally our reason for being, our level of worth. That's why the New Zealand Women's Sevens team had been created, and nothing else would do. It was all our coach talked about. Everything else was just a stepping stone. Nothing else counted.

The whistle blows and the sevens final of the Rio Olympics begins.

We score first, Kayla getting a try, and I think, Yep, this is good. Kayla is the best line-breaker I have ever played next to. We've just got to stick to our game plan, strong threes, use the width.

So much is happening: I miss a tackle early on; a couple of calls don't go our way.

Unfortunately Portia, who is seen by the coach and the team as our answer to everything, gets yellow-carded. I try to convince the ref otherwise but I know it's no good, and Portia goes off. It was an innocent enough mistake and shouldn't matter — we've already had so many cards this tournament. But it's like someone's jammed the communication between us, I don't know if the player next to me has my inside or not, I'm hesitant. At half-time the Aussies are up 10–5.

The second half begins and it's more of the same. Australia gets a free kick right on our line, and straight away we're not sticking to our plan. I've got a player outside me, but Gossy's player has the ball and I'm going, Gossy, Gossy, Gossy? Usually she'd go yep or no, and I'd push off to mine, or just tackle her. It's not a problem, I just need to know. Gossy is one of the best players on the field and the best communicator, but now I hear nothing. I'm stuck. I have no idea what to do, and I turn around and Gossy just kind of dives, and meanwhile the Aussie player literally taps the ball and almost walks in between us. We made it easy, and she gets a try and it's just so uncharacteristic of us to let in a try like that. And usually when the other side gets tries we're like, Yeah, let's go, and we rise to it — but not this time. Something's broken down.

We go into a ruck, and when that happens you've got to trust that the carrier will carry hard, the bridger over the top will support them and then the half will get there to clear it. That's just 101 basics of sevens. But people are running in and I'm two players out from the ruck and three of them are meant to clean it up. I'm all the way over here and I'm looking at the ruck, and I see we can't even secure it, I'm about to run in but if I do, our whole attack will be useless. There's no communication from anyone to say, I've got it. Where's our bond? Where's our trust? And into my head comes treachery: How did we even make the final? This is ridiculous; we are playing ridiculous. I'm imploding too. It's 24–5 to Australia.

Then the Aussies get two more tries.

There must be something I can do or say to flip this around. But there isn't, and we can't. It's as clear as day to me. We don't have the culture where we trust each other and can communicate openly and honestly when shit hits the fan. We are not knitted together. We haven't practised anything that would allow us to snap out of this and fix it together — and there's no training to be done when there's five minutes to go in an Olympic final and we're down by 19 points and no one's talking.

Then Kayla comes back on and scores a try, and there's one minute to go. Portia's back from the yellow and we're in overtime and she scores too, because she's the best in the world and she truly did all she could.

But it's not enough if we aren't all doing it, and the score, there's nothing to be done about it now or ever. It's 24–17 to Australia, and we get not the gold but the silver. And Portia breaks down and I can see she thinks it's all her fault, and I've got my arms around her and I'm going, How can you think it was your fault? It was all of us. But she's distraught. I peel her off the ground, and I'm going, Please, sis, wait till we're in the changing rooms. But she's so upset she doesn't care if the world sees her. I look around and everyone's crying. We're crushed. We've failed in our mission. Our families are in the stands, and they come down and start a haka to us, and it's a great token of love but it makes it worse because, like, Fuck, we let them down as well. And we reply with our haka and we're all crying our whole way through it.

At some point in there I'm gutted because I remember ripping out my fancy mouthguard I had made for me at the Olympic Village, throwing it on the ground in my despair, and I don't know where it is and I'll never get it back.

Then we're back in the changing room and I'm trying to console everyone, when Katty, who's one of our exciting players who was unlucky to miss out on being in the team, walks in and she's like, Shot, guys! I didn't know she was even in Rio. I thought you were in frickin' Wellington, how did you get past security? Like what are you doing here? But it's so her, and it's so random and surprising, and now I cry, because it's the last emotion I can tolerate — this crack-up surprise. Suddenly it's hilarious and we hug and I laugh and I cry and she's like, Oh sorry bro, don't cry. And I'm like, Faar, no, I needed to cry anyway, like you just topped it off, don't worry.

So it's pretty sombre in the changing room, and we're all dragging and no one wants to go out and get the silver. But we have to, and we get through it, and then it's real weird how everyone kind of snaps out of it. Portia, probably because she fell so hard, snaps out of it equally hard and wants to party, but the ones who kind of held it together, we're not ready to be happy yet. And so on the bus back to the village — and I will never forget this — we are absolutely divided. At the back are a bunch of girls, along with the coach, who are partying and yelling, and the coach who for four years has told us we're going to win gold, is now trying to make us feel good about silver. At the front of the bus are the girls who are all really sad and upset and don't want a bar of the back group, and I'm in the middle of the bus, right in the middle of the divided team. We're split. We can't even lose together.

If our culture was strong, if we'd played as a unit, at our full potential, and we still got silver, that would be something completely different. Then you'd have to go, The other team was just better than us. We gave it our all, and they were better. But to lose the gold because you failed to reach your potential, when you know you have the best players but you didn't have the glue — that's why I was so gutted there on that field. That's the taste I will never forget.

————

Ever since I made that first camp in Waiouru in early 2012 I've been like, I'm not going to drink. I'm not going to screw this opportunity up. I'd seen Dad go down and many other talented sportspeople lose themselves to drugs and alcohol, and I wanted to give this other way of life a real shot. It didn't take long for the girls to stop pressuring me to have a drink. Actually, before long they thought I never drank alcohol. Little did they know that drugs and alcohol nearly got me before I found the rugby. I promised myself, I'll drink if I make the Olympics. I made that promise with Tyla Nathan-Wong as well, but her bet was we had to win gold at the Olympics. True to her character, she stuck to her bet. But for me, that night we go to the hotel near the Village, and the coach is shouting everyone, and I have my first drink ever with Goss and Portia and the team-mates I've had for four years of going through all this shit with them. It's a buzz to have a drink together, even if it's bittersweet.

There's a dance floor and a DJ and Niall Williams puts all our medals around her neck and pretends she's Michael Phelps because he's won heaps of medals this Olympics. Ching ching, go the medals. Look at me, I'm Michael Phelps! We're dancing, and everything is hilarious, we're all cracking up. Ching ching! And next morning we wake up and realise our medals are all chipped. It was so funny at the time but it's hard to tell them apart and everyone wants the least-chipped medal.

But in the end, we realise it doesn't matter — we'll take these medals when we go to schools, and the kids will drop them, and those first chips will be just the first of many. I learned with Olympic medals, you either let no one touch it and be real careful, or you let everyone have
a go and accept the dings and the chips that comes with it.

After that weird and emotional day and night, seven out of our fourteen went home, and seven of us stayed on — we physically split this time. We could apply at the Athlete Support Office for tickets to anything we could get our hands on, so we made the most of it. I was leaving the team — I couldn't do another four years of carnage and bad culture. I'm never going to get to be at the Olympics again, I thought.

I got right in behind the hockey girls, the Black Sticks women, and went to all their games that I could, and we bought them Maccas and a couple of bottles of vodka after they came fourth. We saw Valerie Adams win her silver, and I ended up sitting next to Richie McCaw, which I would never have dreamed was possible, and I was thinking, Cool people go to the Olympics. Growing up, I definitely did not think I was one of them.

Me and Tyla spent some time shamelessly Snapchat-stalking Venus and Serena Williams, desperate for a photo with Serena. We'd refresh their stories on our phones: Oh she was at the playground five minutes ago, so we'd run down to the playground but they'd be gone, and we'd refresh our phones and find out where they'd gone next. Then we were just a minute behind them, and eventually we saw the crowd at one end of the dining hall, and we ran over and it was them. Serena was hard to spot, her cap low and head down, facing away, with a strong leave-me-alone vibe coming from her, but Venus was out there swapping Olympic pins. Huri was with us and she was like, Ruby, go and get a photo with her, but I was suddenly a bit shy, like Oh nah, nah, and she was like: Ruby! This is literally the only time in your life you'll ever be able to.

There were so many people, but I pushed my way to the front using all my rugby skills and I got her attention. Venus, have you got a New Zealand pin? I was as polite as you can be while you're elbowing someone out of the way. I'm sorry, she said, in a lovely way. I've already got a New Zealand pin. And before she was even finished, I burst out with, Can I have a photo? And she was like, Of course you can. Oh my gosh! And so the girls got me with her, and straight up that was pretty awesome, and I posted it straight to Instagram. Some of the girls did get a photo with Serena, but she wasn't looking at the camera and she was obviously so over it. It must be hard having such a huge profile and everyone just wants a photo.

My other brush with fame was in the dining hall waiting to use the toast machine, standing there with my floppy, non-toasted bread in my hand, and an older balding man in front of me, he was taking his time, holding me up. I must have been in a hurry, because I partly wanted to be rude and be like, Bro, you're standing right in front of the whole toaster, but then I thought, Come on, Ruby, don't be a dick, he just wants to cook his bread too. And then the man turned around and it was frickin' Rafael Nadal, one of the top tennis players in the world.

Lucky I wasn't rude!

I'm so sorry, he said. Here I was, in your way. Please, put your bread in here. And then while the toast was on we stood there having this convo and he was so incredibly nice. What sport are you doing? he asked me. How are you going? I couldn't believe he even cared.

I noticed that the girls were looking at me, so when the toast was ready I asked him if we could get a photo with him once he'd finished his meal and he said, Of course. We all watched him closely while we ate, making sure we wouldn't miss him as he left . . . and a bit later when he stood up to go, we dropped our meal and ran over to him. His trainer was going, Rafael, no, Rafael, no. But Rafael insisted that he stay for a photo, and so we got this awesome photo, the four of us and him, and his trainer ended up having to take it, which I thought was hilarious. Little moments like that were just gold.

I'll never forget that Venus and Rafael were so awesome. *Of course I want a photo with you.* They weren't too big to take a moment. It was a real cool thing for me to see.

So, as tired as I can sometimes be, I'll always try and give people the time of day if they want a photo, because I know what it means, and it can be something a person will never forget.

And Huri, she was right. If I didn't work my way to the front to ask and take that opportunity, I'd never have had another chance.

———

As the 2016 Olympics campaign wound up, with all its highs and lows, I was conscious of a feeling of being so frickin' proud of myself. I felt like I had lived my values, lived the goals I'd set myself — to act from my heart, to act from love, to never try and be someone I'm not. As well as the pact I'd made with Tyla not to drink until the Olympics, I made a pact with Goss too: if we won gold we would get the Olympic rings tattooed together. Well we didn't win gold, so we didn't get the rings, but it was still such a big moment in our lives. Gossy had a look at a few images and a few other girls heard about us getting a tat to mark the occasion, and we found the one.

I got my first tattoo with seven of my sevens girls: two rugby posts joined by a heartbeat — because, 100 per cent, I will always act from my heart. It felt right to me because it showed that my value of love was at the heart of my identity, and my heart has always been what has powered me through rugby. And it always will.

We might not have won but I had my sanity and my identity. I had my self-love still.

RUBY'S TRAINING BAG
If I act from my heart, I will always be able to look myself in the eye and have self-love.

25. Restart

I was all set to leave the team. I couldn't do this any more — exhaust myself trying to weave together players that I felt were being driven apart by the culture and coach. No way. See ya. But then, the day after the final, our team's assistant coach, Allan Bunting, said he wanted to have a chat. We'd always got on, and I always appreciated his honesty, but because of the culture in the team we weren't tight as, so it was a surprise. Can we go for a drink tonight? I even asked Porsh to come with me 'cos I had no idea where this was gonna go. We met up at the hotel outside the Village and had a beer and he said, What are your plans?

I'm done, I told him. Gotta get on with my life. My relationship's stretched to the frickin' nines from me being away all the time. This was true. My partner at the time found it really hard with me being away so much, and putting first a team of people that weren't always that nice to be around — the rugby life is definitely hard on the families. Also, I told Bunts, I'm not even happy when I play now. I want to do something else. I'll probably go study media or something.

He told me he'd had an offer to go and coach in Japan — he'd played there in his days as a professional rugby player, and spoke

Japanese, better Japanese than he did te reo Māori at the time.

That's what I heard, I said. All the best bro, like, all the best . . . you're gonna do amazing over there. I meant it. His sevens brain was special.

Then he said the thing that changed my whole world: You know the head coach is leaving. I had heard he was applying for the men's coaching role so I had a feeling he would leave. Yeah, I said, wondering what that had to do with anything. Well, what would you say if I applied to be head coach?

It was such a shock to me. Bunts. Head coach of our team. He was probably the one person who would actually speak up for the other players, especially the ones that were more hard-done-by.

And he was like, Maybe I'm too young. Maybe I'm not good enough.

But I was hardly listening. All these things started clicking together in my head — how Bunts runs all the tactics anyway, takes all the training, designs all the moves, always deals with us with honesty — and then I came to. Wait, Bunts — what do you mean you're not good enough? You are the most qualified person in the world to be the coach of this team. Of course you can do it, and who cares if you're only 41 and you're Māori. Not everyone in rugby has to be old and white and bald. I was suddenly so excited I couldn't stop talking. Just apply, and if they don't pick you they're stupid.

OK, he said, I wanted to see what you thought. I've been thinking about it and if I apply I'm going to base it all around Māori culture. I'll put culture at the centre, and we'll have a player-led environment. All the senior players who stay on, I'll make them the leadership group and I won't chop and change it.

This is the kind of thing coaches often say, that they'll include the players, but then they don't really, because it can be quite a scary thing to put your job in the hands of others. But when Bunts said that to me, I don't know why but I knew I could trust him. I knew he was for real. This was the kind of team I wanted to be in. One with a real culture. My eyes were lighting up. I was imagining enjoying being in this team again. Oh my goodness, this is what we needed this whole time. Even at our worst moments during that Olympics final, I'd known beyond certain that our team had all the ingredients — the best players in the world — but there was something wrong with our recipe. This guy's got the recipe. I instantly knew it, and I knew I wanted to follow him into battle.

If we got silver and our culture was like that, just imagine if our relationships and connections were good. We'd get the most goldest gold ever.

Bunts, I told him, if you go for that job and you get it, I'll stay. I'll follow you to the Tokyo Olympics.

He applied, and some time after that he rang me and he was like, I got it!

Life was about to change.

———

Our team is a waka, and we leave mana in our wake.

From that November of 2016, when Bunts officially became Head Coach of the Black Ferns Sevens, we were on a journey together — of him finding out more about who he was as a coach, putting into practice all the instincts and knowledge he had around leadership, and of us learning what it meant to be trusted, have accountability, learning to understand ourselves again as a team.

Straightaway he got me, Niall, Tyla, Gossy, Kelly, Kayla and Portia as his leadership group, and he appointed his best mate, Cory Sweeney, as assistant coach. They've known each other since primary school, and sometimes it's real suss when coaches appoint their friends, but we quickly saw that Cory was humble as, so knowledgeable, was working at a coaching academy, understood the tactics really well, and we saw that altogether the new management team was frickin' unreal.

Bunts got his new leadership group together and straight-up told us: I don't want to take another step forward without your input. How do we work this out together? From that day forward we were part of every decision. For example, one year they couldn't decide between the last two or three contracts to offer, and it was inevitable that someone was going to lose their spot in the team. So they got the whole leadership group in and they were like, This is the situation. They told us their perspective on the team as a whole, the balance they were looking for, so we could understand the overview of why someone needed to be replaced. Everything we might have said behind their backs, bitching to each other with only a bit of the information available to us, we said directly to management and were listened to and responded to, and we left that room upset but knowing that the right decision had been made for the plan they had for the team. Coaches never usually do that.

The other genius part of our leadership group was that we were completely different people but we all knew ourselves well enough to speak up for what we believed in. This is so important, because if everyone is too similar or if people with different views aren't strong enough to speak up when it counts, you just get the same views and group-think takes over. The fear of disagreement or hurting feelings becomes stronger than sticking up for what's right, and that is a dangerous space. Our group was strong and had firm opinions and had the ability to hit each other up. We could chat through every friction and even though we all had different values, it actually brought us closer together after the honest conversations.

———

Relationships are such fascinating things. They are such an important part of life, but sometimes we get lost in life instead of learning how we like to have relationships with others — how do we love, how do we like to be loved, what makes us feel valued, how do we communicate with different people in our lives? We are constantly reviewing our performances at work or school, but not in our relationships, like How could I have done that conversation better? All these things are so important but often don't get much thought.

I've learned that figuring out myself, learning about where I'm from, who I am, what makes me tick, has made me able to serve my relationships far better. I can also create good relationships and safe spaces a lot quicker now that I can identify what I value in myself and therefore in other people.

Allan Bunting, Bunts, is one of those people I can so easily create a safe space with. He values clear, open, honest communication, and immediately. If there were ever any whispers or conversations about someone or a situation, straight away he would set up a conversation about it, even if it screwed up the schedule. To me, if you wait for a more convenient time, the problem simmers away and becomes far bigger. Bunts and I agreed on the importance of honesty and of facing the harder conversations head-on. It goes without saying that neither of us would make good managers who have to keep everything ticking along so that all appointments happen on time. I know it's not everyone's cup of tea, because not everyone values these things above all else. But I do.

I have always wanted to be a part of the greatest team on the planet, and when I strive to be the greatest player on the planet my definition of greatness is very different to others and I know this. To me, greatness is not breaking try-scoring records or being top of the tackle stats or getting the most caps. Those things *are* great and they *are* incredible. But to me, the greatest player stands up when there are no cameras and when they can hide behind comfort but they choose not to . . . when everything seems to be going great but they still choose to make the room uncomfortable and say what needs to be said. They make the players next to them not only feel safe to express themselves, but able to trust them in the most incredible pressure-filled moments. When they are struggling, they come to you and they don't feel like they have to suffer alone. When we win on the field, we celebrate together. When we lose, we hold our heads up because we did everything we could and we had every conversation we needed to. To me, true greatness is felt in a team and it is in a look in the eye and in the hug you know is always there for you, day or night.

A friend and coach, Crystal Kaua, once told me that we don't suffer from the things that come out — we suffer from the things we hold in. If we hold something in, it will explode out in terrible ways — addiction, violence, suicide. It rots people from the inside out. I believe that the real road to mental health or fitness is the constant journey of figuring out how to express our emotions in a way that doesn't hurt ourselves or others around us. This is more important to me than the rugby. To be the greatest team is life-changing.

———

Bunts used to tell us that his whole thing was to coach so well and so hard that his role as a coach would become redundant. A huge selfless call to make by a coach. That's what it has to be on the field, because when we get to that point it's just us. The coaches have helped us with everything they can up to that white line, but after that, we've got to take responsibility. We can do this. We are unleashed. We are responsible. Even at our biggest games, even at Tokyo, Bunts will be running the water out for us at half-time, and that's it — he won't talk in any of our huddles, he lets us do the talking. Trusting us to know our jobs, trusting us to trust each other. Sometimes he even walks away, and that can't be easy. But that's how much he trusts us.

Bunts letting us take the huddles was extremely uncomfortable at the beginning. We all have specific areas of the game to lead, but there's still a learning process to know what to say in the heat of the moment when you are extremely fatigued and emotional. But this is a whole other level of leadership awareness. You go from worrying only about yourself in a team huddle — getting a water, waiting for the coach to say something that might help — to constantly being aware of every aspect of the game because you need to have the answers now, not the coach. How long do we go, how is our depth on attack . . . I need to tell Goss to take the kick for touch at our next penalty because they aren't even contesting in the lineout . . . Why are we slipping off tackles today? The growth we had as leaders just from Bunts' trust was quite incredible. He really was doing exactly what he told me he would, that night in Rio.

True leadership is the opposite of individualism, the opposite of one person standing above the rest. It's an encompassing, inclusive thing. I never like the top-down way of leading. Even if I've been here for years, I shouldn't walk around like I'm a better human than a newbie or treat them badly. I love to do things through conversations and mutual agreement. In our team, it's either unanimous or we need to talk more. And if you can't say it up-front, then you shouldn't be saying it behind anyone's back. I always work hard to make sure that we, as players, have an open platform to share things and be up-front. As a leadership group you get to know much more than the average player, and I always want to pass on as much as I can to the rest of the team — after all, we're representing the whole team with our decisions and discussions. And some things we are actually unable to lead and need help with from other players. Like selection, for example — how do players want to find out that they haven't made the team? As leaders we often make the team, so speaking on behalf of those who don't make it can't be done accurately so we will ask other players for help.

Rugby's image is very macho and tough and, probably

because it's been such a predominantly male domain, it's not always obvious that what actually drives the players is emotion. In our team, we all took personality tests one time — everyone, from players right through to team management — and they showed that we are all emotional people, every single one of us. This fits with what the great All Blacks and Black Ferns coach Wayne Smith said — that you have to get the whole team to emotionally buy in to the process, the great undertaking that you're all part of.

We're all very different people but we all fight with our hearts full. We all fell in love with the concept of the black jersey. You could even say it's a romantic idea — the pure emotion of representing your country. I reckon even those old-school staunch rugby players still felt that in their hearts.

So in our team we acknowledge this — we're all emotional people. We all feel a lot. And we use that knowledge: if we can buy in to our process with our shared emotions, we become formidable.

What I saw with Bunts was that he understood all this — that the essence of a team is its culture and its bond, and he threw himself into helping us develop those things. For me, it was what came naturally anyway. It was what I'd always wanted. A family full of good people making the right choices in life. We were a team again. In this new environment we grew to understand that while we're all very different people, we're all human beings and we all share the same goal: to be the best team in the world.

Ninety per cent of the women in our team are Māori or Pacific Island. Bunts himself is Māori. In fact, it was funny because when we arrived at the Olympics in Rio we were so colourful we altered the ratio of the New Zealand team overall — it had been tipped towards Pākehā but when the sevens teams arrived we made the ratio real pleasing to everyone.

The thing about Māori and Samoan and other Pacific cultures is: everything's for the family. It's why people go to gangs, right, so they can feel they belong. So if this team becomes our family — a family outside of our family — we will do just about anything for it. Bunts took that Māori identity and put it at the heart of the team, totally culturally accepting and welcoming to all. He used te reo when he coached us, but more than that he connected us to something that's a whole lot bigger than rugby — so we could represent not ourselves as individuals, but our culture and our ethnicity.

His idea of the team as a waka is a Māori metaphor and made sense to all of us — the waka is what we make together: mind, body, culture. It is quite a common theme in teams now, but back then not many people had done it; Bunts may have been one of the first in a professional team. He has since been approached by other professional coaches to help them follow the same theme. The tauihu is the prow that cuts through the water with puhoro —speed and dexterity — guiding us, leading us through unknown waters. We paddle together, our strength nothing without the others. And in our wake we leave mana. And that means our footprint on this earth, the thing that is left once we've passed.

Every single day we would talk about these things in our team meetings. All teams have important guiding ideas and metaphors they use, but the cool thing about us is that it was cultural, it was deeper, it was literally about who we were. It was the story of our team, but it was also everyone's personal story. And for me that was engulfing because if I'm going to dedicate my life to something it has to mean something. We mucked up in Rio, but where are we going to go next? Where's the waka headed?

I don't have a drop of Māori blood in me, but man I felt *New Zealand*, part of this powerful culture that we were creating together where people can be themselves and still belong. Tahi, rua, toru were our calls, our haka our full expression of us, of respect for our opponents, of love for all who love us. Ka pai when we did something good, and tino pai when we really smoked it.

When Bunts said Tino pai, you knew you'd done a really good job.

I'm here to make New Zealand great. I'm a Kiwi. I honour the Māori side of Aotearoa. I am a New Zealander and I'm proud, and Māori culture is part of my country's culture, therefore it's part of what I'm representing, so I respect and love that too.

People often comment on how they love to watch us because of our obvious closeness as a team, and the joy we have towards our game and each other. What you're seeing is real, but not simple. We've built that through having tough times, through not being afraid of honesty — whether giving or receiving. We're all different people, but what you're seeing is the team culture that we've built, and that's a real thing.

There's nowhere I would rather be. Straight up.

———

And so my career changed. In December that year, just a few weeks after Rio, we went to the Dubai Sevens and we won. We were back to our winning ways. But most importantly — win or lose, our culture was fun again.

Of course, we didn't win all the time. Not immediately. In 2017 we came third in Sydney, but then won in Las Vegas and again in Kitakyushu, Japan. For me, though, I was growing in confidence. I was happy with what the new coaching team was bringing, as well as my own growth as a player, and 2017 was the year when I really began to feel secure in my position in the team. I felt like I could focus on sorting out my routine, on understanding my strengths. *Let's sort out everything*. It had taken years to get to that point, but at last I knew without a doubt that I deserved to be there.

Then the fifteens coaches came knocking. They had been in contact with a few of us sevens players, saying they wanted to bring us in and if we just missed the last two tours of that season's World Series we would make the fifteens World Cup team. I was torn. Shit, I wanted to go. The Black Ferns has always been a goal — long before sevens was even a thing it was always fifteens. But it didn't really sit right with me. I mean I knew I could if I wanted to, I backed myself, but I just wanted to be present and really experience being a Black Fern. I wanted more fifteens prep, I wanted to maybe play a bit of club and do a National Provincial Competition (NPC) season again, do it properly. I had also just come into my own in the sevens team, I had a really good grip on how it all worked and I was playing awesome.

I went to Bunts for a chat, and without saying it directly to me I knew he wanted me to stay and help lead. So I never got back to the fifteens coaches, I decided to stay in sevens and use it as an opportunity to grow as a leader within the team. With Goss, Kelly, Portia and others all headed to the fifteens World Cup, half our leadership had gone. I and Tyla Nathan-Wong and Niall Williams were going to have to step up big-time.

That ended up being a huge year for me. There was so much chat in the media about how all of our stars had left our team, and it fuelled me even more to show the world that our team had so many unknown stars still to be revealed.

Everyone stepped up. It was hands down the break-out season for Michaela Blyde as well, who finally got her time to shine. In Canada in May, and then again in France in June, we won even without our most 'famous players', making us the winners of the World Series. Those wins shone a light on our culture and on the depth of our team. We were the undisputed champions again, and the superstars underneath the superstars had got their moment.

It hadn't been easy to overcome my earlier feelings, but I'm so glad I got over it. It was the right decision, and it gave me a lot of confidence. That year, I won New Zealand Women's Sevens Player of the Year and was nominated for World Rugby Player, along with the incredible Michaela Blyde who was top try and point scorer that season. Bunts did what probably no other coach would have done and let a group of us go to the World Rugby awards in Monaco, the weekend before the Dubai tournament, and we were so proud having two of us nominated from the New Zealand team. Mini won it, as she would the following year. I was so proud of her.

For me, being New Zealand Player of the Year in 2017 was a huge honour and a privilege but it honestly hadn't been a goal of mine. My goal was the same as it had always been: to be part of the best rugby sevens team in the world — on-field and off-field, in our play, and within our community and culture. I had also heard from reliable sources that the panel choosing the New Zealand Women's Sevens Player of the Year hadn't actually watched much sevens, and even though I was grateful to win it, to me Mini should've won it or at least been nominated. She had just won World Rugby Player of the Year but wasn't even nominated for the New Zealand awards. And that's what I said in my acceptance speech: I called them out for not nominating Mini. I must've hit a nerve, 'cos I was never nominated again for the New Zealand award, even after winning World Rugby Player of the Year two years later.

————

Great leadership may not be what you assume. It's not someone who knows everything, who knows all the answers, and stands above the rest. A great leader creates an environment where it's safe and easy for everyone to be their best selves, so that you can find the person who has the best answer for the team. To bloom. In that environment, we can see exactly what everyone's made of. So in our team, everyone's a good rugby player but, like, What is Ruby really good at when she's herself? What is Portia really good at when she's herself? What is Gossy really good at when she's herself? Leadership is about bringing out the natural strengths and differences in people.

Gossy is our captain and when she blooms there's no one who works harder. She never shies away from any physical challenge, she's the fittest, she's an absolute workhorse, she's doing the extras, she's going and finding different ways to do stuff, extremely self-sufficient. Her actions speak to me of true greatitude for her talent and opportunities.

But she hates conflict, and I love a good conflict — well, I don't exactly love conflict but I do welcome opportunities to talk through differences. I'm the culture leader, and definitely the leader in the team who drives all the off-field stuff. So Gossy will come to me if she sees any kind of problem or situation that's difficult between players, or if someone is going through something hard, and often I'll already have had someone come to me in tears, or be talking to the people involved. And at the same time, I will go to Gossy if I'm unsure whether we need to step in and often she will say, No Rubes, don't worry about it, that's all good. And gosh I appreciate that honesty from her.

To me, our leadership group is so effective because we're not even trying to be leaders, we're just being ourselves — the best version of ourselves — and so our powers combine. The best captain or the best leader does not have every single answer. They don't think they know everything or have to do everything themselves. They have the ability and the humility to ask for help, and to acknowledge and call on others' strengths in collaboration with their own.

We have a word that encapsulates our ideas about leadership: rangatiratanga, which is a traditional Māori philosophy and practice to do with people governing themselves, with the idea that leadership is as strong as the collective strengths of each individual in the team.

I love these ideas. I've always found my happiness within a team, with the relationships I've made there, with that sense of being on a collective journey. It's hard to know whether rugby has informed Ruby, or Ruby has informed rugby, but I think it's both: the culture I've found in rugby has been the perfect environment for me to develop and grow the parts of myself that come naturally, and to see how those things — the honesty, the hard conversations, the love — contribute to our success on-field, playing the game we all love.

Everyone talks about the pressure of the high-stakes games, but to me — and I know this is weird to say — that's the easy part. The easy part is going out and looking cool and playing a game we're trained to play. The hard part lies behind closed doors: the training where we tick every box there is to tick so that we're ready for whatever our opponents bring; the difficult, honest conversations; the culture-building so we're truly unbreakable as a team. That's the hard stuff.

RUBY'S TRAINING BAG
Our team is a waka, and we
leave mana in our wake.

2018

26. Mump
in the road

We were set for a huge year in 2018. We not only had the five tournaments in the 2018 World Series, but there were also two additions — the Commonwealth Games, opening early April on the Gold Coast in Queensland, and the Rugby World Cup Sevens in July in San Francisco.

We'd already lost to Australia in Dubai in December, and then for the next tournament, in January, we were in Sydney — and again, Australia totally spanked us: 31–0. A record win against us. They completely took us by surprise, changing up their defence from passive to incredibly aggressive, with a line speed they had never had before. It would have been easy to start blaming each other or to blame the ref, but the truth was we just weren't expecting it. But even for this, our worst defeat, I was still happy to be there, still felt a sense of true joy in this game, this team. I didn't mind because I've learned the hard way that losing in a good culture is way better than winning in a bad one.

———

That defeat turned out really good for us because we studied
it so hard that by the next time we played Aussie, at the
Commonwealth Games, we were ready. That defence change
was their best card and they'd already played it. If they'd kept
it a surprise till the Commonwealth Games, which I would have
thought was a more important tournament, they could have
beaten us there. No one remembers them beating us in Sydney,
but everyone remembers who won at the Commonwealth Games.

But when I say 'we' beat them at the Commonwealth Games,
I mean the team. Not me. I wasn't there. Because somehow, from
somebody somewhere, I'd picked up an unwanted extra.

It was such a landmark, us playing at the Commonwealth
Games. Men's sevens had been in the Games six times already,
but 2018 was the first time ever that women's sevens was
included. It was a huge moment.

After our loss in Sydney we'd been training the hardest we
ever had under Bunts. Our level of fitness was really good, and we
were feeling the difference in us, the buzz. The Commonwealth
Games was the next best thing to the Olympics. Three weeks
before going into the Games village we went to the Sunshine
Coast for our final training push.

We were all sleeping together marae-style in the lounge of
one of our apartments — I'd set up the mattresses like that just
because it was so fun, I loved being on tour with this team — but
then I woke up one morning, about ten days into the training
camp, and I felt a lump in my throat and a weird feeling in my
body. Maybe I feel sick? The Commonwealth Games was right
there in front of us. Shakira Baker was next to me, and I asked her
to feel the lump. Sis, what is this? Should I be worried? Nah, nah,
all good. That was what I wanted to hear. I decided I was all good
and kept going with everything.

But then I started to feel real crook. Maybe it's the flu? That
would mean I had to isolate. Shit. This really wasn't the time to
get sick. Within a couple of days my symptoms had worsened

and I had to take a day off training. The physio, Nic, did some research and she said, You've got the symptoms of mumps. Fever, weak, dizzy, swollen throat feeling like something was stuck in it. She said it was unlikely, but her face wasn't very convincing.

The Commonwealth team doctor came out to our hotel to assess me. She had her stethoscope and she put it in her ears and listened to my chest. She felt the lump, which was getting big by this stage, and she took the stethoscope out of her ears and put it around her neck. She sat back and looked at me. I'm pretty sure you have the mumps, she said.

What does that mean? We had a week before we were to go into the Games village; two weeks before the Games began. I was frantically doing mathematics in my head — how long does the mumps last, how long am I contagious for, the first game's on this date, when can I . . .? And the doctor's saying, Look, you have to isolate, it's really contagious, we'll monitor you, you're going to have to stay in this room and not talk to anyone.

So there I was in a room all by myself, every day getting worse, terrible headaches, and at the same time becoming more and more worried and mad. I need to train. I've got to play.

I was determined not to show how bad I was feeling, and it worked because the doctors and coaches were all like, You should be feeling way worse . . .

No one had actually said, You're not playing. No one wanted to break my heart.

I wasn't getting better. I got worse in that room, but I was still pretending I felt fine. I was still convinced I would be playing at the Games.

How are you today? Nic would ask.

Sweet as, Nic, just did some push-ups.

I was forcing myself to keep doing my analysis, to eat, to tick the boxes.

Then one day I wake up and it's just different. I feel like I'm in the Sahara Desert. My body is sore and the lump is huge and

I can't talk properly, and when I do talk I sound drunk. It hurts to talk but I'm still telling Nic, I'm fine! Let me train!

Should I ask for help? Headache almost unbearable, throat squashed, it hurts to move. Faar, I didn't know anything about the mumps, I thought it was just a little thing, but I am feeling really out of sorts. But I am still so convinced that if they need me to tackle someone, I can.

Then that night things get a whole lot worse. That night has no beginning and no end. My whole body is now racked with extreme pain, and fever has removed me from reality. It's hard to describe the pain, it feels all over but it's coming from the inside. It's not like a sore arm and you hold your arm, it's like the inside of my body is acid. Every position is uncomfortable. I feel faint, I begin to vomit uncontrollably and I try to move but now my vision has gone. When I open my eyes it feels like piercing needles.

What the frick, am I blind?

I try to crawl to the bathroom, feeling my way along the ground, but I keep losing consciousness, and when I come to I'm on the floor, I'm on the bottom of the shower with spew by my mouth, I'm leaning on the toilet, going in and out of consciousness. I honestly don't even know which way is up. I have a moment of strength and I pull myself up to the sink and I force myself to open my eyes. I look in the mirror. It stings and tears stream down my face. I'm not crying, it's the pain and the spewing making my eyes struggle. I can hardly see, or hold myself up, but I say in a muffled, coarse voice to no one but myself, Ruby you are getting through this. This is not going to get you. I fall back down and the coolness of the bathroom tiles is momentarily comforting, then I'm out again.

I am locked in this hotel room and no one can get in because I have the key, and Nic has already done her last check for the night and of course I told her I was fine, and now I am blind. I told her I would message if I needed anything but I can't see to find my phone, and even if I could there's no way I could look at the light of the screen to actually text her. The whole function of my body is closing down.

Nic? Nic? I try to call for help, but even trying to yell all I can muster is a coarse whisper and it is far too late. No one is coming until the morning. You're gonna be fine, don't be stupid, you're gonna get through this. I somehow make it back to the bed. The only way I can find respite from the pain is to sit there with my eyes closed. As still as I can. Don't move. If I even move or try to open my eyes, the pain comes blinding in.

For hours all I can think is please someone come to the door . . . please, somebody, come to the door.

Finally. At last. There's a knock. Ruby? It's Nic. Ruby, open up.

I can't move or call out. I'm trying so hard to yell back but only the whisper is coming out.

And at last, after she's run down and got a key from reception, she opens the door. Nic, I say, my voice scraping out of my throat, I can't see. Nic, I'm sorry. She sees the state of the room, the state of me, and she freaks out. I'm going, It's not your fault. I couldn't ring you . . . She's calling the ambulance, and I am trying to hold still because if I move it is just pain everywhere.

The ambulance guys arrive, and then Brad, our strength and conditioning coach, arrives and I tell him, B-Rad, bro, I can't see, I can't see, and he's like, It's all good, don't worry, and I can't open my eyes, I don't understand why the pain in my eyes is so piercing, but I can hear him and he helps me into the ambulance, and I'm like, Brad I'm so sorry, because it's my fault I let myself get to this state. He's sent in the ambulance with me because he's already had mumps so is seen as less at risk. Of course, even in as much pain as I'm in they ask if I can get on to a stretcher but there's no way. I tell them they don't need a stretcher, I still think I can play. But with the help of Brad I know I can get down to the ambulance. My head pounds the whole way, my eyes squeezed shut.

I am rushed into the hospital and I hear the doctors say, She needs an emergency lumbar puncture, and Brad's like, Bro, you're gonna get a bit of a needle in your back, but don't worry I'm right here. I am lying on an operating table and he's holding my hand (he tells me later that when the huge needle appeared it was more like I was holding *his* hand). I'm so grateful to have a familiar voice there with me. And then I feel something get jabbed into my back. It hurts but it doesn't matter because my whole body is in pain anyway. And I feel everything draining out of my spine.

I wake up in a hospital bed and then the doctor comes in and starts using big words like meningitis and encephalitis. Your body has a viral infection so has pushed too much body fluid into your brain and your spinal cord, your brain has swollen and as a result created extreme pressure in your spine and on your eyes, and that's why you couldn't see.

In my big effort to show everyone I could play, I had put myself in real danger. I didn't realise that if you don't tell the doctor how sick you are, you could be risking your life. But it wasn't even that I wasn't telling anyone how bad it was getting — I had literally fooled myself into thinking I was untouchable, until my whole body went into shock with the meningitis.

———

Lesson learned, you might say: You need to speak up when you're sore. But I haven't learned my lesson yet. As soon as I am conscious, I'm back to counting the days till game day, going What's the day? How many days until captain's run, until game day. I turn on the TV in front of my hospital bed and the Commonwealth Games are playing. Every day I'm watching, trying to get there.

Meanwhile, I don't realise how much drama I've caused. All the rest of the team are in quarantine, unable to go into the

Games village until they've got the all-clear (luckily no one else gets sick). And then I'm still drifting in and out of sleep, and suddenly my partner at the time is sitting by my bed and I cry because, thank frick, it has all been so scary and I was staying alone in the hospital at night.

Rob Waddell, Olympic legend and the Chef de Mission of the New Zealand Commonwealth Games team at the time, visits me and brings me all these things that the athletes from the wider team have signed and sent. Meanwhile, no one has actually told me I'm not going to be playing. In my mind, I've got six days. I'm still planning. Bunts messages to say he's coming to visit, and I tell him I'll meet him in the cafe.

Really? You can stay in the bed and rest.

Yeah, nah sweet-as, I'm all good.

I'm not supposed to, but I pull out all my drips in my arm and somehow get down to the cafe, nauseous-as, but holding it all in, sitting there as casual as I can manage, pretending that I didn't just about die.

Bunts doesn't tell me till later, but he has actually come to say, Your dream's over, you're not in the team. Maybe I kind of knew, but I wasn't going to let him say it.

He's sitting there with flowers and a balloon. I haven't eaten for days but I order a smoothie and pretend it's enjoyable to sip at.

How are you? he goes. He's surprised because he's been told I'm bedridden.

Yeah, bro, I'm all good, I say. Like, I don't know what they're telling you, and yeah it was scary and I probably should have told Nic earlier, but nah, sweet. How's training? What's the go?

His face. He's real confused. I've lost about 10 kg but the way I'm sitting he can't exactly tell. I haven't looked in a mirror for days and I don't look as good as I think I do, but me and him, we have a connection, so if I say I can play, he listens and does all he can to make it happen, and while I don't quite say I can play I'm not giving him anything, and then he's like, Oh OK, far out, I'll tell them that you're feeling alright, eh? And I'm like, Yeah, hard out!

He leaves all confused, without the heart to tell me I need to stay in hospital. I sit there with my half-drunk smoothie and wave and wait for him to be out of sight. Then as soon as he's gone I walk quickly into the cafe toilets and a few mouthfuls of the smoothie come up. I eventually make it back to my room and the nurses are all upset that I left the bed. They hook me back up to my IV, all the while telling me that this is where I need to be to get better. But I'm not listening and I tell them, You don't know me.

I've had a little energy kick talking to Bunts, so when the nurses have gone I say to my partner, Come on, let's break out of here. Do you have a car? She does, so I'm like Let's go.

I take out the IV drips again, get changed out of the hospital gown and sneak out of my room. In my head, I'm still playing in the Commonwealth Games. If I can just sneak back into the team, I'll have a shot. *It's all mental, it's all mental, it's all mental.*

I make it outside and I'm fighting the nausea, and in my head I'm walking like a hero, but really I'm hobbling, like almost crawling. My partner is on the phone to the Com Games head doctor and I'm saying, Tell him we're all good. And then, just as we reach the car, I go to lean on it, and I pass out, miss the car and wake up on the ground with the rest of my smoothie on the ground next to me.

Fuck, fuck, it's happening again. I can't control myself. The vomit is pouring out my mouth like a hose, spattering everything around me. And when it stops at last, I take stock. I'm on all fours bent over the bushes at the side of the car park. I stare at those bushes, at the bark around them, at the concrete of the car park where my head is now resting, at the vomit. And finally it hits me.

Ruby, you're not going to play in the Commonwealth Games. You actually can't even get into a car.

This is it.

The first thing that comes to mind is my team. I've gotta tell my team I'm not going to play with them.

Days ago I could have avoided this whole friggin' situation, if I'd just told Nic what I actually felt. Far out! But here I am at last, with my forehead on the concrete, admitting it to myself, and I am so sad. So gutted. I've tried so hard. But now I have to go back to the hospital.

I know what I have to do, and after some rest I ask to go to the team meeting before they get on the bus that will finally take them to their accommodation for the Com Games. I didn't realise it but because of me the team isn't going into the village now. When I hobble into the room with my team-mates waiting, I realise how little I've become. The idea of me tackling an international women's rugby player right now is laughable. And for them, it was maybe a couple of weeks since they'd seen me, and they were all like, Oh my gosh. And they realised it too: *She actually can't play.*

I'm so sorry but I can't come, I tell them. We are all crying. My people, my partner, even the doctors have all been sympathetic but I know they can't fully understand. This is one of those moments where no one else in the world can actually understand the gravity of your situation except your team-mates. That's why you become so close. That's why they become your family away from home. They know how much I have put into this campaign, into this team and this moment. They know how hard it is for me to say goodbye. It was actually so comforting and therapeutic to address them, knowing that they understood what I was saying. You hear me, I say to my girls. I love you all, go and do the business.

It's massive, and then I get to walk them out to the bus, and they do the haka to me, and I'm standing there with my fat mumps face trying not to cry, and then they drive off. This is it. This is the end.

———

I flew home after that, rather than staying on to watch. I just wanted to get better. Now I had accepted how sick I was, I knew I needed to go home and focus on being healthy again. I ended up watching the Commonwealth Games final — which was an unreal, historic game that we won in the last second — with the other girls who didn't make the team. That was another level of comfort, like, far out, none of these girls made it either, I felt really connected with them. I was still not back to my proper weight, so they all came round to my house and it was a really cool moment watching it together. Then the team won and when they arrived back with the Commonwealth Games medals we got to haka them at the airport. We'd won the first-ever women's sevens Commonwealth Games gold, so it turned into this beautiful experience.

But it comes back to that truth — that you never know till you're actually on the field that you're going to play. Anything can happen. I had found it so hard to accept. And then the Japan tournament of the World Series was the very next weekend after the Commonwealth Games, and when I got on the plane home from the Gold Coast I was actually thinking, If I go home now I can make Japan . . .

But then Huia Rudi Harding (Huz) got called up for Japan instead. They hadn't even considered me, and the doctors still wouldn't be quiet about how the meningitis can turn life-threatening, how I'd had a lucky escape. You need to put your weight back on, give your body time to recover . . .

Then they said, You'll be lucky if you make the World Cup.

The World Cup that year was in San Francisco all the way in July. This was April. No frickin' way. I wasn't having a bar of it. As soon as I could, my boots were back on and I was training. I reached out to everyone who could possibly help me — my doctor, my psychologist, my natural healer. My natural healer was an intuitive counsellor and she said I had been attacked by an evil energy, and honestly that was the best way I'd had the whole experience explained to me. She said I needed a few cleansing sessions. After I'd reached out to all my people and my resources, I felt fantastic — when you've been down so low, even a 20 per cent improvement feels so good. I'd been back for a couple of weeks when our team doc at the time came down to check on me. We were doing a standard sprint session, 100-metre sprints. And 17 to 18 seconds is a good pace for a single rep — even 18 to 20 seconds would have been good in my returning state. But I saw him there watching and I thought, Bro, you know what? Watch this — and almost every single rep I was hitting 14, with a couple of 15-second reps.

The physios and coaches were timing me and they were like, What the frick, because these were PBs for me. Back in the gym I was hitting big targets too, hip-thrusting over 200 kg. Put me on the friggin' plane, I was begging them. Let me go to Canada. The Canada tournament was 12–13 May — not quite two months from when I first got sick.

I don't know if scientifically or medically I was over the illness, but mentally I was. I was just so determined. I trialled again, and that was it, I was back in the team. They agreed to let me play Canada. The doctors and physios were like, Well, just take it easy . . . but there was no way. I was back in the starting line-up and I was destroying people, I was like, Bro, get out of my way!

We won the Canada tournament, setting a new record winning margin against Aussie, then we went to France and had the same domination there. And by the time we were heading for the World Cup, I was in full stride.

RUBY'S TRAINING BAG
I reach out to everyone who can possibly
help me when I'm feeling down.

27. Breathing space

Back near the beginning, in around 2013, my sports psychologist, David Galbraith, told me that when you're at the kick-off and the whistle's about to blow, you should be able to take one breath and be calm. What the heck, bro? I thought he was crazy for thinking that's possible. It wasn't that long after my debut in Fiji, and I'll never forget the nerves I felt in the changing room before that first game started, my sense of almost panic as I looked around, desperate for guidance, not knowing how to deal with that moment of such intense nerves and pressure. In those early years I had lots of moments like that. I knew I had the ability, but I was just frazzled in those moments.

The time that's worst for me, when my nerves are screaming and I just want to freak out, is that period just before we play a game, when we're back in the changing room after completing our warm up. The warm-up itself is fine. It's physical, I can lose myself in it. But now the music starts playing, which means there's only six minutes before we're playing, and all that's left is to change into my sevens jersey before we run out to play. Six minutes. My heart rate's going up. *Oh my gosh, oh my gosh. It's really happening.*

I've seen many athletes crumble under that pressure and I didn't want it to happen to me. I knew that to be successful in my sport, I had to learn to deal with pressure.

I'd tried so many things. Visualisation was huge for me in my first World Series season while on tour. In my room in the days leading up to the game, I used to put my boots on and hold a rugby ball while lying on my bed and mentally go through an entire game, including the whole build-up of the changing rooms. My body would physically flinch as I imagined myself tackling and sprinting. My heart rate would race, as I was trying to get used to being in that state. Other senior players would watch highlight reels of themselves doing great things the night before a game, or even in the changing room before playing. I tried that too, but I felt a bit weird watching myself over and over again like that.

But this concept of the breath really intrigued me. While I couldn't immediately compute what the psychologist had told me back then about the one breath, he had given me a clue. The word 'calm' — I needed to find a way to be calm in the madness of my mind. Some players struggle to get aroused enough for a game. They need to do visualisation to get pumped up or get aggressive. I'm the opposite. My energy is always high, I'm always pumped-up inside, so my work then becomes tuning into that high energy, while being calm. DG would call this mindset the ninja-monk — calm but deadly.

So I set out on a journey, learning to meditate so that at any moment I can find that calm place in myself; and, crucially, learning how to harness my breath. I was so lucky to have the help of my psychologist and breath coach for that. I have grown to love the breath. It's the function in my body that I can most easily take control of, and so the power that it has over mind, body and emotion is massive. Breath truly is my go-to, 100 per cent, and I believe we should all be taught how to breathe, like monks are taught from as young as five years old. It's the only autonomous function of the body that we have the power to control. Our heart pumps our blood without our control, our cells regenerate without our control, etc. but with our breath, even though we breathe without thinking, if we focus in on controlling it we can have a huge influence on how our bodies respond to different situations.

——

With practice, I have learned how to become calm, even in those intense six minutes just before a game starts.

I take my first long, slow breath, letting my body know I am choosing to be calm in this moment. I initiate my focus for that game, saying what I need, and my mantra is: I am calm . . . and nearly always that brings me down straight away. I pick up my jersey, I hold the front and I breathe it in — the power of the calmness, the moment, breathe in everything that I'm feeling. Then I breathe it out, long and slow and I let it all go — the stress, the worry, the negative. I am calm. And I'm moving towards a state where I'm so calm that I don't even remember saying the 'm', and it's like, I-am-cal . . . and then I'm gone. I'm calm. It is done.

This process is all about truth. It's not an effect that comes out of nowhere. I have to believe myself, I have to trust myself, because in those moments whère I could freak out, I have to know the truth of this. I have to have already made a pathway to this state; I need to know what this state feels like. I need to meditate and practise all that stuff outside of footy too so that when I come in here, when I'm preparing to run on to the field, I know exactly what it feels like and therefore that is my truth and it just is. I am calm.

My focuses for games will change, but the calmness never does. And another thing that will never change is my final thought before I play, which will probably shock some people, especially opposition that I am always aggressive towards — *I am of love*. That's a whole-hearted belief and it's bigger than rugby. I know it is the truth because I try and live it every day. That is my value; that is the essence of me as a person and, no matter what happens, I'm going to make decisions out of love. Love for the jersey, for the legacy, for my family, for myself getting through all I've been through and all I strive to be, for the people who are making this game happen, for my amazing life where I am constantly pinching myself, for the amazing people I've crossed paths with, for my body that gets me through the most incredible moments, for the most high one blessing us with this life, for every human everywhere, and for the little girl watching who I'm about to give the show of her life to.

On the field this means that I love my team. Therefore, if you're not on my team I have to tackle you as hard as I can, because I'm here to win for them. I don't stand up here in front of my team and say, I promise I'll try and win for you. None of that. I'm doing this because I love them and I love our purpose, I mean what I say, and I'm about to show you what that means. It also means that whatever happens on the field, I leave it there. When I cross that white line at the end, forgiveness and love is who I am striving to be, and so it gives me this sense that no matter what happens and no matter what I do, it's always of love and therefore I can't actually get it wrong.

One last breath of love, I breathe all of that in all the way and sometimes hold it a bit, then breathe out and release everything that will get in the way of this moment of unconditional love. And then I smile.

If I'm having a rough day, I might do my breaths again once I've put on the jersey, or when I'm walking out to the field, or even sometimes on the field, but usually I'm in a good place and I'm sweet.

The unexpected will always happen, but I can focus and control how I react.

This process is not about simply holding the pressure at bay or ignoring it. I'm not denying it's there — I acknowledge it, I take control of it. In those pressured situations the biochemical reaction of stress will always be there, and I understand what it feels like, but I can choose how to regulate that emotion: am I nervous or am I excited? This is so important — the words we choose are directly linked to our feelings and our behaviour. Our brains have always been designed to protect us, right from primitive times we are wired to seek out the negative threats; like if we are being hunted, if we are being segregated, we will seek out all the dangers around us. So if you do not consciously decide to focus on a more positive mindset, your mind will default to think negative. I've lived this. Before running out, if you aren't used to it then you will easily focus on the crowd, on the pressure, on making a mistake. So it's up to me what I choose to focus on. If I can change the language that I focus on in my head, I can change how I think; if I change how I think, I change how I feel; and if I change how I feel, I change what I do.

So: not nervous. Not stressed. But excited. Inspired. Energised. Honoured. That's my switch. I let go of my stress and I find my readiness. I find my excitement. *There's no one else I would ever put forward for this role, because I'm perfect for this, and the person I am, deeper than the rugby, is perfect for this as well. I do not have to go to war with guns, all I have to do is win this battle of a sport I love. How lucky am I to feel this pressure? What a privilege this pressure is.*

Oh man, this is awesome. I'm so excited to be here.

I understand what my psychologist said all those years ago. The whistle is about to go, I take my last breath and I'm there, I'm clear, I'm calm, I'm done. It is done. It's done before I even get to the game. I understand, and I will use that in life, not just in rugby. But I would never have been taught that if it wasn't for rugby.

I breathe. It's done. I run onto the field.

28. World Cup half-full

I had watched the 2013 Sevens World Cup from my sofa in Christchurch, still crippled from rupturing my ACL. All I could do was promise myself, The next one. I don't care what it takes, I'm going to be there. And now at last, here I was — with my team, despite the mumps, despite missing out on the Commonwealth Games.

The 2018 World Cup was held at AT&T Park in San Francisco, a huge baseball stadium transformed into a grand rugby field. Sevens has had massive growth in the USA in recent years, both men's and women's, with both of their sevens teams coming from nowhere into the top three. We knew they were going to be a massive challenge, and that even just playing USA in the USA is part of that challenge — they're a really proud nation, hearty, the most patriotic people, and when their team was playing it felt like everyone in that bloody stand was on their side.

In sevens you have to respect each game like it's a final. Even at the start of the pool games you can't take anything for granted. Whether you're playing China, Fiji, Aussie or whoever, you have to treat it like it's everything, because teams do step up when they play us.

It's the biggest compliment — they see the black jersey and they play out of their skins. It means we never have an easy game, and we know that if we let up for a single second, they will beat us. It makes them play better, and it makes us play better too. That's the spirit of the game.

We return that respect by playing them as hard as we can. And as a result we can beat a team 30–0 and it could have been one of the hardest games. People find it hard to understand and it is hard to explain — it's a feeling.

We played USA in the semi-final at the 2018 Sevens Rugby World Cup, definitely the hardest game because every time they did anything great the crowd would just roar. That game started to get close. They were putting it all out there but we dug our toes in. The feeling we had, it was like we've done so much prep, we've played the same game with the same-size field, the same-size ball so many times we can read it.

We saw how they defended our free kick, so when we get our opportunity Kelly looks at me and calls a move that we have done many times, which requires us to both get our timing off each other perfectly. Kelly creates a little hole for me but I have to hit it at the right speed and not give away my movement too early. I go through like a knife through butter because Kelly times her pop-pass with precision and there's just the sweeper to beat. I can calculate that with my speed and the speed she's going, she doesn't have me and I'm going to score. It's a weird thing, that flow, that absolute knowing. Usually when I make a break I'll call out Portia's name to see where she is, but I know I don't need to this time. I get the try, just at half-time. Despite the crowd, we beat them 26–21.

——

Australia played France in the other semi. We'd had this thing with Aussie all year — they beat us in Sydney, we beat them at

the Commonwealth Games, we smoked them up in Canada.
We expected them to beat France, and I was looking forward to
beating them again in the final. But at the very last minute one of
the French players got around the Australian captain, went all the
way and scored a try on full-time, winning for France. Pure shock
on all our faces. So it was France we would face in the final.

The French are an awesome side and they never give up, it
was definitely not an easy game as everyone had to work right
up to the final whistle. But that day, France just had no chance.
Again I don't know how to explain the feeling, but we were going
to win. It was already done. We had three tries and the score was
15–0 at half-time, and we were just warming up. And by the final
whistle it was 29–0.

I was on the sideline in the last minute of the game with
Portia and we were just looking at each other like, Man, we've
done something pretty awesome here. I was thinking back to Rio
2016 and our mess there, and I was looking at my team-mates
in awe, going What the heck are we doing? Who are we? We'd
completely stomped over everyone.

In that moment we were unbreakable as a team, and
unstoppable on the field.

Usually, whether you win or lose, it's like *I could have done
more*, but that tournament was pretty near perfect: 29–0 in
a World Cup final. That was a huge moment in my career.
Wow, I thought, this is us at our peak.

Most of the people in the starting line-up had been playing
together since that first Fiji debut back in 2012. *We've changed
so much*. When I re-watch the World Cup games, I see our
confidence, I see how many different angles we take. Back in
2012, we knew the rules but now we had so much experience and
depth. Honestly, I could just sit here and watch it all day.

———

You've got to have a tactical edge, and for me it's the brain stuff, the analysis — understanding the rules, understanding the refs, studying my opponents, knowing everything about the way they play. What do they do? Do they kick or not? It's like I know them.

Before the World Cup I watched all my opponents' games and I learned all their calls — I do this before every game we play. One of my favourite things to do — and it's a little bit psycho — is when they're all lined up to kick off and they yell 'one', I go: It's going right forward! And the look on the kicker's face is priceless. *She knows our call!*

Confidence lies in your preparation, so for me that's the ultimate preparation. And in that moment, whether their kick's awesome and they get it back, or not, I am a more confident player than they are. It's purely a head thing. We don't have time to set up in response, we still have to hold our space, but the pure joy I get from the kicker freaking out gives me that one-up. To me, we haven't even started the game and it's 1–0.

These days we're given so much to help us with this aspect of the game. After every single game, after I've done my ice bath, had my shower and eaten, I grab my iPad — we're each given one for this purpose — and I study the game we've just played.

The availability we have now is just crazy. I can use Instagram to contact a ref if I want to know more about why they made a particular call. I try and get into their head to see what they're seeing.

Of course, I try my best to be very respectful about this. I don't ask straight after a game because for me there's too much emotion straight after, and I also try not to come across as challenging — simply trying to understand their opinion. Spectators will always yell at the ref for getting things wrong, and I used to get mad sometimes myself. But aside from rules, you need to know what they're seeing, what they're looking for. It's so much more complex than right or wrong or the wording of the rule book — it's how your ref is interpreting it that's important.

For me, this comes back to greatitude. I remember when having access to these tools was just a dream, so my great action is that I'm going to make use of them, watch games, do analysis, know everything. Create my edge.

RUBY'S TRAINING BAG
I take control of the pressure. I let go of
my stress and I find my excitement.

29. Straight down

nd then 2019 struck. During 2018 I thought I had it all; my rugby was amazing, I'd just cracked how it all works. At first it seemed awesome — we won our first tournament of the year. But after that it was like dominoes tumbling unchecked. First, Allan Bunting had a major health crisis and had to take time out from the team. I was so close to Bunts and my rugby world fell apart, I felt like I was grieving inside but I knew he would want me to take care of the girls. Second, one of our team took it even harder than I did and she had to leave for a while too. I was so scared I was going to lose them both forever. But third, I was left by my partner of seven years. I wasn't expecting it at all, and my heart was broken. All the joy vanished from my life and it was like the whole world — all the things we'd planned for and worked towards — ended without warning when she told me she loved me but she wasn't in love with me any more. Please remember that there are always two sides to every story, but at the time I was shaken and completely lost.

Heartbreak. Since shortly after the 2016 Olympics I'd been working with NZR on their HeadFirst programme, helping raise understanding of mental health among rugby players. At some point after I started doing that work I kind of joked to myself, like I think I'm alright at this whole mental fitness thing. But imagine if I had a real hard mental health challenge? What would I find? Is what I preach actually legit?

I was about to find out.

It wasn't a nasty break-up. No one cheated or said bad words, but it was just a terrible shock. She explained that she wasn't happy living the way we were any more. I was away a lot; she wanted to do her own thing. She was being honest, and I applaud her for that. I asked if we could get relationship counselling but she was done. She moved into a property we owned in a different city, and I stayed on renting in Tauranga where we had begun building a new home.

If you really loved someone, you wouldn't just leave, would you? This kept going back and forth in my head. And voices that came straight from the shallow grave of my childhood also started up. Unlovable. Unworthy. Wrong. All my fault. No one will ever really be there for me.

I had to put into practice all the things I had been preaching. I was in such a vulnerable moment with the accumulation of losing all these loved ones at once. Part of me could have gone into self-destruct, but I now knew there was another way. I was in the middle of a really important stage of my life, and I'd seen what happens when you waste it. I needed to get through this.

First I reached out to a couple of my closest friends, drove out to their place, told them and cried and cried. Leaning on all the safe spaces I had created. Then a little while later I got together a group of players I felt close and safe with within the team, and I told them and I couldn't stop crying. *Bear with me because this is going to be hard to say* . . . Half of them started crying too, and to be honest it was actually nice to finally share with them what I had been going through and I was so grateful I had this circle in place. I knew I could do that in the team —

whenever I am struggling with something, I get team-mates together that I trust and know I can lean on and I ask for help and I share. It's important to show if you are struggling as a leader in a team environment so that other players know it's OK for them to do the same.

And I experienced the truth of setting things up in the good times so that they're ready for you in the tough times. Do the work when you're going well, because there will come a time when it's not going well.

I wrote a lot in my journal. I am loveable. I am loveable. There was one day when I wrote that over and over again, my tears hitting the page. I didn't believe it; I needed to believe it.

It was a strange time and my super-power of being able to sleep forever left me — I was getting three to four hours in at night and still training all day. Other times I paid too much attention to silly things, like random people messaging me, giving me compliments. So I just tried to be self-aware, and stay focused on myself.

Every single morning, before I headed out for training, I watched Louie Schwartzberg's video about gratitude, from Everyone Matters: *Today is a gift, it's the only gift that you have right now, and the only appropriate response is gratefulness . . . Open your heart . . .* Even on the hardest days, that set me up so lovely.

On the outside I probably looked fine — I was doing my job as well as ever, I turned up, I smiled when I was supposed to, I carried on. I could actually still perform my rugby skills really well, like rugby was the easy bit. But inside myself I was numb. If we played and we won, or if we played and we lost, I didn't really care. I'd never asked for any mental health leave before, but I asked to be excused from our March tour to go get some family time in because I was struggling. However, the stand-in coaching team said I had to stay because the team needed me.

I learned the deep truth of something I'd always said — the off-field affects you. Your whole being. Of course I talked to my psychologist David Galbraith, DG, who's known me from the beginning of this journey, and he was real upset for me. But he gave me a list of things to do to help me through and he never judged anything I said. Shit it's so good to have people you feel safe enough to share with. Each time that I explained how I felt to those I trusted, it became easier to do. My friends consoled me; but DG really helped me out too. Both kinds of help are important.

I still had months of sadness to go, but that was a huge step along the way. I felt like me and my ex-partner both held ourselves well with the way it ended, and that's a reflection of us as people. But no matter how well a break-up goes, they ain't ever easy. To everyone who's gone through one or is going through one, you are a hero to me.

———

That year, I really felt like I went to the University of Ruby. I realised that to truly love those around me fully, wholeheartedly, safely and in a healthy way, the key is to actually love me, too. Then I can unconditionally offer love without subconsciously searching for validation or permission, or only offering love that comes with conditions.

Love is such an important word to define for yourself. Love, the feeling, is not always enough. I learned this from Dad — I learned that just because someone loves you, it doesn't mean they know *how* to love you or that they can love you the way you want to be loved. I feel like it's so important to have an awareness of how you love and how you like to be loved — to ask, How could I have done this bit of loving better? You have to know it's hard sometimes.

You have to put in the work, communicate and make sure that it's working for both of you, and it takes both of you to give and to take, to be honest and to have respect. And if you're struggling, let's sit down and talk about it. Love is worth fighting for.

———

Sometimes we don't want to bother dealing with tough things. We sweep the issues under the carpet. We avoid the honest, straight-up conversation. We think, I'll do it later. But these things can fester and grow. There will come a time when we are tested; and at that time, if we haven't dealt with all those things, they will come out. In this aspect of life, there is no difference between the off-field and the on-field.

For me it's those games, those really high-intensity, high-pressure games where we're going into overtime and the next team to score wins the game, and if I've done my work on being a really good person, on preparing as best I can outside of my rugby, in those huge moments in the game it almost feels like nothing is too big. I know I'm a good person, I know I've prepped, I know I'm supposed to be here and I know I can do this. But I feel like if I've got any insecurities about what it takes to be a rugby player, that's when it comes out, that's when I drop the ball.

It's the same with ordinary life. So when my partner and the coach who believed in me the most left me it was hard, but I knew what to do, and I fought my insecurity with all the tools at my disposal.

People are always talking about being grateful, and it seems so easy when you're living life and you're happy as. *Today I'm fine and it's a great day, so woo!* But that's when you should be working on stuff too, practising your values, getting clear about your identity, because if you don't, then when the shit hits the fan, when you're struggling in life, it's so much harder. I do that work when life is good and I'm happy. It's cumulative. It's my groundwork.

———

In among the sadness, I learned that I was a finalist again for the World Rugby Sevens Player of the Year. And not just me. Our Black Ferns sevens players took up all three spots in the nomination list: me, our captain Sarah Hirini (Gossy) and our vice-captain Tyla Nathan-Wong. It was pretty cool for all three spots to be from Aotearoa, so it meant heaps. It was such a cool moment because we'd all debuted together in Fiji, we had all re-committed after Rio, we had all been through so much. I love them dearly.

We flew to Japan together with tickets to the men's World Cup final — that year between England and South Africa — and we were put up in a five-star hotel right next to the Tokyo Tower. Our fellow Black Fern mate, who had also played with us in Fiji in 2012, Kendra Cocksedge was nominated for the fifteens Rugby Player of the Year so we were all hanging out together along with every other rugby star in world.

The next night was the World Rugby awards dinner. Ty was in a dress, Gossy in a Māori korowai and I was in a white trouser suit, so we all looked real cool. At our table was Melodie Robinson, someone I've always looked up to as a role model in media — a former Black Fern, she's had so many firsts as a female commentator and sports journalist. Being the generation I am, I missed all the crap around being a female in the media, but Mel is open about the harassment and bullying she used to get. I feel like she went through all this muck so I could have a sweet-as run.

So I'm enjoying talking to her when suddenly the presentations begin, and the sevens are one of the first, and I'm getting ready to clap for my captain or vice-captain, both deserve it and I associate those two with representing our team with all those bloody awards. Then the guy goes — Ruby Tui! And all I can think is, Are you sure? Everyone's saying, Ruby, it's you. Are you sure? Are you sure you don't want to give it to Gossy, or

Ty? They're my main girls on the field and I think they should probably have it. But yeah nah, they bloody said my name.

When I accept the award — World Rugby Sevens Player of the Year, just like Mere Baker promised me a decade before — I tell the crowd that this is not even a competition. We are all from the greatest team in the world and any of us could stand up here and get this, especially my captains. There are no individual awards in a team sport. This I mean from the bottom of my heart.

But the coolest part of the night happens later on, after the awards are over. The others want to go out and celebrate, but I'm still not completely back on track. This is November, and the year has been so long and hard. I'm just going to go to bed, I tell them. A little later comes a knock at my door, and Gossy, Ty and Kendra come in.

Come on, Ruby.

Nah, it's all good.

But then Gossy sits on the end of my bed and she gives me the best captain's talk I've ever had from her. Ruby, you've just been through one of the hardest times of your life. Now look at you. You're the best. You're World Rugby Sevens Player of the Year and you're telling me you're not going to celebrate this moment?

I mutter something.

She goes on, So get up and get changed.

The other two are on the same waka: Yeah, bloody come Rubes.

And it's a moment for me. I've been so down in the dumps, but look at where I'm standing right now. I am literally on top of the world, not the bottom like I was thinking. Bro, I say, massive speech sis. You got me up. And she, Kendra and Ty are all cheering. So I go out after all and we have a really good night — hang with some of the All Blacks boys, doing karaoke. And next morning we have teppanyaki with a couple of other rugby girls and laugh over our night. I'm so grateful Goss and the girls gave me that.

———

So 2019 was a hard year, but an important year. The team was rocked when Bunts left, but the other coaches stepped up and while we lost to Canada in April and to the USA in June, we won enough tournament points overall to still win the World Series. When Bunts came back, he and Cory were appointed co-coaches — the perfect balance, the perfect duo — and that arrangement stood all the way through to the Tokyo Olympics.

Near the end of that year, in December, we were in South Africa playing the first-ever Women's World Series tournament in that country, which we ended up winning, when I got an email to say that my new house, the one being built in Tauranga, was ready. My house.

As soon as we were back from tour I drove to see it. This frickin' brand-new house. I walked in and there was no furniture, just the sense of newness, waiting for me to fill it. I lay down in the middle of the carpet and I absorbed it. Tears came to my eyes, and I was happy. Look what I can do. This is me; I did this. I'm still worthy, I'm still loveable because the most important person I need to know I love right now is me.

RUBY'S TRAINING BAG
Set things up in the good times so that those
tools are ready for you in the tough times.

30. Les' be honest

When you love a person and they love you, it's beautiful.
Nothing else matters.

I had boyfriends all through high school and then
when I moved to Christchurch, somewhere in those turbulent
first years I met a girl and I thought, Yeah I like this. To start with
I was embarrassed and I struggled to talk about it. Once I started
to love myself more it became easier to accept, and I'm lucky that
the people I love accept me too.

One day my Aunty Tala, the one who was always there for
me, came down to Christchurch for a family funeral and I was
busy helping with that, attending all the services and singing
songs. I didn't bring my girlfriend at the time at all, because we
were quite new anyway — it would have been the same with a
new boyfriend — and I didn't know how to bring it up or tell my
aunty. Then on her last day as she was leaving I gave her a hug
and a kiss goodbye, Love you, Aunty . . . and she squeezed me in
and said in my ear, Next time you bring your girlfriend to come
and meet me ay? How the heck she even knew, I have no idea.

It just wasn't an issue. And for myself, I realised it doesn't
even matter. If you are sharing love with someone, the only thing

that matters is how you are treated in that love. Whoever that 'somebody' is, it's no one's business if you don't want it to be. I found liberation in accepting that myself.

I don't ever want to be put in a box. People say, You've got a girlfriend? You're a lesbian. Then they say, Oh, you've had boyfriends? You're bisexual. I don't know why people are so caught up with drawing a line in the sand. When I told my mum, I didn't 'come out' — I just said, I've got a girlfriend. And once she knew she was still going to get a grandkid, that was it. She's loved my girlfriends just as she put up with my boyfriends.

I just love who I love. I have no problem screaming from the rooftops that I love a girl. But I'm not interested in being put in a box just to ease someone's comprehension. I think the focus should be, Who are you? What makes you beautiful? How are you going to spread love in this world?

My mentality is, if you have a wonderful, beautiful relationship with a guy, beautiful! If you have a wonderful, beautiful relationship with a girl, beautiful! For me, it's not based on gender — it's based on the person. A word I use if people need it to understand better is 'pansexual' — for me, it takes away all the boxes to do with gender and sexuality, and just puts the focus on the love. As long as I'm not hurting anyone.

In many cultures there is a binary gender focus on men and women and nothing else, but in some indigenous cultures, including Samoa's, they have others, like the fa'afafine. I know there's a big focus most places on gender and sexual identity, and at some stages of your life it might seem like the most overwhelming part of your life — but that's where I encourage people to look into themselves, where they are from, what they are about, who they are, what's meaningful to them, because then you become strong enough to understand that it's not the biggest thing. There are so many horrible things in this world, and I am just not convinced that spreading love with the same gender is one of them.

I'm half Samoan, and obviously the church played a big part in my upbringing. I definitely believe that there is a higher spiritual energy around us, whatever people feel comfortable calling it — the universe, God, Allah — the power that makes the sun go up and the karma go round and round. I like to call it the Highest Power. I would probably need to write another whole book to explain my beliefs, but I absolutely engage in giving thanks, saying grace and praying for those who have passed on. But I love and respect all my people who have very specific religions, and there are a lot of them. I think sometimes people of the church get a hard time, but I know that the church has helped and saved so many hurt people. I love church too. Whatever you believe, however you want to spread healthy love, that's beautiful. One day I asked one of my very religious friends that I consider family, straight up: Sis, be honest, what do you think about me having a girlfriend?, and without any hesitation she just looked at me and said, Sis, only God can judge you, no one else. I completely agree with that: God's people's words aren't always the same as God's words, they're still trying to get through things themselves and just do the best with what they've been taught. Only the Highest Power can judge, and I have always lived with love and peace for others, and I have been blessed beyond belief in my short life.

I just cannot agree that how someone spreads love is something we need to focus all this hate energy into, and I would feel like that even if I had a boyfriend. It's just a waste of everyone's energy. Let God be the judge. If you are a good person and you are spreading love, that's all that matters.

Since 2019 I have been sharing my life with a beautiful woman, Dani. I work hard every day to love her as best I can and we communicate openly and honestly so that we can grow each day alongside each other in a healthy way. I am proud to say I am in a happy relationship that does not include physical, verbal or emotional abuse. If either of us have an issue with anything, big or small, we make time to communicate in a safe way without judgement and work through it together. This will sound like a given for most people, but for me it's such an important thing. Having a healthy relationship is one of the things I am proud of most in my life. I am so grateful for Dani's beautiful, kind soul and I love her so much.

31. Final-ly

Meanwhile, our team was on another dominating rampage. We won Dubai and Capetown in 2019, Hamilton 2020, Sydney 2020. We were well on track to peak at the Olympics in Tokyo in July 2020. But then Covid hit and the rug was pulled from under our feet, as it was for the whole world. It will always be one of those moments in history — everyone will remember where they were when their first lockdown started.

The 2020 Olympics were postponed. A lot of my team were hit hard, mentally, with the postponement. Not me, though. It felt like nothing compared with what I'd just been through, having people I love walk out, and I just thought that, given everything, this was inevitable. I was starting to understand why I went through 2019 — I could stand strong in 2020. To be honest, I didn't think the Olympics would even go ahead in 2021.

When we went into lockdown I trained hard throughout. Afterwards, with international competition still so elusive, a few of us were released to play New Zealand club rugby and so I went back to my beloved fifteens for a season. I got to go back to grass-roots footy where I started and help the Auckland Ponsonby

Fillies — coached by one of my idols, Linda Itunu — win their
first women's club comp in 27 years. I went on to play for
Counties Manukau for FPC (the Farah Palmer Cup) and we came
equal top two of the ladder for the North Island competition.
Being a part of both of these teams absolutely filled my cup
and I don't think the players knew how much they were giving
my soul.

Then in December 2020, with the Olympics looking like
a real possibility for 2021, we all came back to sevens.

———

Since Rio, every day I feel the fire burn in me. But when
training started back up in 2021, the fire was just raging, the Rio
redemption fire. I remember thinking after the 2016 Olympics,
Was there more I could have done? What else could I have done?
There was no way I was going to be thinking that after Tokyo.
I couldn't let myself get too comfortable, thinking I was doing
enough, becoming complacent.

So I messaged Bunts: I need more.

Sweet, he messaged back. See you in the morning.

Just like he had done in 2013 meeting me and Honey on the
Mount Maunganui beach before the sun was up, he had my back.
It means a lot when a coach buys in to your crazy intentions
to get better. I hate early mornings, so morning trainings were
the perfect uncomfortable — just what I needed. And this time,
because we're professional, it didn't have to be 5.30 any more. We
met at 7 and used the hour before our team meeting began.

I'd had some shoulder issues niggling away for months, to
the extent that I had to sit out of contact work during training
for the whole six months leading up to Tokyo. So those sessions
with Bunts, just simple catch and pass, repetitive stuff, helped
me learn to pass without being scared of the pain. I even taught
myself to change the way I passed left to right so that my arm

wouldn't swing through the pain, but around it. I was the first player to get to work every day, with only Bunts being there when I arrived some days, and often the very last to leave. With all this resource around me that I never had in the last campaign, my great action, my greatitude, was going to be to use every part of it.

It was perfect. We met every training day up until we left for our journey to the Olympics.

But while training was going well, the build-up to the Olympics at the beginning of 2021 was hard and horrible for our team. In the few months leading up to the Olympics we had four close deaths in a row within the team, including our captain losing her mum. Bunts could've freaked out and forced everyone to train more, but he stayed true to his values and he let everyone go — go and be with family. It meant we had a lot of people away, and our captain and her closest two friends — that's half of our leadership group — had to leave for a few months. Bunts didn't stress about it and neither did we; it was the right thing to do. And it made me realise even more why I went through 2019. That was one of the biggest things Covid forced us to do — look at our lives and at what was truly important to us, and one of those was family. As athletes we say we are doing it for our family, but the reality is that our families have to adjust and make sacrifices for us. In choosing to be athletes, we often have to be selfish with our time and commitments.

As a team we were doing everything we could to attend every tangi (funeral) we could, even with all the travel required and the Covid protocols we had to follow. Then another leader in our team, Niall Williams (Niz), went down with a devastating injury and was ruled out of the Tokyo Olympics. I was having flashbacks to Rio . . . of all the girls that should've made it but didn't. Sport can be so cruel. I missed Niz and her fiery spirit so much in Tokyo.

Through all this heartbreak we were allowed to feel, and Bunts made us a safe space to share and be real about everything.

Leading up to Tokyo it was truly family first and rugby second, and this paid dividends when we had to come together in the big moments.

———

For ages, every international tournament we tried to get to we were told no, but finally in June we made it to Townsville, Australia, to play in the Oceania — a Covid-era tournament with only ourselves, Aussie and Fiji. It was a shock, getting reminded of the fierce physicality of international sevens. It was in that game against Fiji where I got a knee to my forehead and ended up with blood pouring down my face. Seven stitches later, I've got a scar I'll have for the rest of my life. I love my scar. I don't care that it goes down the front of my forehead. It's a manifestation of all the scars inside me, of all my challenges and effort, gratitude and healing. I wear it with pride.

The world was reeling from Covid. We got stuck in Townsville with a lockdown, and then when we finally made it out, on our way to Tokyo half the team got stuck in Brisbane for another lockdown. Finally we arrived in the Olympic Village where the virus had already taken out a couple of athletes, so the feeling couldn't have been more different than Rio. High alert. Masks, plastic partitions, no mixing between the teams from different countries.

But we're here.

———

Tokyo Olympics, 2021. The stands are empty. The big question the journalists are asking is, What's it like to have no crowds? Bro, that's how we started. We're used to it. In my first-ever game in the black jersey, in Fiji, there were just a few hundred Fijians, all yelling for Fiji. In my World Series debut in China the stadium was vast but there was no one in it. In those days you could drop a ball and no one in the public would ever know — no audience, no TV coverage, no social media attention. It wasn't until we played at Twickenham Stadium in 2015 — where we played right after a men's game — that we had a different experience. The crowd was deafening. I remember one of the girls screaming in my face and I couldn't hear anything.

Over the years of my career, the game has grown and grown — until in Sydney in 2018, the year we got smoked, it was packed out for all our games. We were warming up and this half-cut idiot was yelling, Who won gold at the Olympics? Who got yellow carded, Portia? — yelling it right at Portia. It was so hard to stay focused and not retaliate; my weakness is definitely when someone comes at somebody I love. They knew our names, they knew our worst moments and they weren't quiet about letting us know.

Then in 2019 and 2020 there were two sevens events in Hamilton — the first, the Fast Four, was an exhibition match; the second was New Zealand's first-ever sanctioned men's and women's sevens tournament as part of the World Series. Both those events were next-level for me. To play in front of a sold-out home crowd, to do a haka to a crowd who understands what a haka is. Tens of thousands of Kiwis screaming the place down. For me it was the connection of everything — the black jersey, the haka, our culture, our journey.

After the Fast Four, which we won, we walked around meeting fans and of course they're all dressed up because that's part of the sevens culture too. One group had dressed up as us, with black clothes and cut-out faces — and one of them had chosen to be me. What the heck! I gave her my medal from that day, because seeing her was like a different kind of achievement. The following year we beat Canada in the final and won the first New Zealand trophy of the World Series, and we saw the same group of fans — to me, they were tangible proof that we'd grown the women's game right here in Aotearoa. What a buzz.

So we've played in empty *and* packed stadiums. Getting to

Tokyo and seeing those ghostly, empty stands wasn't a big thing. *Oh, this again.*

———

I remember back to Rio, and I think someone actually said it out loud in the changing room: *We're going to get a medal, no matter what happens.* There was this young, innocent, naive happiness about that. But this time, there's none of that for me. Nah, we're not here for silver. The gold fell through our hands in Rio; it's not happening again. We've changed our coach, our management, the way we run this team. Our hearts and our souls have been poured in. We're here to give our best, together.

Our first pool game is Kenya again, and it's sweet and we win 29–7. Everything is going to plan.

We rest, warm up, everything's fine. Next is Great Britain and they come out fiery. I drop the ball, right in front of the posts, a play I've done a thousand times. It's a knock-on, they get a scrum and we know that's where they love to attack. Shucks, and they score. All good, we can get away with one; I had to flush it. I catch the ball and give Portia a long left–right pass, down her front like she usually likes because she's really fast, and she drops it too. Shit, I think, what have I started here? Me and Portia look at each other and we're scared of what Gossy's going to say because we're her right-hand people and this is basics. Great Britain score again. OK, 14–0 is fine. We've been here many times before . . . but they score again. That's three tries in four minutes, and then at last Michaela gets the ball and gets one try then another, so we go into half-time 21–12. Even though Porsh and I have been avoiding it, I catch Gossy's eye and, like I thought, it's not good. She gives me a pukana look. And all the years of building that trust and communication mean that we can have our whole conversation in one second: Bro! Not good enough. Sis, I agree with you. That was rubbish. We were terrible. I'll fix it real quick.

She rightly lets the team know how that this first half wasn't good enough, but we already know. But now it's time for the second half, and this is the time to roll our sleeves up. Years of training have taught us that this beautiful game is not over till it's over. We're always up for a challenge, so let's bloody go.

We get into our groove and Tyla shoots through a gap and gets a try and with a minute to go we're just two points behind. Great Britain gets a player yellow-carded and in the nick of time Michaela gets her hat-trick, and we win on the hooter: 26–21. As I told Sky Sport, there wasn't enough hand-sanitiser in the whole of Japan to clean up that performance of ours.

To me, that experience of being so far down happened for a reason. The other team can be winning at half-time, I don't even care. Whatever happens, we will win. That was the feeling that swept over me, and it was almost terrifying, to be honest. I gulped because, despite my confidence, I knew nothing was going to be easy. *This is going to happen again.* Frick, Great Britain aren't even in the top three teams and we let that almost happen. Nothing's standard. The teams that no one expected to turn up have turned up, and I was so grateful to Great Britain for showing us that.

Next day, Russia is our last pool game and we win 33–0. By a strange scheduling quirk, we play them again that same day in the quarter-final and beat them again, 36–0. Two games to go — a semi, and hopefully a final. But still I know deep down that our finals day — if we get it — isn't going to be easy.

RUBY'S TRAINING BAG
Complacency will eat your dreams
from the inside out.

32. Gold you so

There's nothing better than being in a multiple-day sevens tournament and saying, Just one more day.

We're up against Fiji in the semi-final. Fiji making it to the semi was a shock. No Canada, no Australia, no USA. None of the other medallists from Rio. Fiji was so far undefeated. We watched them dismantle Canada — the world's number-two team — in their quarter-final, and we knew that our semi-final game against them was going to be huge. Anything could happen. They were the sleeping giant of sevens rugby.

I'd always thought if Fiji got half the resources we do they would take over the whole world. Well this time they'd got stuck in Australia over Covid, and while it must have been hard, missing family while Fiji was battling Covid, there was a silver lining for them — they had never in their lives trained and eaten so well for so long, worked combinations out as much as they had for the last four months, and I saw that had made them dangerous. A force to be reckoned with.

Also, they had pressure. Sevens is their national game and earlier that same week their men's team had won gold in their comp. Their whole country would be watching us, hoping for a repeat.

I knew we could win — but if we made mistakes they would get us.

And right from the beginning they play crazy, crazy, crazy — they're a whirlwind and straight away they are right on top of us. We score first, but then they come right back and get a conversion and they're leading 7–5. Our game-plan is to secure rucks early on, but there are signs we're a bit rattled and we're not imposing our pattern. Things aren't happening the way we thought. It's going to be a long day at the office, but I'm confident that at seven minutes we'll have settled down and will have the upper hand. I assume we're fitter than them and if we follow our game-plan and set rucks, making them work back, they'll be out. And sure enough, with 30 seconds to go before half-time, after our third ruck, that's what seems to be happening. Now's our time.

Tyla offloads to me at halfway, and now I'm running for the line, with three Fijians in pursuit. A couple of them fall back, but their No. 11, Alowesi Nakoci, is still on my tail. I'm not worried. I don't know how many times I've played Fiji, and they don't usually chase you to the end. Always, always they run out of gas. So now I'm like, Sweet, I'll just put this ball down over the line and . . . But suddenly in a split-second it flashes in my head that, shit, she chased me all the way, in fact she's still here, and in that same split-second — *What is this?* — she tackles me and punches her hand into the ball so that it dislodges from my grip as I dive over the line.

Such a cool, try-saving moment for Fiji. As upset as I am, because I know how crucial a try before half-time is for momentum, I can't help but feel how awesome, how determined that was — the kind of moment we play sevens for. *Don't ever disrespect Fiji like that again*, I think to myself.

I pick myself up. Alowesi is still bent over, gasping — she's just given everything — and I go over to her and tap her on the back and say, Bro, that was frickin' awesome, don't stop. Because it was. But now I have to rejoin my team huddle and reality sets in. It's half-time, and usually we score just before half-time and then, *boom*, we're in control. But oh my gosh, I single-handedly gave that control to Fiji. It was a crucial mistake in the game. It could have been 12–7, but it's 5–7. I just took a comfortable but hard win and turned it into a neck-and-neck.

I'm walking across the field, back to the team. All the voices want to come into my head — you're terrible, you let the team down, you don't deserve the accolades that say you're one of the best in the world, how dare you believe any of the praise. They are pushing at me, but I know I can't let them. If I let them in, I'm gone. I'm borderline. I need to drop this so quick. *Fuck!* And I yell that swear word strongly and sharply, and then that's it. That's me. I had to release the energy. No more. I reach my team and they all know exactly what I'm feeling. They know I dipped into that zone. Alena Saili comes and brings me the water bottle and puts her hand on my arm, and I'm not going to pretend I don't feel shit because I really do, everyone can see it, they know, they understand me, they know me as a person, I'm not a dick, I'm not a psycho, but I just need that little second, that hand on the arm, that water bottle.

This is where all those relationships you make off the field are really important. This moment, right here. I need love and I need alofa, because I know I fucked up. Often in teams with bad cultures, no one comes and gives you a drink, no one looks at you; someone might even be like, *Good one*, sarcastic. If a person's already internally fighting their own thoughts, that is so hard, especially in such a high-pressure moment. So it's moments like this, in this huddle, with this team, that I am really grateful for. All our years of honest conversations with each and every one of these girls has built the trust that gets us through moments like this.

And even in the most terrible situation, which to me this is, we can still process the situation we are in. We can tell that Fiji are really out of their comfort zone now. Their coach is in the middle of their group doing all the talking. I see lots of physical cues that show me they have played really well but are emotionally just hanging in there. Whereas we have played terribly, are behind — and yet mentally, we are there. We know what to do.

Our coaches, I can tell they really want to step into our huddle and talk. They can see as clear as day what we need to do, but they don't step in because so can we. They've built this self-leadership culture and it's the way we roll, and it's so good that they don't step in because it shows they trust us. We know how to do our own talking.

We turn to the job ahead of us.

The second half. We need to score. Portia gets a try and it's converted and now we're leading 12–7. But not for long, as Fiji scores and now it's even, 12–12. Bloody good on them. As I run back after that try, I meet Gossy's eyes and say, Now we work, sis. And she replies with the same. Now we work, sis. It means are you with me? Heck yes, always. We've had that moment many times in games, and you have to have all the assurance and conviction in your reply. *Now we work*. Let's see what we're all made of. OK, Fiji, you want to be in the top four, you want to be in with the big guns, now let's see what really happens in the last three minutes of the second half of the semi-final at the Olympics.

We're all exhausted, but we just have to score once and we will win. Everyone's on edge.

We take our time to set up a final hit, a final killer blow. For it to be the final play, we have to score with less than 30 seconds to go. We're at 41 seconds remaining. Kelly passes to Stacey and she's heading for the line and now there's 36 seconds to go. Usually we just stand under the post and wait for the time and then *boom* and we win the game . . . but not this time, not with this Olympic Fiji super-team. Fiji is chasing; no one ever chases us this much. Thirty-five seconds, 34, 33 . . . And with their

No. 3 coming at her, Stacey's forced to score. From there we get 30 seconds to convert but then Fiji has another chance to get the ball back in play. People at home maybe thought we'd won at that point, but me, Gossy, Kelly, we knew. We haven't won yet.

We miss our conversion — Tyla hits the post, and even though we're now 17–12, we know we're still vulnerable, and then in overtime it happens — Fiji gets a try, the score goes to 17–17 and if they can convert it, they'll get the two points and the game will be over and it will be theirs. Seventeen all, kick to come.

I just cannot accept that they are going to win. This has to stay a draw so we can go to extra time. They have 30 seconds from the time of the try to get the ball over the posts. But they're doing this huge celebration down on the line that takes 10 to 15 seconds and I'm counting. Does the kicker realise she needs to get her ass back here? I don't take my eyes off the kicker.

It's all on her. Can you imagine the pressure? She has to kick from the sideline, the hardest angle under any circumstances, and she is absolutely out on her feet.

This whole time I stay with her. I watch her body language and I say to the ref, Hey, from when you score the try to when you kick the try, you've got 30 seconds. What's the time?

I say it loud enough that the Fijian player will hear it, just to make sure she knows I'm counting. Like, Not only do you have to slot the hardest kick in the game probably in your career, but now you've only got six seconds to do it in. The ref says, You know the rules, and she looks at me like Can you piss off, Ruby? But I need her to say, *She's got six seconds left, same as everyone else*, and she says it. The Fijian hears, and she looks up at the scoreboard and it says 6, 5, 4. She looks worried. She looks rushed and unstable. She doesn't have the time to prep. And I know there is no way she's going to get that over. She drops her head, her form goes out the window and when her boot meets the ball she completely shanks it off to the left. The score stays at 17-all, and we're going in to overtime.

And I'm like, Here we go. *Now* we work. You can push us, but we're going to win this now. We've had so many on-the-hooter wins, we've had so many on-the-hooter losses, we've had so many overtimes. I can't even tell you how many times we've been in this situation and I know Fiji has never been in this situation. They are in overtime against the best team in the world, and that is an extremely uncomfortable situation. The pressure is almost tangible; if you let it in, you're done. It's beyond fitness, or skill, or game-plan. It's about knowing how to deal with immense pressure — pressure that's on you so thick you can taste it and feel it like the humidity of the day.

Extra time is golden point — whoever scores first will win. Fiji only need the ball once so let's not give it to them. I feel so alive in this moment. These are the moments you start to live for as a sevens player at the top of your game. This is what we trained for, so let's go. It's a toss to see who kicks off. We want to receive. We lose the toss. And now we're at this huge moment. We're kicking off and we know that as soon as they get the ball in their hands, all hell will break loose. We have to get our hands back on that ball.

Theresa Fitzpatrick and I make the call to Tyla for the same kick we've had the whole game, a kick to Mini. But I hear Stace scream at me that she wants the kick. I look at her, she's dead serious as she says it again. The mana in her voice — I just know Stace is going to get this ball back. Wait! I say to Tyla and Theresa — Sis, cancel, kick it to Stace. Now Ty has to get this on the money . . . a huge moment but she knows the pressure too well and she does, and Stacey leaps and the Fijian 2 and 3 both leap, all reaching, reaching, but Stacey leaps higher. She snatches that ball back, that wonderful energy, and we've stolen the restart. This is the moment that probably wins us this game. At last we're all playing properly. Carry, carry and the Fijians are going offside and can't keep up. And then we're right down in front of the line and Gayle Broughton grabs it from the ruck and pushes the

Fijians out of her way and takes it over: 22–17, and we're through to the final.

The Fijian team is devastated, rightly so. This was the best Fijian team I have ever played. The last twelve months, they had worked so hard and they've shocked almost everyone. They were so close. They'll go on to beat Great Britain and win the bronze.

And now we have a couple of hours before we have to do it all again in the final, against France, who have just beaten Great Britain. But I am certain no game could be harder than the Fiji one. No one else could have beaten them. The game we've just played, that was like the final of the Olympics.

——

I'm pretty set in my routine between games. Refuel, shower, recover, nap, analysis. Everyone's a bit different and we all respect each other's way of doing things. Some people might go for a quiet walk in the stadium or use recovery machines, but I love to nap, and I've learned to be able to nap in the middle of noise. I set my alarm and then I wake up and do analysis — we all get an iPad loaded with the game we've just played, and the game of the team we're about to play. I stay low-key and just build up slowly. I take a couple of notes and boom — my focus shifts to this next team.

But this time things aren't going to plan. I am so sore. Something has happened to my left arm. That shoulder has been giving me grief all year, and towards the end of the Fiji game it was hard to even catch the ball. I iced it, took heaps of painkillers, and took refuge in my nap, but when I woke up, geez.

I'm sitting upright on the physio bed trying to stay still while Kate, our physio, straps up my left elbow as tight as the tape will safely allow so that it won't move.

Bunts comes past and taps my left shoulder. Rubes, are you all good? His voice is caring, encouraging but worried.

I can't move my neck but I turn my torso towards him.

I'm all good.

Are you sure? He's trying to tell me it's OK to say no, but he knows I won't.

I'm all good.

The truth is I can't really move the top left half of my body. My neck's jammed; it feels like it's connected to my shoulder problem. My elbow is completely black with bruising, and I've subluxed my wrist from the semi, which I don't end up getting an X-ray on till we're back in New Zealand. All France need to do is hit my left shoulder a few times and I'll be toast.

Kate finishes up — she's strapped my elbow into a slightly bent position, immobilised but still useful, so I can pass and tackle. This is definitely the closest I've been to not being able to play. My arm. My neck. I feel like the tape is holding me together.

All I have to do is start the game. Bunts can take me off if I get hit. Just get through the beginning so Goss can look to her left and see me just like she has since our debut together in 2012, and so Theresa can hear me yelling from her right. So they feel at ease. I can carry the pressure of starting. I have to turn up for my team for the Olympic dream just one more time so they don't have to worry about a last-minute change. I've got their back till the end. No matter what. I chuckle to myself as I look at the bulk of tape Kate's stuck to my arm. Taking this off later is gonna hurt.

But I would rather get run over by a car in this hobbling state than suffer an Olympic final loss again. The fire is burning so strong. Let's go.

———

Pain is part of contact sport. It's part of all sport because any physical action can cause your muscles to burn and throb. But rugby is definitely next-level in the toll it takes on your body, and over time I've learned a lot about the different kinds of damage

— the pain you can't play through, and the pain where it's about
pushing through using your mental strength. Your hands are
bleeding from calluses, your feet are bleeding from blisters,
but those aren't actual injuries in rugby. When I first started I
might've thought I couldn't run with blisters, but blisters aren't
going to break your damn foot. Like, what are you willing to
push through? You have to go when your body says you can't. It's
very rare that a top rugby player in a top team is at full capacity.
You've always got a pulled this or a broken that. I find myself
saying to younger players, Look after your body. But I'm aware of
the contradiction between care, and determination to play at all
costs.

If you want something different than everyone else, you
have to do things different than everyone else. So figuring out the
balance of your different is very important.

I found this in my journal:

> Champions feel pain too, but their
> breaking point is not of this
> world
>
> Greatness comes to those who take it
>
> PATHWAY ONE
> 1- No Excuses
> 2- No Give Up Talk
> 3- No Seeking Re-assurance

On the day of an Olympic final, when you've already been
playing for two days, everyone's going to be sore as heck, bruised,
probably bleeding somewhere. On that final day, it's not who's
the fastest or the strongest, it's who can pull up the best feeling.
It's a big mind play. So I deal with this pain the same way I deal
with pressure. I sink down into myself through all the burning

bits and the throbbing bits, down past all that. I acknowledge it, and it's like noise: I'm through it and past it. I leave it behind, and I focus.

There's no way I'm not going to be on that starting line.

I look at my subs, Risi (Risaleaana Pouri-Lane) and Alena. I hope they're ready to play some minutes. I'll just go till there's nothing in the tank. So I line up with the girls, and I've got Gossy on my right and Theresa on my left, and I have the poker face so France won't know how vulnerable I am. Let's go. Next minute, my left shoulder is hit three times in a row by some of the strongest, most-determined women on the planet, and it's like they know. Halfway through the first half, their utility back, Camille Grassineau, a great player, hits me perfectly, hard and fast right in the left arm. It was such a good hit she even says sorry to me in English as she runs off. And now I'm struggling and Bunts does the right thing and pulls me off. But I started. I did my job.

Our half-time lead is 19–5. Looks good, but I wouldn't confidently tell myself it's indisputable until it's one minute to go and we're winning by two tries; the job's not done till it's done. And then, with four and half minutes to go, the French score again. It's 19–12. We don't want it any closer than that, and Bunts puts me back on.

I may be half-crippled, but I know how to close out a big game. And with just over two minutes to go, our team does it: we create the opportunity and Tyla grabs it and gets a try right between the posts, and then converts it, and there we are within my confidence zone — with a minute to go, we're ahead by 14 magical points.

Then it's full-time and the hooter goes but the ball is still in play. I'm dancing on the edge: on one side is celebration and losing it; on the other is — the game is still on. Stay here, stay here, I tell myself. I stay in the rugby mindset. I've got to stay focused, methodical. Scrum. Scrum first, always. *Stay in it.*

Everyone does their job. Ball gets put in, let my opposite overdo it but stay composed, Tyla passes to Kelly. Kelly kicks the ball out. Wait. Ruby, wait. Whistle goes.

Now.

We finish with 26–12 and we've done it.

We've won gold.

———

Everyone wants to be happy, but happy is different for every person. You need to figure out what the frick happiness even means. For me, on the journey that began when I learned what made me unhappy, I've learned that what makes me happy is the absolute pursuit of the best I can be, of a team that works together, of a team that is the best in the world. Of gold, as a symbol of all that. Of being present in every moment of the journey of that. So when that final whistle blows it is incredible and I've never felt anything like it — to win an Olympic gold, yes. It is every emotion, every single emotion, all at once, a magical storm, all good, all bad, a tsunami of tears down my face. *Ruby, just look up to the heavens and embrace this moment.* It doesn't even feel like I'm breathing. I am floating and time has stood still and this moment, this moment, is all there is.

But it's not just the win. This moment contains it all. It contains the whole journey, my absolute pursuit, staying true to my values and holding fast, content with every single decision good and bad, and it's the joys of this incredible odyssey and all that's been won and lost along the way, and the women who are no longer in the team, and the ones who have been there all along. Stan Walker's 'Aotearoa' is blasting through the stadium. Of the seven players the coach put on to close out that game, six of us have been together since that first camp at Waiouru: Tyla Nathan-Wong, Sarah Hirini (Gossy), Portia Woodman, Gayle Broughton, Michaela Blyde, me. And Kelly Brazier has been with us since 2013. Three of us — me, Portia, Gossy — debuted together in Fiji. We are all still here.

I'm last off the field, last back to the changing rooms, and it couldn't be more different to Rio. I start a chant, Tyla's going to have a dri-i-ink! Because she always vowed she wouldn't have a single drink till we'd won gold. We're cracking up. We're getting changed as quick as we can because we want our medals. So we're taking off our Adidas gear and pulling on our Peak uniforms — they're the sponsor of the Olympic team — and that's when I feel it: the solid little object I stowed in my pants pocket. It's there. I'd forgotten. I'm going to do it.

And we line up and we're laughing and singing, so sweaty still in our clean clothes, and the guy is telling us we go out last because we won gold, and everything is just great news to us.

I bend my head for the gold medal as Risi puts it around my neck. My head is bent, but my heart is open to the heavens. And I reach into my pocket and I feel for that object: my silver medal from Rio — and this, this is the moment I have visualised.

In the lead-up to the Olympics I have been taking my silver medal with me everywhere, looking at it every day, touching it, a tangible reminder of the journey I was on, of my pursuit. I love the silver because it tells me you can have everything on paper, the best players in the world, and you still might not be ready.

It's all chipped, it looks terrible, and that's the journey. People are looking for this beautiful pristine gold medal, but it's the niggly, disintegrated, chipped silver medal that I actually learned everything from. So I packed it, because I had this vision: *imagine being on the podium holding the silver that got me here and holding the gold that I finally got.* It was a pretty out-the-gate vision, and yet it's obvious — the silver is such a huge part of getting the gold.

So I pull it out, and the woman next to me who, because I'm No. 1 and at the end of our row, is from the French team, says, What's that? And I say, Bro, this is the reason I'm here. I've got the gold around my neck and the silver in my right hand and I'm looking at them both, thinking, I did it. This was my exact vision. I have them side by side, one in each hand, and I'm like, This is life, this battered, tattered, second place from when we had the best players but we hadn't done the work together, and then this pristine gold, beautiful treasure, everything we've worked for. We could not have got the gold without the silver. Look at all we've learned. I think back to the jersey ceremony the night before our first game at this Olympics, where every single one of us spoke from her heart — open, honest, authentic, connected — and I felt then that the stars had aligned and it was our moment and our time.

Then we turn and face the flag and it's the anthem, and we laugh afterwards 'cos it's honestly the worst singing we've ever done, but I just sing my heart out and I look at the sky like I always do when I'm singing the anthem because the sky's always there, showing me the bigger picture.

There's no audience, no crowd noise. There are cameras everywhere and everyone's posing with each other, with Bunts, hugging, Gee brings a Māori flag out of nowhere. But I just want to stay in the moment, to breathe in that moment, and I lie down on the grass and feel my whole body against the earth, the grass between my fingers, the huge volume of the stadium's vast emptiness, and the weight of the gold on my chest. This is the moment.

RUBY'S TRAINING BAG
Winning is a moment that contains the
entire journey of the pursuit.

PART THREE

COMMUNICATION

There's a saying: All the greatest ideas and inventions are in the graveyard. Not actualised. Never expressed.

The number one thing that old people say is not, I wish I hadn't done that, but I wish I *had* done that. Regret is one of the worst feelings in the world: I never did this, I never tried at this, I never said that.

So I encourage myself to not leave things unsaid, and to never go to sleep wondering if I should have said this or communicated that.

Take the risk. Take the chance, because life is what you make it.

At 30 I'm still learning about how to live my life. I could easily have not made it this far. I could have gone to jail. I could have ended up as head honcho of some drug house. I could have cut my own life short when I was still a child.

Out of my gratitude for my life, I want to communicate my story, the things I've learned so far.

I'm still only just starting, still growing so much.

Take the risk. You are known purely through your communication. It's how you make your place in the world.

It's all anyone knows of you. You could be the most beautiful person, or you might need help — how you communicate determines your relationships with others, and it's the gateway to connection. And connection is what life's all about.

Communication breaks down barriers. It unites the world.

This means so much to me, because when I was very young, I learned about how *not* to communicate. If you're yelling or screaming or swearing or cussing out someone, you've lost the ability to communicate. That's not mature, adult, effective communication. It's not even a conversation any more. It's a battle. If you're having an argument and the emotion is winning, it's probably not the best time to talk. It's like yelling at the ref in the middle of the game — it's not usually the time or the place where you're going to be listened to, or get a productive outcome. Better to wait until you can reflect, get your thoughts in order, lower your voice.

I've learned the value of communicating well. Like anything, I have to practise — I make mistakes, I improve, and all the time I get clearer about what I want to communicate.

Take the risk.

33. Finding your meaning

Our lives, our traumas, things that have happened to us, they can be extremely hard to face. To be 'straight up' and look ourselves in the mirror and acknowledge things that have rocked us takes huge courage. But once I look my life in the eye, I lose the shame around what I went through, the things that are so heavy to carry. Not only that, but I can see my pain and I can use it to help find meaning in my life.

I was once embarrassed at school about staying at the Women's Refuge; I would lie about it because it was so shameful. But now I work with the Women's Refuge whenever I can and I donate to them often. Now I can show other kids who may be living with abuse or escaping from it at the refuge that it doesn't mean you're at a dead end. You can choose another path, the path of a good healthy relationship; you can stop the intergenerational hurt. Your trauma doesn't have to be your tragedy.

When I was near the end of high school I was very close to a young boy — I had a huge crush on him and he took a big liking to me. He was into cars and he dated younger girls, but I still liked hanging with him when it was just us. We were the same year in high school and we hung out a lot. At one stage, after he'd had a big fight with his mum, I picked him up and he lived with me at Mum's place for a few months.

We were really close. But towards the end of that time he was changing in ways I found unsettling. He was posting weird stuff online, hanging with younger and younger friend groups and doing really dangerous things to be cool. We had a couple of arguments, and then I left Greymouth for uni and stopped talking to him. One day at uni, I was in The Warehouse in Christchurch when I saw him again. He looked bad, almost like he was homeless, and he was with a much younger kid. We kind of made eye contact and I could have said hi, I could have asked why he was doing all that weird stuff, but I was still holding a grudge against him for embarrassing me with his behaviour. I was too proud, so I didn't say hi. I didn't say anything. And not long after that, I got a text from a mutual friend telling me he'd killed himself. I felt so guilty and upset. His suicide really blindsided me and messed me up. At that time I wasn't as good as I am now with safe spaces and sharing, so I was just internalising everything and I didn't understand why I was feeling so much. I pushed those feelings down for a long time.

My friend's death was a massive seismic shift for me. I was actually shocked at how much it affected me. With suicide you never know who the waves will hit. A depressed person may think no one will care (I know this, from my experience of those feelings), but it's often the opposite. It could be the baker they bought their sandwich from every day; it could be old school friends they used to hang out with — all these people will feel it and wonder if there was something they could have said or done to help, and they will have to work through that guilt. When someone so familiar to you passes, it's like a part of you passes too.

But from this pain and hurt I learned how important it is to check in on your friends and create safe spaces. I always try to give people the time of day, no matter who they are. I remember myself not saying hi to my old friend — I see that Warehouse aisle, me holding my grudge, turning away — and that's why I say hi to old friends if I see them pass within earshot, and why I sometimes talk to people for a bit too long. I'm constantly getting told by managers to finish up talking to the crowds after games, but I know how precious connections are. Connections can reset us, refill our cups and often save us. My dear friend taught me that.

———

From this pain I also found purpose. As my public profile grew I wanted to do what I could to promote mental health. So when Nathan Price asked me to be part of HeadFirst, a new online mental health programme to support mental fitness in the rugby community, I didn't hesitate. It was the perfect opportunity to honour my friend and to turn the pain into something positive.

This was just at the time that Instagram was gaining ground, so my video clips were getting noticed and it became known that I wanted to help people in that space.

Another thing I committed to was what I call my Mental Health Mondays. Every single Monday, unless I'm assembled with my team, I post something on my social media that promotes mental health. It's a simple thing, but it's one of the ways I live my values.

———

Everyone's journey is different and difficult in its own way. For me there were the years of uncertainty with contracts, the Rio campaign that was so hard when the team wasn't getting along, not to mention my injuries, my personal struggles, my successes and failures. I had struggled with mental fitness so much, and watched people I love struggle too. But from that pain I learned to speak up about mental health and to not be ashamed about it. Shame is the lowest-vibrating energy we can have, and it is so dangerous to our spirit. I learned to speak up when I need to, and to take opportunities to grow when I'm in a good head space because it's so hard when your mental fitness is low.

I know some people find it hard to talk about these things, but I'm trying to model that it's life, it's reality. I know it can be hard to be straight up with yourself and what has happened to you, and there will be times in your life that are hard because of things in your past or things that happen in your present. We can't change what life sends to us — there will always be things we don't see coming. We can only control the way we deal with them.

Learning to nurture your mental health can be such a cool journey — it can take you from hurting to meaning. It starts with knowing your identity and knowing your values, and that's going to help you in every area of your life.

RUBY'S TRAINING BAG
We can't change what life sends to us — we can only control the way we deal with it.

34. Be the change you want to see

I've never had it as a goal to have people look up to me or be inspired by me. I never used to take social media very seriously as a thing in itself — like, I certainly never worried over how many followers I had or anything like that. But finding ways to communicate what I believe in and what is important has become an important part of my life.

I think of myself at ten, getting mad at someone saying that I could be a Black Fern, not knowing what was even possible. And now here I am wearing that black jersey, and I know how people see me when I'm in it — like, when we wear that jersey we are the closest thing to a superhero for some kids, even though I'm just me when I take it off. But that's what the black jersey gives us, and I realise now that these two things combined — the black jersey, and social media — are very powerful tools to grow women's rugby.

———

Back before we had much support or resources, a couple of years before Rio, us players had to run all our socials. Tyla, Kay and myself started the New Zealand Sevens Instagram account and made our own content, and got the New Zealand Men's sevens to do content so we could post it as well. We knew the value of having direct connection with our followers. I also saw the value in getting media promotion of our team right. I asked for help but it never came, so I just elected myself as the player/media manager of our team. I knew that professional rugby teams have media managers to support the players (luckily we have one now), and when you're a player at a promo alone it can be quite daunting. I used to stand there as Portia would do long content pieces, asking the media people if she was going to get a break soon. One time I went with three of our team members down to a live broadcast. The presenter didn't even know the name of our team and called us the Silver Ferns off-air, and I had to educate him and let him know what competitions we had coming up. He had no idea I was a player myself, but I was so glad I was there that day.

———

I also studied for a media degree at the University of Canterbury as I had always wanted to help push women's sport. I started out writing pieces for local Christchurch papers about women's rugby club games, anything for experience. My dream was absolutely to commentate the Black Ferns live, to help communicate to the world how entertaining women's rugby can be. With the help of Melodie Robinson and Scotty Stevenson I got my foot in the door. I kept turning up and taking opportunities, and one day I found myself commentating the mighty Black Ferns next to Ken Laban. I couldn't believe it . . . I was so happy.

Then, on the first weekend of February 2018, I became the first-ever female to commentate an all-male World Sevens Series Tournament at FMG Stadium in Hamilton. That was also next to Ken and it was such a buzz, a real achievement for me personally and, to me, a statement that times were changing.

I remember after the Black Ferns game Ken was saying good job to me, and then started saying something about an invoice. I shook my head. What, girl? he said. You aren't getting paid for this?! I'd never asked for money before — this gig was a dream of mine and to me, they were doing me a favour letting me go live on the mic. I could hardly believe they did, really.

Insert into my life Dan Sing from WeAreTenzing, which is a talent and influencer management agency. Dan and his colleague Brooke Howard-Smith have completely changed my life when it comes to my off-field opportunities. I used to just do favours for people and companies, but as my profile grew it was getting so hard to keep on top of it. Dan and Brooke taught me how to shine my values into my brand, how to use social media instead of letting it use me. Dan is now my manager and is always in my corner looking out for me, filtering everything to allow me to be more present and to enter only into collaborations that align with the person I want to be. In fact, you wouldn't be reading this book if it wasn't for him. He has helped me communicate better to the world so that I can connect with people better. He has shown me ways I can be the change I want to see in the world. I will forever be grateful for him.

———

With Dan's help, I came to understand how I can harness social media and my public profile to promote the things that matter to me, including mental health awareness and empowering women.

Understanding what I want to achieve helps me create meaningful content in my social media posts. Before I did this work with Dan I'd be like, I've got nothing to post. Now it could be something really simple — for instance, I might tell people that I've had a massive week of training, and for my wellbeing I need to relax, so I'm going to light this candle and sit quiet for a moment . . . It's kind of simple and funny, but it highlights the importance of taking care of your mental health, and it offers a positive experience for people.

I have learned that I can grow women's rugby by sharing my love of the sport. Through my media work as a sports commentator, I can show people a confident, brown face in that setting — I'm going to look good, I'm going to be confident, and I'm going to have good things to say. Connecting with an audience is a real buzz for me.

I love the contrast between the way I look on the field — out there busting my gut, my body going through all sorts — and the way I look when I get my hair and make-up done, when I get all dressed up. Me and the other rugby women dress up and go out and I see the looks on people's faces, like, What the heck? And I'm like, Yeah, we have a job that makes us sweat and bleed, but we can do this, too.

Or I spend two hours getting everything done, hair, make-up, wardrobe, and then I'm in the TV studio with two opinionated ex-All Blacks talking about what the All Blacks could have done better — and sometimes it's a mission, but I do it because I want people to see a strong, confident brown woman holding her own — and I do, I go out there and kill it. And actually I belong there because I'm the only current professional player sitting on that panel. I want to see more brown female faces out there. It makes me so happy to see other sisters doing it too.

So that's another huge part of my identity — empowering women. I love being a woman, so let's celebrate all the good things that we've got going on.

———

Opportunities for connection can come out of the blue. An interview I did following our pool game against Russia at the Tokyo Olympics was off-the-cuff, fun, completely random.

I didn't even know what the BBC was — I thought it might mean 'Better Be Clear' but it turned out to be one of the largest broadcasters in the world, and the interview went viral. It was fun, and I gave the moment of connection my full focus, and then didn't give it another thought.

I didn't notice the attention that interview got for a while. Then I looked for it online so I could send it to my cousins — I'd used Samoan during the interview and I wanted to know if I'd said it right. Did I pronounce it right? Did I do a good job? Sometimes I can't find my interviews online but this was different, like — it was everywhere! I got so many messages from people all over the world and did so many interviews with broadcasters in different countries just because of this.

I guess it shows that if you're authentic, and always turn up with your whole self, and be present in this journey we call life, anything can happen.

———

Nutrition as an athlete has always been a massive part of the journey. After many one-day tournaments in the early days of my career, playing up to six games in one day while trying to put on weight, I found that having protein shakes after every game was taking a toll on my gut. Even at a two-day tournament I was having them with breakfast, again after each of the three games and then again at night. It was too much. I was bloated, gassy, nauseous and extremely uncomfortable, just when I needed to be at my peak.

There had to be another way. I experimented with my diet, and I eventually figured out that dairy was the issue. I started looking around. I was encouraged not to cut dairy by my professional advisors, as dairy is such a good source of protein and that's what I needed to gain weight. I found out that I'm not completely dairy-intolerant, I just can't handle the daily amounts we were having. But surely there were other forms of protein — and indeed it turns out there is protein powder that has absolutely no dairy in it. That's common knowledge now, but when I first started out this type of protein was very rare and hard to come by.

It's extremely hard as an elite athlete to find new supplements that work, because I can't just go to any old shop and trial everything on the shelves. As an Olympic athlete in this country, I have to be careful: every supplement that passes my lips must be batch-tested so there's proof from a licensed tester that it contains no banned substances.

I started researching. At that time I found there was a whopping *one single* product in the whole of New Zealand that was plant-based and already batch-tested for me to try. The difference was immediate — straight away I felt lighter and stronger, and no longer nauseous during tournaments. But it was difficult to get them to understand the seriousness of the ongoing batch-testing requirements.

So I started being proactive. I was thinking about my brand and what I believe in, and it was clear that nutrition is a massive part of mental wellbeing. I emailed for years, trying to get a company to support me on my journey, but I couldn't get anyone to make the right protein for me while providing the certificates I needed. This communicated to me that, once again, if I wanted this change to happen I was going to have to do it myself. So what did I do? I created my own plant-based protein powder.

I went through a whole process working with a nutritionist to develop a formula that really worked for me and my training loads. Dani and a couple of friends were my first samplers, as I couldn't taste it myself until it had been batch-tested. And then finally it was ready — my own product. I had to wait a bit longer, but at last I got an email with the batch-test certificate. All good to go.

———

So I started taking my own pea protein powder, and honestly it was amazing. My digestion was great. I felt lighter in my tummy but more powerful — lighter on my feet, faster. Oh man, what had I been doing for all those years?

I won gold on my own protein powder.

There were still some issues with the product around taste, and it's a work in progress, but the results for me are undeniable. It was funny, though: before the Olympics I'd often had trouble getting manufacturers to reply to my emails, but after I got back to New Zealand — armed not only with my gold medal but also with the profile I gained after my interview with the BBC that went viral — I found that people were more ready to help me.

Through my own journey of being ignored and now having my own product, I just want to open people's minds about what they're eating, and the value of good nutrition to both mental and physical fitness. If you're not getting what you need, go out there and try different things like I did; experiment with what works for you and what doesn't; maybe invent your own product or favourite recipe and see how it helps. I love the product that I have created with a team of people I trust, and I can't wait to share that part of my journey with you too.

RUBY'S TRAINING BAG
If you're authentic, and always turn up with
your whole self, anything can happen.

Epilogue: Pursuit

The hugeness of my Samoan family's journey to New Zealand really came home to me when, in 2018, I visited Samoa for a family reunion. Dad couldn't come for paperwork reasons, but a whole group of us went, and Aunty Tala took us to the house she and my dad were born in, in our village in the Palauli region on the island of Savai'i.

It was so different to the world I grew up in. There's lots of beauty there of course, in the people, in the land, but the fale where they lived freaked me out, to be honest — old and so gloomy, very run-down now. My cousin Hemi James and I were chuckling because we couldn't believe it. This was where Dad lived for almost the first decade of his life.

It was January when we were there, the middle of sevens season, so I had to keep training. I told my family there that I was going for a run and they looked me up and down and asked if I was going to wear shorts. It was over 30 degrees, and very humid. Of course I was going to wear shorts!

But in that very traditional place, it wasn't that simple. If a female from the family was seen in shorts, the family could be fined, so my grandad's wife instructed me to wear an 'ie or lavalava, the traditional sarong-like formal wear. It sits from your belly button all the way down to your ankles. I thought she was joking. She was not.

My older cousin Teri, who plays women's rugby in Australia, joined me and we both put on our lavalavas, and off we ran into the sweltering heat. With every step, the lavalava pulled and dragged at my legs. As we ran through the countryside, over bridges with missing pieces and jagged metal sticking out of crumbling concrete, villagers staring at us as we appeared to be running for no particular reason, the chaffing between my legs from the sweat under the lavalava reached its peak. I began to understand why Grandad moved to New Zealand. He came in the pursuit of opportunity — not for himself, but for us who came after.

There was no way I would be pulling on a national rugby jersey with the name Tui on the back, and going to the Olympics, if Grandad had not brought us all to New Zealand. I am so grateful to Grandad every day, for the vision that meant his grandkids could grow up with all these opportunities.

Everything I do shows my appreciation, my greatitude, for what he made possible.

I wear this Tui name on my back with so much pride. I'm part of the first generation of my New Zealand Samoan family to not have the traumatic shock of moving countries, moving cultures. How dare I not strive for greatness, how dare I not make the most of my life, when my grandparents, my aunties and uncles, my dad, went through so much to get here to this land of opportunity?

———

Just as I look back on how Grandad's decisions have shaped my life, I also see how I've been shaped by the things that happened to me. As a woman now, I honour the little girl who got through so much.

I've been back to Canvastown a couple of times, to that lonely house beside the ever-flowing river. Where I saw my mum struggle, and where I was at the lowest point in my life.

The first time was hard. I was in my early twenties and alone that day, and the place seemed dark and miserable. It reminded me too much of how alone I'd felt there as a kid. But I was on a bit of a mission and it felt important to revisit the location of the hardest times of my childhood memories. I drove the winding, skinny country road with its blind corners. It wasn't as scary as it had seemed when I was a kid, but I still felt a bit bitter about how Mum made me walk to school that day.

Visiting the place where I vividly remembered wanting to commit suicide was difficult. This was a place of suffering, but there was a healing power in going there. It was like swallowing a big vitamin pill — uncomfortable, but once it's down you end up healthier. I realised I no longer had anything to fear.

The second time I went back it was much easier. I took my partner, Dani, who was really patient and understanding. She waited in the car while I looked in again at the property. It was overgrown and still sad, but *I* felt different. Bigger. I stood taller. My growth compared with the sameness of the house was undeniable. Revisiting places can show you your growth, like looking at an old photo. Thank you, I said out loud. This place had taught me so much. I understood that a strong, determined little girl made it out of this house, and that strong little girl helped me achieve such tremendous goals. She got me through some big moments in my adulthood.

Thank you, Ruby. I love you, Ruby.

That little girl, she had no choice. I was trapped, getting told bad things, getting yelled at, watching my mum get abused; but there was just something in me that went, I don't want to be that person. I don't want that life. I want to be a good person and I want to do the right thing.

There had to be an alternative. Because I grew up with my

feet in two worlds, I knew it. I knew there was another way to love. There's another way to do this. I'm grateful that the little sis — my younger self — got through all that and understood the possibility of something different. I went out and I found my other way — I found a life that I loved and I felt safe and celebrated in, and I chose that.

I'm still choosing that. I'm on my journey. It's a lifelong pursuit — of being the person I want to be, of staying true to my values, of all my opportunities, of my brand, my family, my still-unfolding rugby career where I get to play fifteens again. Of having a family with Dani. I'm here on the journey right now, and I always will be.

———

I hold no hate or resentment towards anyone — even my dad's choice of alcohol above anything else in his life, including me; Mum and her depression, when she was unable to stick up for me; my brother's dad and his atrocious behaviour. Those things were all horrible, but I have the choice to do better. I feel like it's really cool that I can say: That all sucks, but I'm not carrying any of it. It's not my burden. I choose to do life differently.

There was a time when I did carry it. I remember in my first years of high school, I used that word *hate* quite a bit. I'd say *I hate him*, talking about Dane's dad, or even about this idiot who was in my class: hate, hate, hate. And it's true that when I voiced those feelings, used that word, beat someone up with my words, thought I was cooler than someone, I'd get a little hit, a tiny hit of satisfaction. But it just leaves ugliness. It doesn't really satisfy. It's like the rope that takes you quickly to a dead end.

What's the other path? What's the other way? I knew I had to learn and grow and heal myself. Blame and anger have no place in healing and I choose to heal.

I'm not a completely healed saint. Sometimes I struggle

to put my ego aside. Sometimes I struggle to step back from aggression. Sometimes I feel those little materialistic pleasures, like when someone says something cool about me, or I get more followers online — those things edge in, want to take up space.

But they're not my pursuit, not my true journey. My pursuit is of what's real and meaningful. I followed the little light of possibility of another way that glowed in my mind even when I was a kid — so tiny at times and so dim — and I've seen it explode. I've seen it shine right into my life, and that's what I'll never stop living for.

I love sevens. It's been a dream job, and we've grown it to be that: paid to train, paid to play. It's such a great set-up. The sport has come a long way since the day I got that Go 4 Gold pamphlet and was blown away by the promise of a contract. I'm one of the rare people in New Zealand who have lived that journey, who have gone from there to here. I'm there for the team and I'll turn up and I'm fit and I'm fast and I'm determined and I listen and I'm coachable. But I'm also one of the hungriest rugby players — hungry for growth, holistic growth.

I've been in so many memorable extra-time wins — two of my favourites are the 2020 Auckland women's club-rugby final with the Ponsonby Fillies and the Olympic semi-final. Rugby is a metaphor for life. Never give up. Fight right till the end of the game, because there's always more to get. If I surround myself with the right people, if I align my whole life with my values, there will be more — more to give, more to find, so much further to go.

Since writing this book I have played in the first-ever premier women's Super Rugby Aupiki competition for the Chiefs Manawa (yes, we won). I have played my debut game for the Black Ferns fifteens next to Kendra Cocksedge, who became the most capped Black Fern in history in that same game (the same Kendra who was there alongside me when we won that women's rugby club competition in 2010). I have done so many things that I never thought were possible when my career first started.

That horrible life that I brushed up against when I was younger, I saw where that path leads. If that life was a rope and I was pulling myself along on it, I know what would happen. I've seen it. With Meredith and Hailey, I saw the dead end. But this other life, this path I'm on now, if I pull *this* rope, I pull and pull and I still haven't seen all it has to give me. I'm learning, I'm growing. This rope doesn't end. The more I pull, the more there is.

The game's still on.

The beautiful sky is the limit.

Ruby's poem
For the sevens sisters

I take one game at a time
I do too much all the time
And in my time I've known three places.
The tip top of the world, the rock bottom and every half time in
    between.

I'm the roughest, toughest, nittiest, grittiest, prettiest rugby lover
    you'll ever see.
I'm a lady, I have class. I lift more than you so I have a nice ass.
I make moments that make me and I always make the pass.

My blood, my skin is thick; my shut, my kill is quick
And my world-class Black outfit is louder, prouder and will
    always make yours sour.

I train to keep winning tomorrow.
Others sit back on today.
Oh, and hey. If I call her Sister, get the fuck out of her way.

The call-out

This book almost didn't happen. I was hesitant, I was nervous, I was uncomfortable. But then something happened. I went to my local bookshop to check out other books on female sportspeople, in particular women's rugby players. I knew there were lots of books on All Blacks, but I wanted to read a book about a woman or a Black Fern to see how they approached this whole autobiography thing.

I stood in the sports section, and I searched and searched. I pulled out book after book, but there wasn't a single biography on a Kiwi female athlete in the whole section. I eventually found an autobiography of Billie Jean King, a famous white American tennis player who did amazing things, but that was it.

I pictured a young brown female sportsperson walking in there and seeing herself nowhere, not belonging in the book world. My eyes welled up right there in the bookshop. *I have to do this.*

But more than that — *we* have to do this. This is a call-out to all the women's rugby players with incredible stories. It will be hard, but it will be worth it. I look forward to walking into the bookshop and seeing your books on the shelves.

I could call on so many women with amazing stories — Crystal Kaua and Honey Hireme-Smiler, to name just two. But this is a special call-out to the girls I stood next to on the field when that final whistle blew and we'd claimed the first-ever Olympic gold in New Zealand's national sport. We had been playing rugby together in the national set-up for a decade. The seven of us would often start a game together, but it was very rare for us all to be on the field at the end. But there we were, and we had just finished the most important game of our careers — together.

Tyla Nathan-Wong (Ty)

Smaller than everyone else on the field, but always makes the tackle. I watched her go from never kicking before to being the best in the world. She carries her family's mana and determination with her wherever she goes. Her family have always been the loudest supporters of her and she tries to make them proud every day. She is kind and always speaks so well — such a good ambassador for our game. She truly has felt like my actual little sister all these years: annoying as at times, but if anyone ever picked on her they had me to deal with.

Gayle Broughton (Gee Fizz)

If the world knew her story they would have even more love and adoration for her than they already have. Gee will light up any room and can give Chris Brown a run for his money with her dance moves. But what I love most about Gee is her heart, she just wants to love everyone around her and never wants anyone to feel left out or alone. She makes everyone feel welcome and ensures they have a good time. A special human that I will always be there for.

Michaela Blyde (Mini)

She's had a tough old journey in this team too, and we've been through a lot together and had some gut-punching conversations over the years. But her amazing work ethic made sure she never gave up the fight, all the way to being named the top sevens player in the world — twice. An amazing athlete, but more importantly a wonderful and honest friend, who loves puns.

Kelly Brazier (Kell Bell)

I've known her the longest out of everyone in the Black Ferns Sevens and she has always impressed the world on the footy field. But my favourite part of being Kell's friend has been her growth off the field as a friend and a person; she is so loving, loyal and gentle with those she cares for. Her silly side has always been the most fun, and her caring heart is huge. Seeing her become such an amazing mum has inspired me to think about starting a family of my own.

Portia Woodman (P, Porsh)

The ultimate figure in women's rugby, and one of my favourite characters I have got to know over the years. Super-humble and so easy to get along with. Radiates a beautiful aura in every room and so proudly represents her culture, inspiring us all to do the same. Just a beautiful person inside and out. I love this woman so much and will probably keep turning up to her house for cuppas that go on far too long for many years to come.

Sarah Hirini (Gossy)

The hardest worker in every way, but off the field she is actually the sweetest person you will ever meet. She is always caring for others and offering help to anyone who needs it. I don't think I will ever find someone I fit so perfectly with on the field. Playing next to Goss is like knowing the back of my hand. We haven't always agreed on everything but we've always been honest and that is why (I've never told her this) she is hands-down the best captain I've ever had in my career.

Acknowledgements

Being straight up with myself and who I am wasn't easy; it took so many people.

Thank you to Allen & Unwin for your patience in putting this together. Jenny, Kathy and Leanne, I appreciate all your work and time here. Thanks also to my editor Teresa, the proofreaders, the designer and the rest of the team at A&U.

To Margie, thank you for the hours upon hours of connection that brought this book to life. And thanks to Pip.

To Dani, thank you for being such a beautiful spirit and coming with me on this journey. You see my worst days as well as my best, and you always have my back no matter what. Here's to our next chapter together.

Thank you so much to my manager Dan and his family, Rani and Frankie, for opening my eyes to my true potential in life and what I stand for.

Thank you to my grandparents and all my cousins and uncles and aunties, you saved me without knowing it.

Thank you to my mum for being the bravest person I've met, and for getting through everything and showing me that it's possible.

Thank you to my dad for making sure I know how to give love even when it is hard. Thank you for getting through everything in your life so that I can have this one.

Thank you to my siblings, Lesh, Dane and Nikki, for only ever making me feel like your sister — you three are the most precious gifts to my heart.

Thank you to every single fan of women's rugby: you have changed my life and the lives of many more players to come. This game is the greatest thing in the world to me, so thank you for making it great. To everyone who's watched a women's game and supported it in some way, thank you for growing something so special with me. Huge thanks also to the media decision-makers, photographers and videographers who have focused their lenses on women's rugby — especially Rachael Whareaitu.

To every player I have ever played the game next to, you have helped grow and shape me in so many ways, thank you.

To my sevens sisters, all of you, holy shit, look what we did! I love you all so much. Wherever you are reading this, I send you all my love and I forever will. Thank you for choosing me to stand next to, and if you ever think of me please message and I'll do the same.

To my coaches and teachers who believed in me, far out, it meant heaps. Thank you to Bunts and your family, Alexis, Nikita, Ngakaunui, Miharo and Uekaha, for changing women's rugby and creating a space where I could really spread my wings in my career.

And to everyone out there on their journey to being straight up with themselves too: you are my heroes. Thank you for wanting to choose a better way too.

About the author

Ruby Tui is a professional rugby player. She won an Olympic silver medal in 2016 and a Rugby World Cup Sevens title in 2018. She was named Black Ferns Sevens Player of the Year in 2017 and World Rugby Sevens player of the Year in 2019. She went on to win gold at the 2020 Tokyo Olympics (held in 2021). In 2022 she won the inaugural Super Rugby Aupiki competition with the Chiefs Manawa and then made her debut for the Black Ferns, helping them win the 2022 Pacific Four Series.

Off the field, Ruby is a regular commentator for Sky TV and is passionate about promoting healthy environments for Kiwi kids and speaking up about mental health within the sporting community. Creating change through speaking out on public issues, and demonstrating motivation and gratitude to her peers, is how she would like to leave her mark. Ruby is the current ambassador for the HeadFirst initiative.

@rubytui